OREIMO

4

Story by
Tsukasa Fushimi

Art by
Sakura Ikeda

Character design by
Hiro Kanzaki

Based on the light novel series by
Tsukasa Fushimi

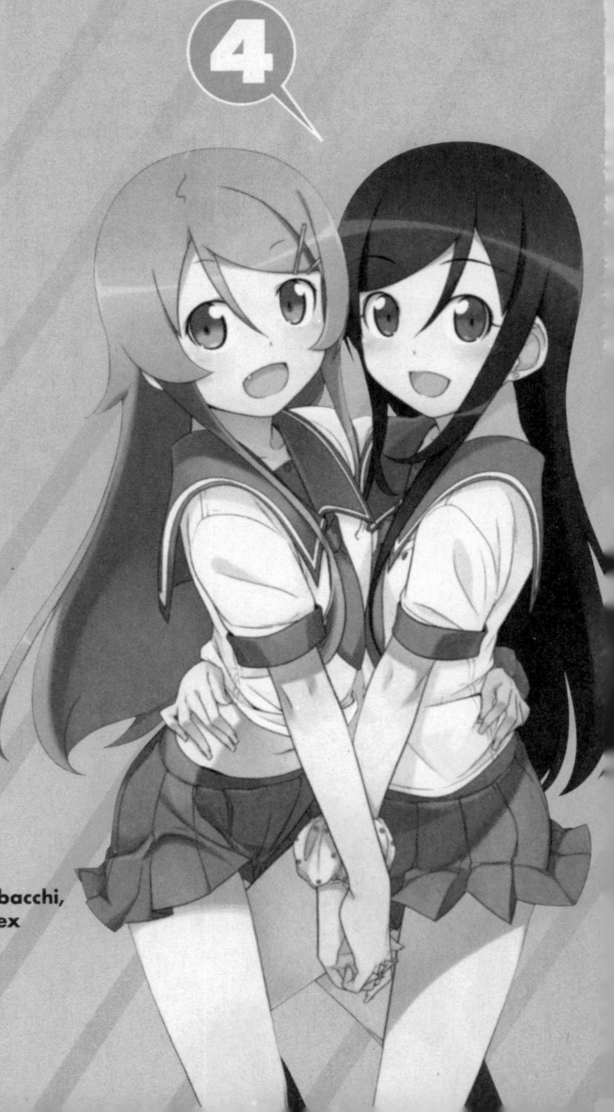

Translation
Michael Gombos

Editor
Jemiah Jefferson

Lettering and touchup
Susan Daigle-Leach

Special thanks to
Carl Gustav Horn, Lia Ribacchi, and E. J. Rivera at Aniplex

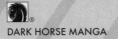

DARK HORSE MANGA

TABLE OF CONTENTS

もくじ

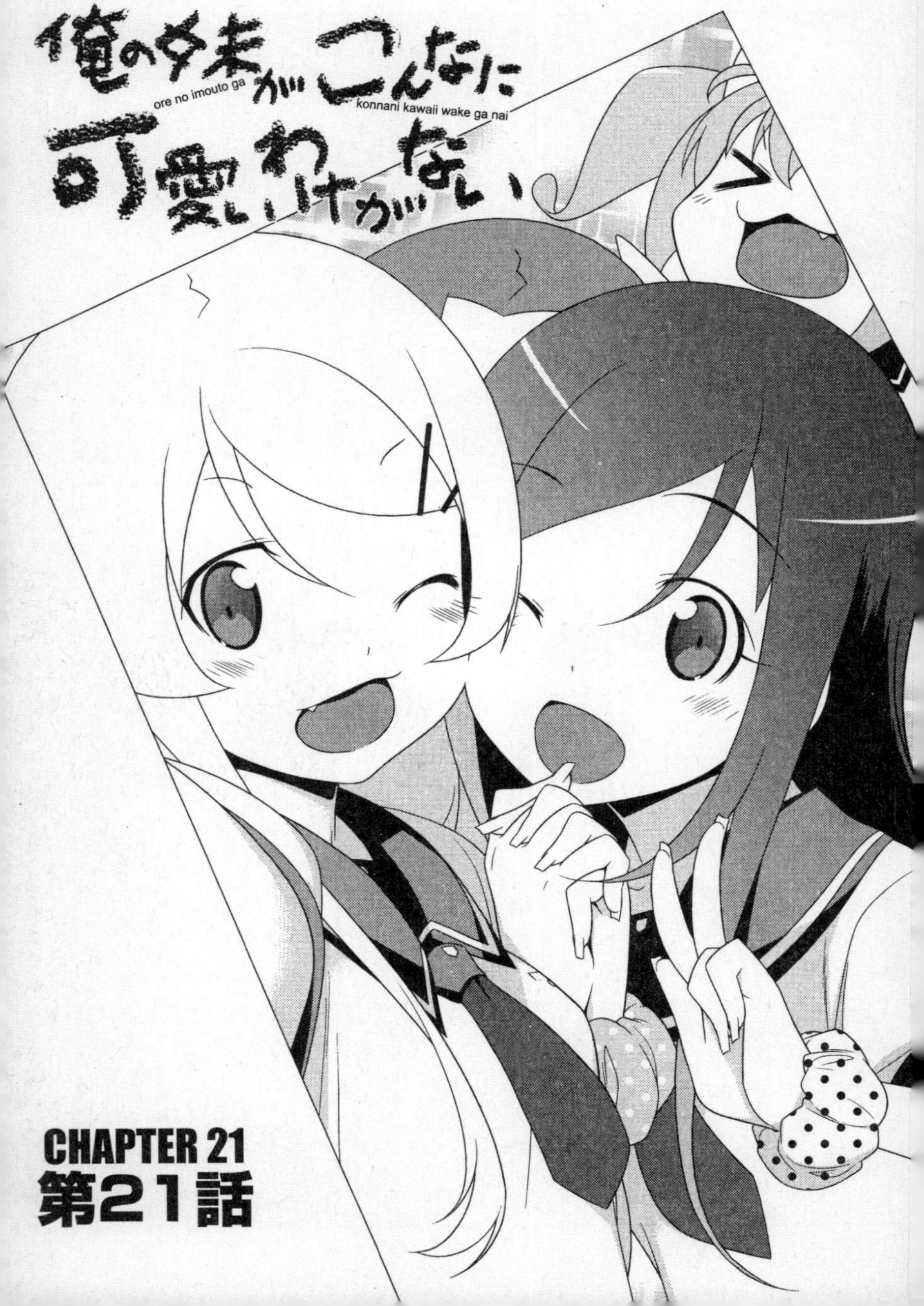
俺の妹がこんなに可愛いわけがない
ore no imouto ga konnani kawaii wake ga nai
CHAPTER 21
第21話

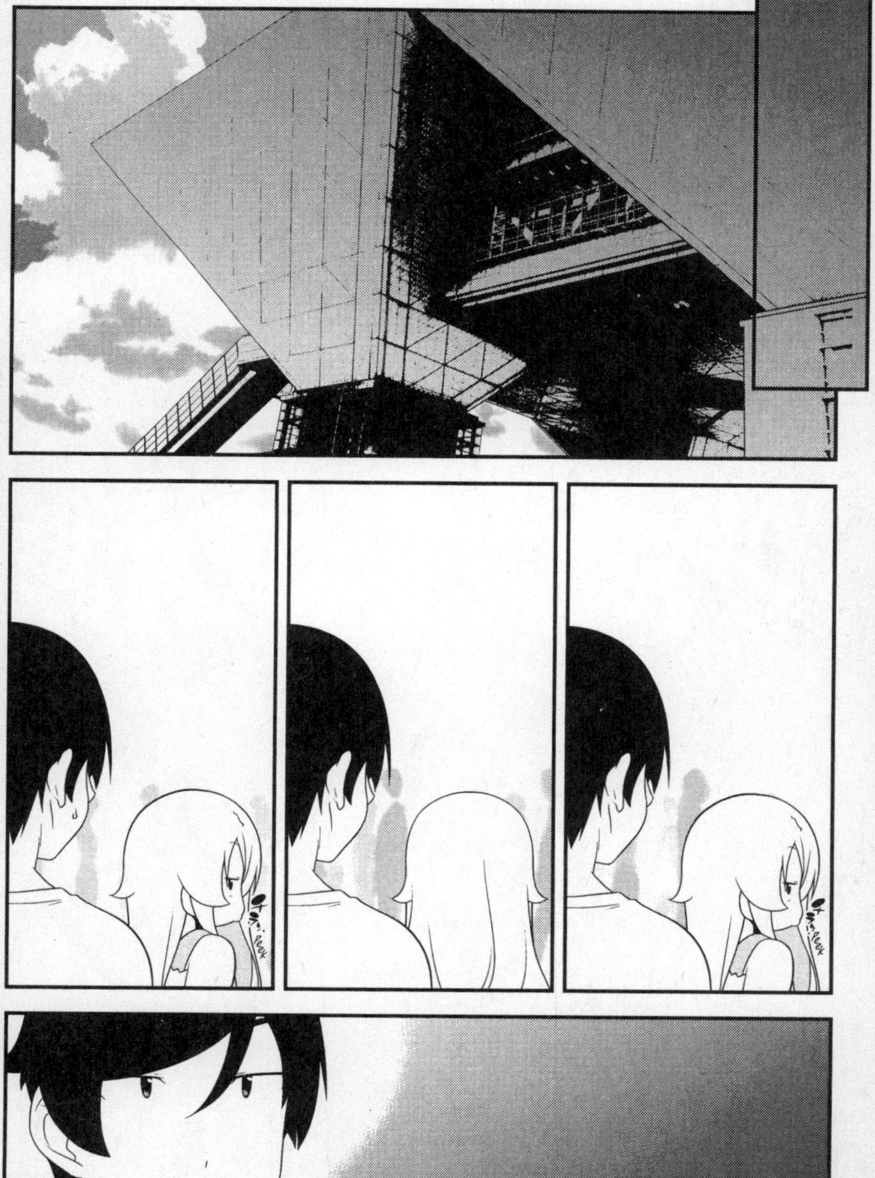
peek
peek

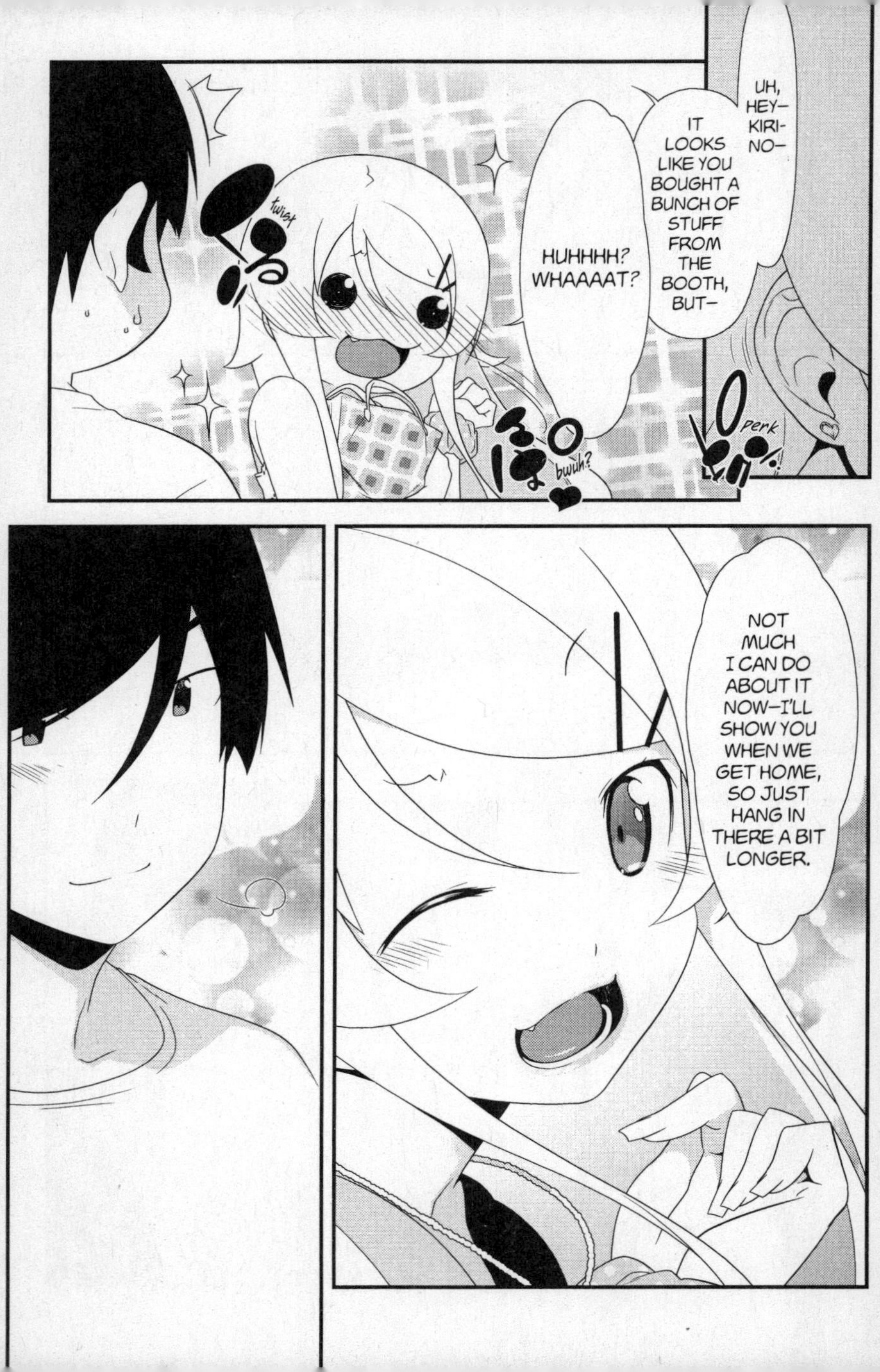
UH, HEY-KIRI-NO-
perk
IT LOOKS LIKE YOU BOUGHT A BUNCH OF STUFF FROM THE BOOTH, BUT-
HUHHHH? WHAAAAT?
bwuh?
twist
NOT MUCH I CAN DO ABOUT IT NOW-I'LL SHOW YOU WHEN WE GET HOME, SO JUST HANG IN THERE A BIT LONGER.

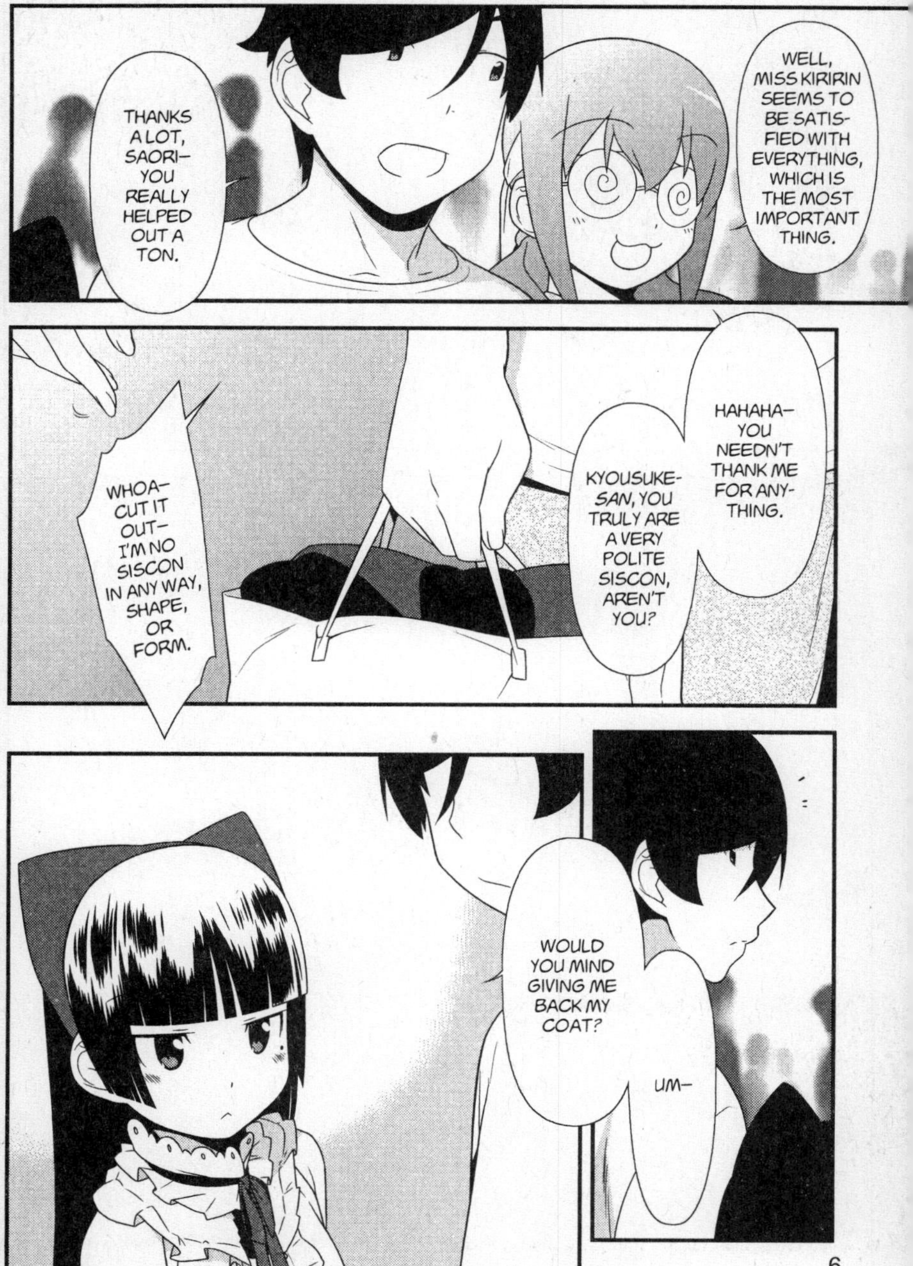
WELL, MISS KIRIRIN SEEMS TO BE SATIS-FIED WITH EVERYTHING, WHICH IS THE MOST IMPORTANT THING.
THANKS A LOT, SAORI-YOU REALLY HELPED OUT A TON.
HAHAHA-YOU NEEDN'T THANK ME FOR ANY-THING.
KYOUSUKE-SAN, YOU TRULY ARE A VERY POLITE SISCON, AREN'T YOU?
WHOA-CUT IT OUT-I'M NO SISCON IN ANY WAY, SHAPE, OR FORM.
UM-
WOULD YOU MIND GIVING ME BACK MY COAT?

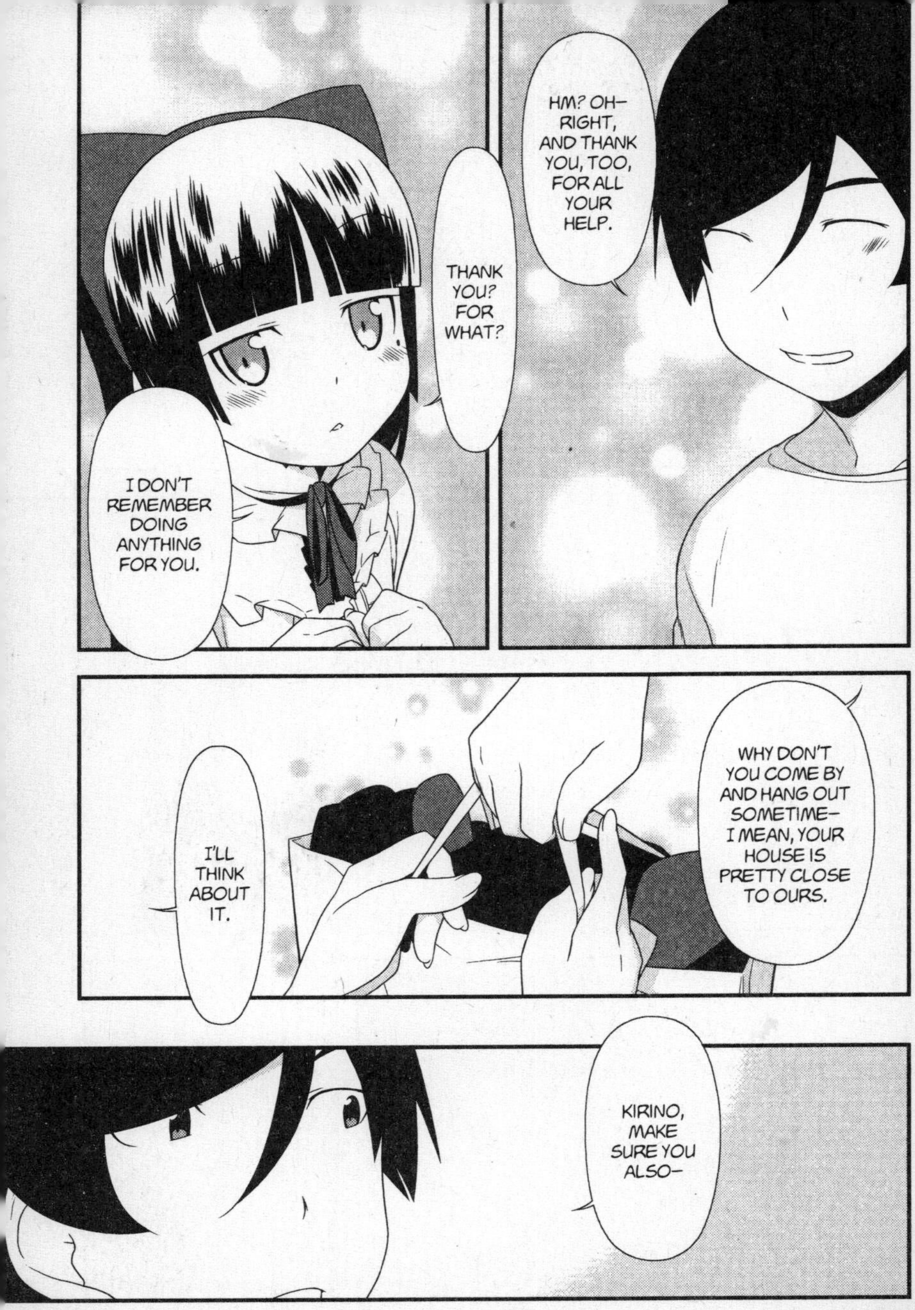
HM? OH— RIGHT, AND THANK YOU, TOO, FOR ALL YOUR HELP.
THANK YOU? FOR WHAT?
I DON'T REMEMBER DOING ANYTHING FOR YOU.
WHY DON'T YOU COME BY AND HANG OUT SOMETIME— I MEAN, YOUR HOUSE IS PRETTY CLOSE TO OURS.
I'LL THINK ABOUT IT.
KIRINO, MAKE SURE YOU ALSO—

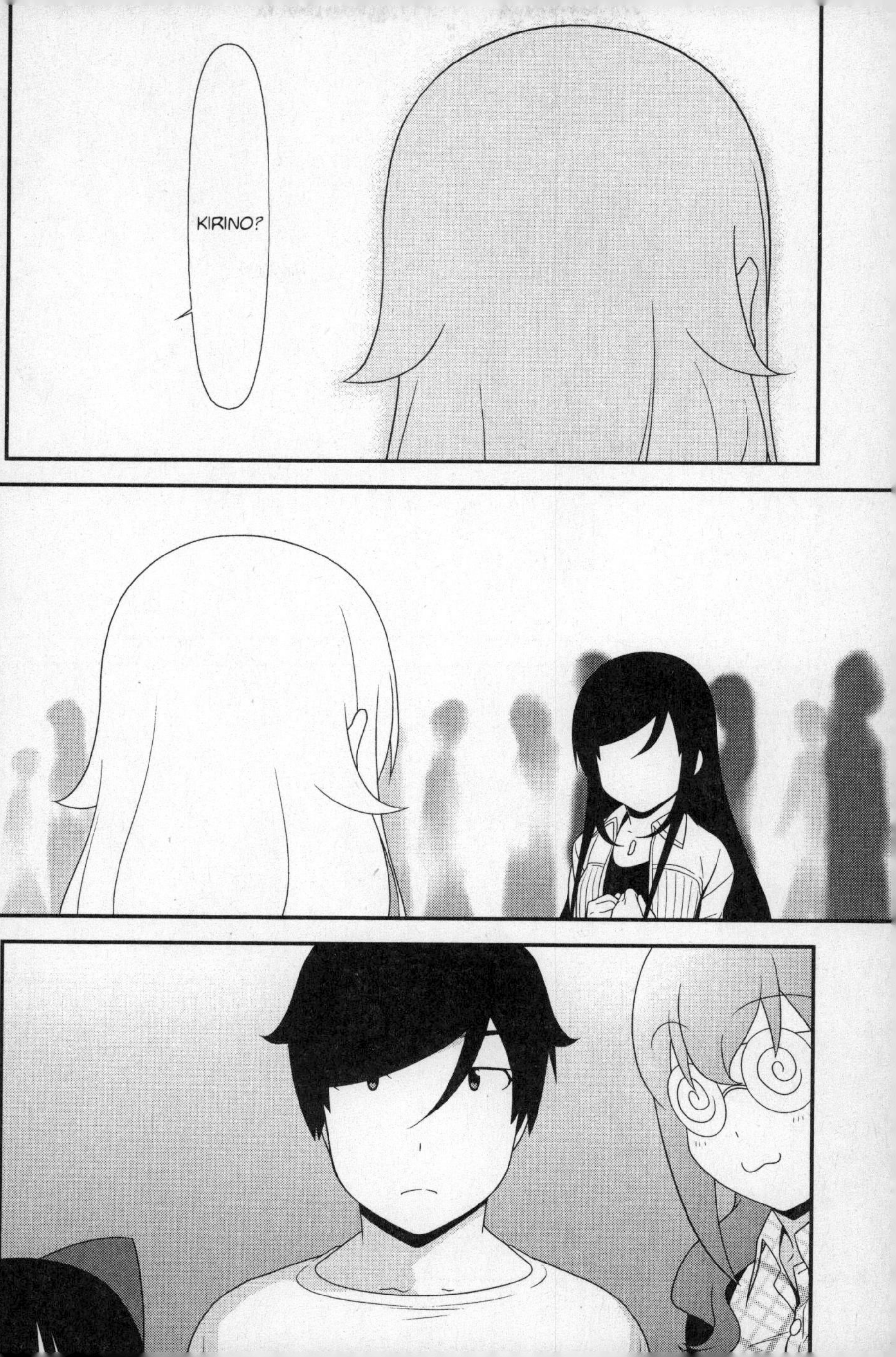
KIRINO?

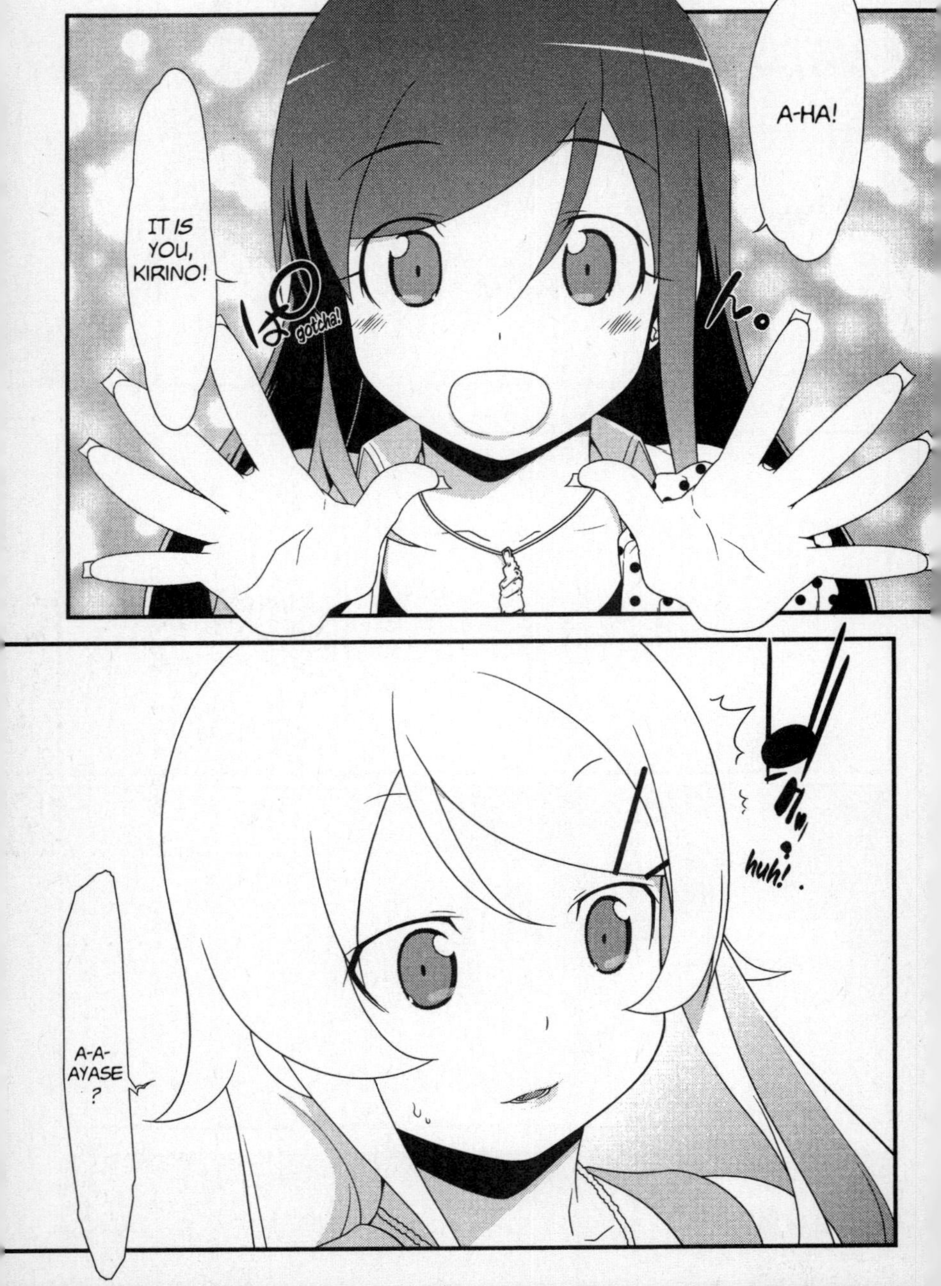
A-HA!
IT IS YOU, KIRINO!
gotcha!
huh!
A-A-AYASE?

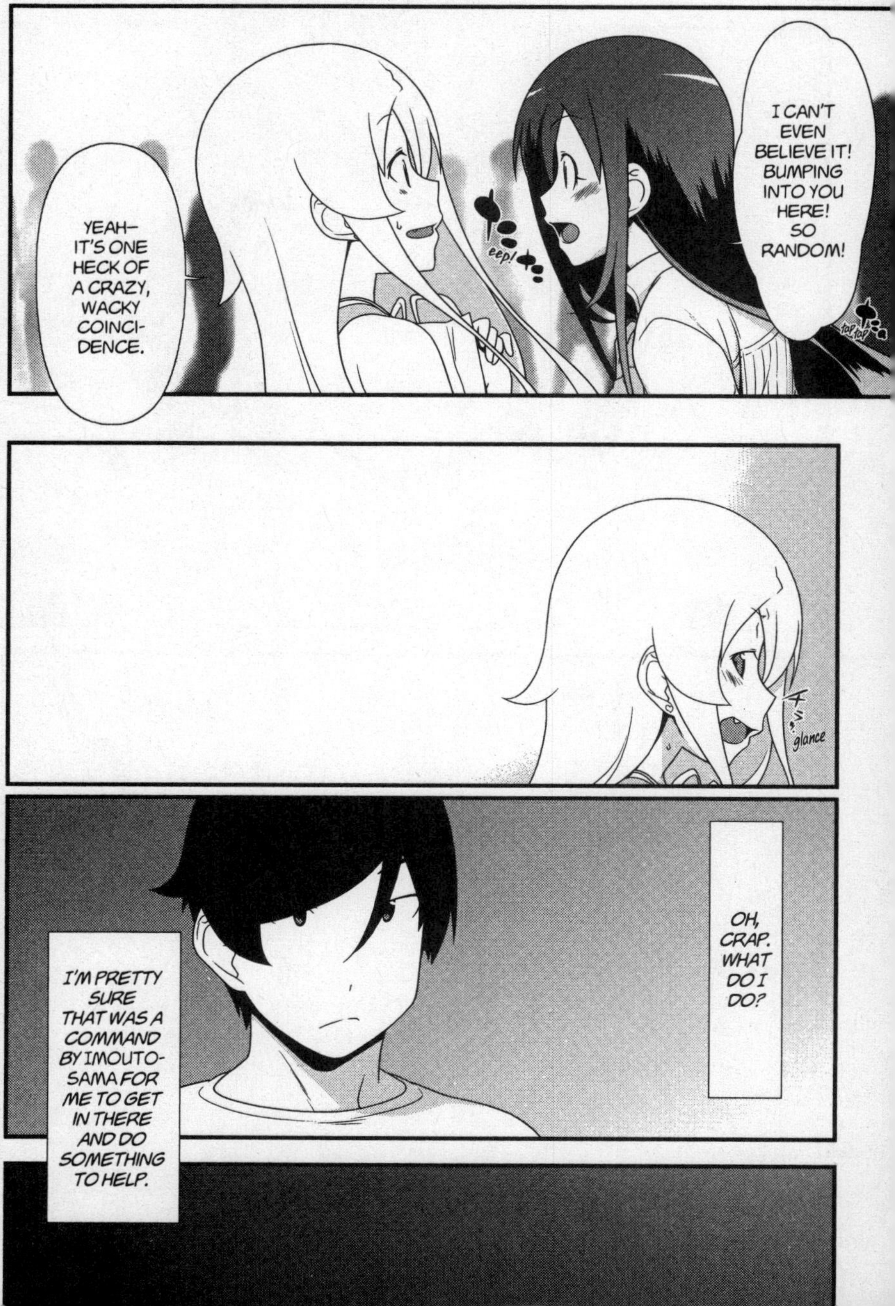
I CAN'T EVEN BELIEVE IT! BUMPING INTO YOU HERE! SO RANDOM!
tap tap
eep!
YEAH— IT'S ONE HECK OF A CRAZY, WACKY COINCIDENCE.
glance
OH, CRAP. WHAT DO I DO?
I'M PRETTY SURE THAT WAS A COMMAND BY IMOUTO-SAMA FOR ME TO GET IN THERE AND DO SOMETHING TO HELP.

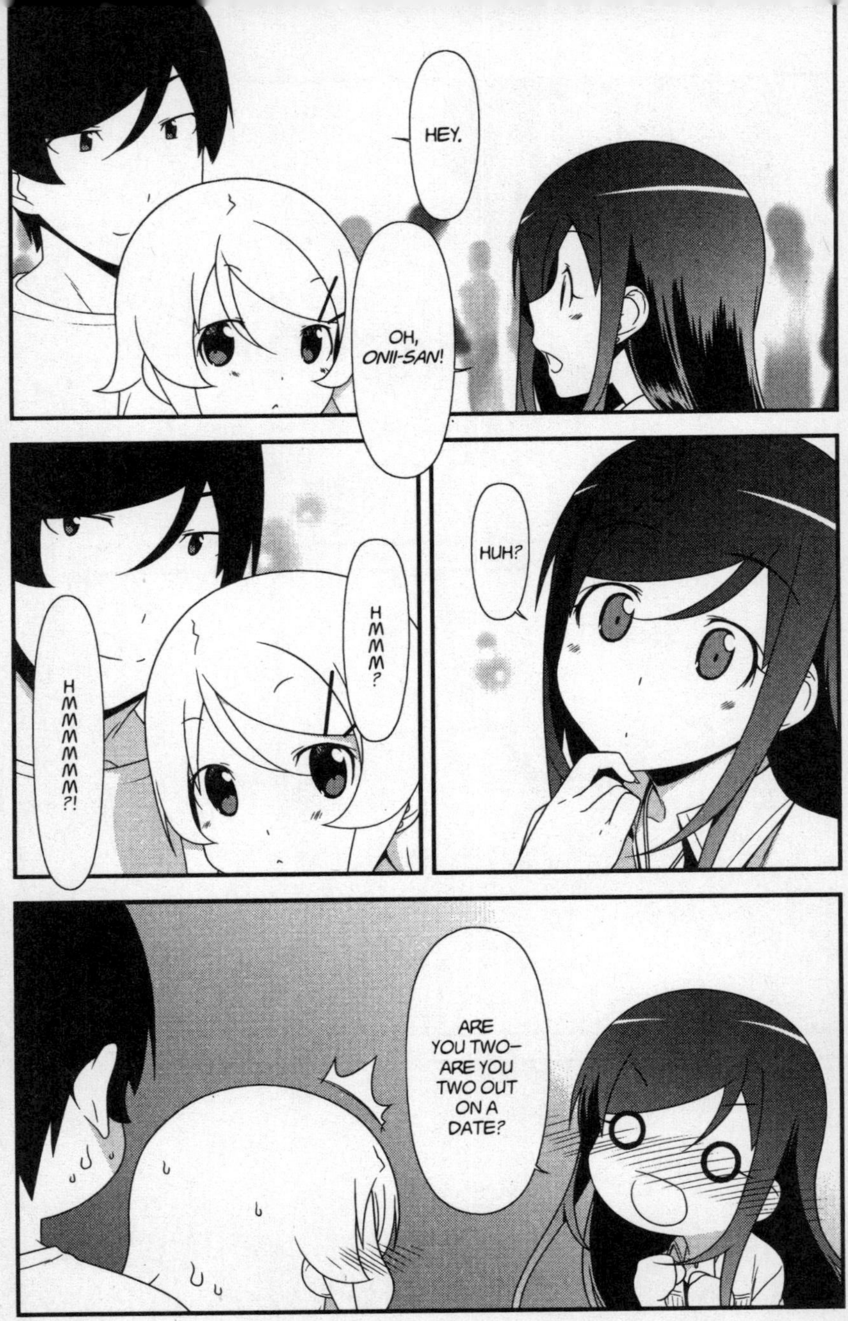
HEY.
OH, ONII-SAN!
HUH?
HMMM?
HMMMMMMMM?!
ARE YOU TWO—ARE YOU TWO OUT ON A DATE?

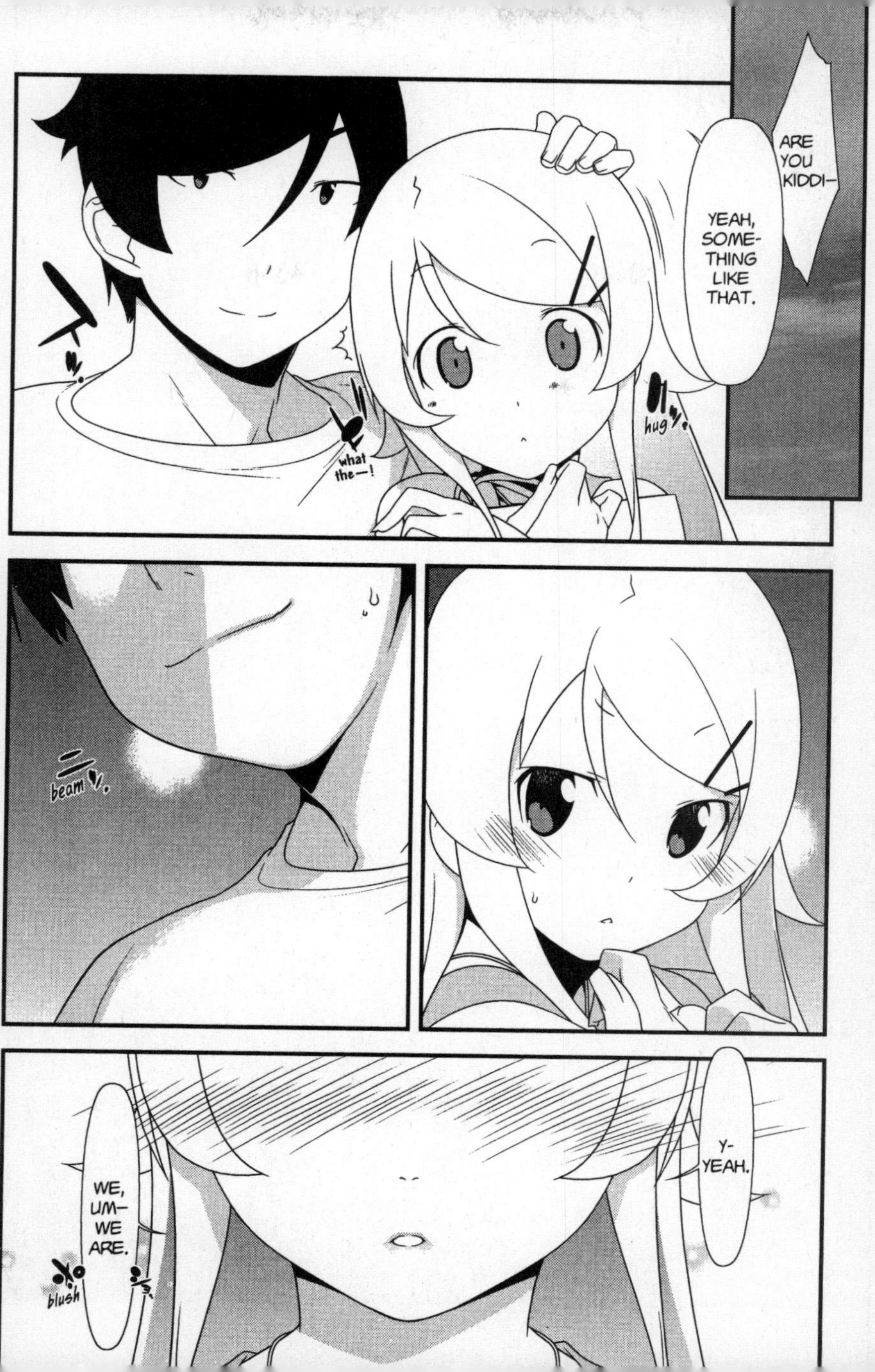
ARE YOU KIDDI—
YEAH, SOMETHING LIKE THAT.
hug
what the—!
beam
Y-YEAH.
WE, UM— WE ARE.
blush

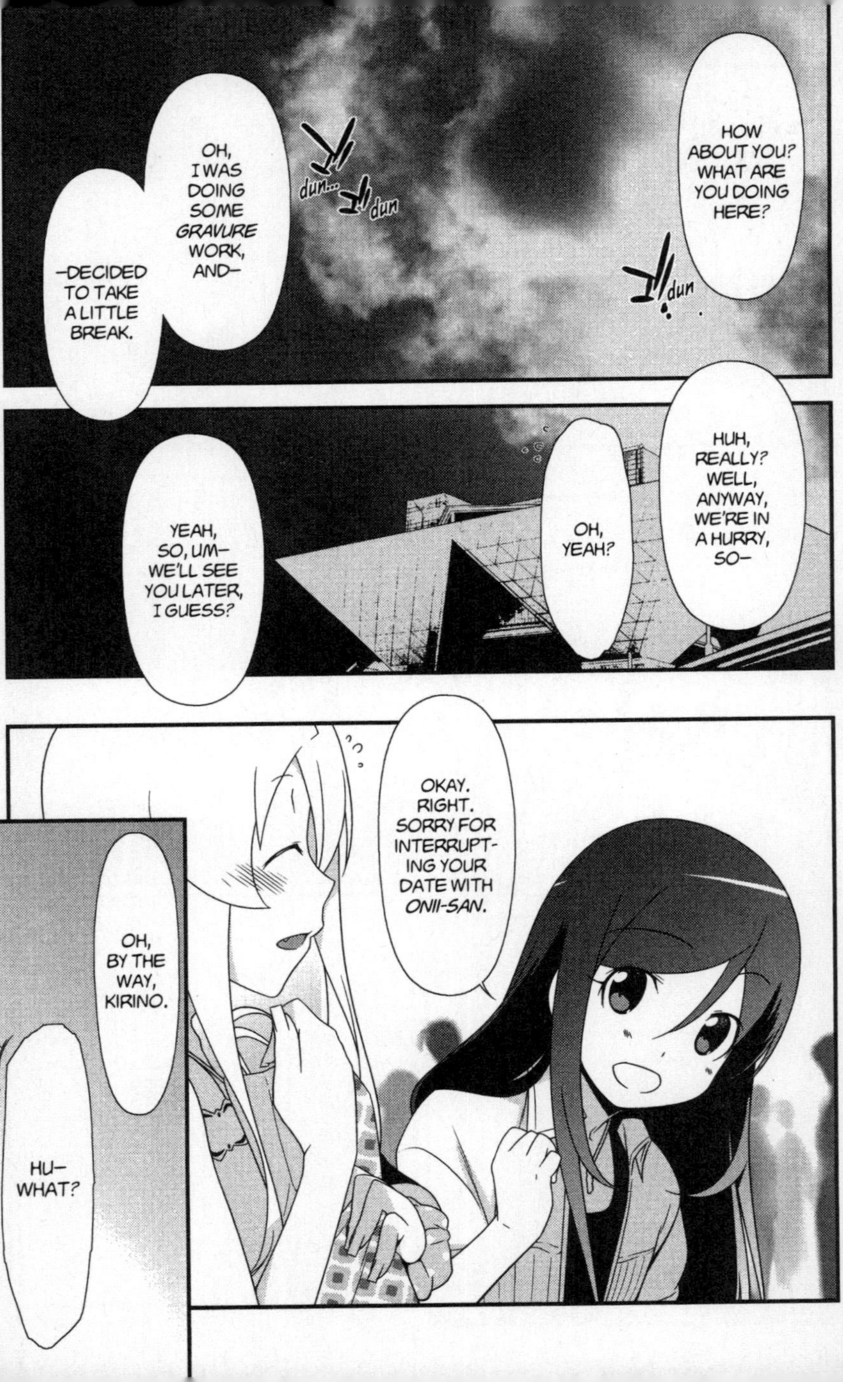
HOW ABOUT YOU? WHAT ARE YOU DOING HERE?
dun
dun... dun
OH, I WAS DOING SOME GRAVURE WORK, AND—
—DECIDED TO TAKE A LITTLE BREAK.
HUH, REALLY? WELL, ANYWAY, WE'RE IN A HURRY, SO—
OH, YEAH?
YEAH, SO, UM— WE'LL SEE YOU LATER, I GUESS?
OKAY. RIGHT. SORRY FOR INTERRUPTING YOUR DATE WITH ONII-SAN.
OH, BY THE WAY, KIRINO.
HU— WHAT?

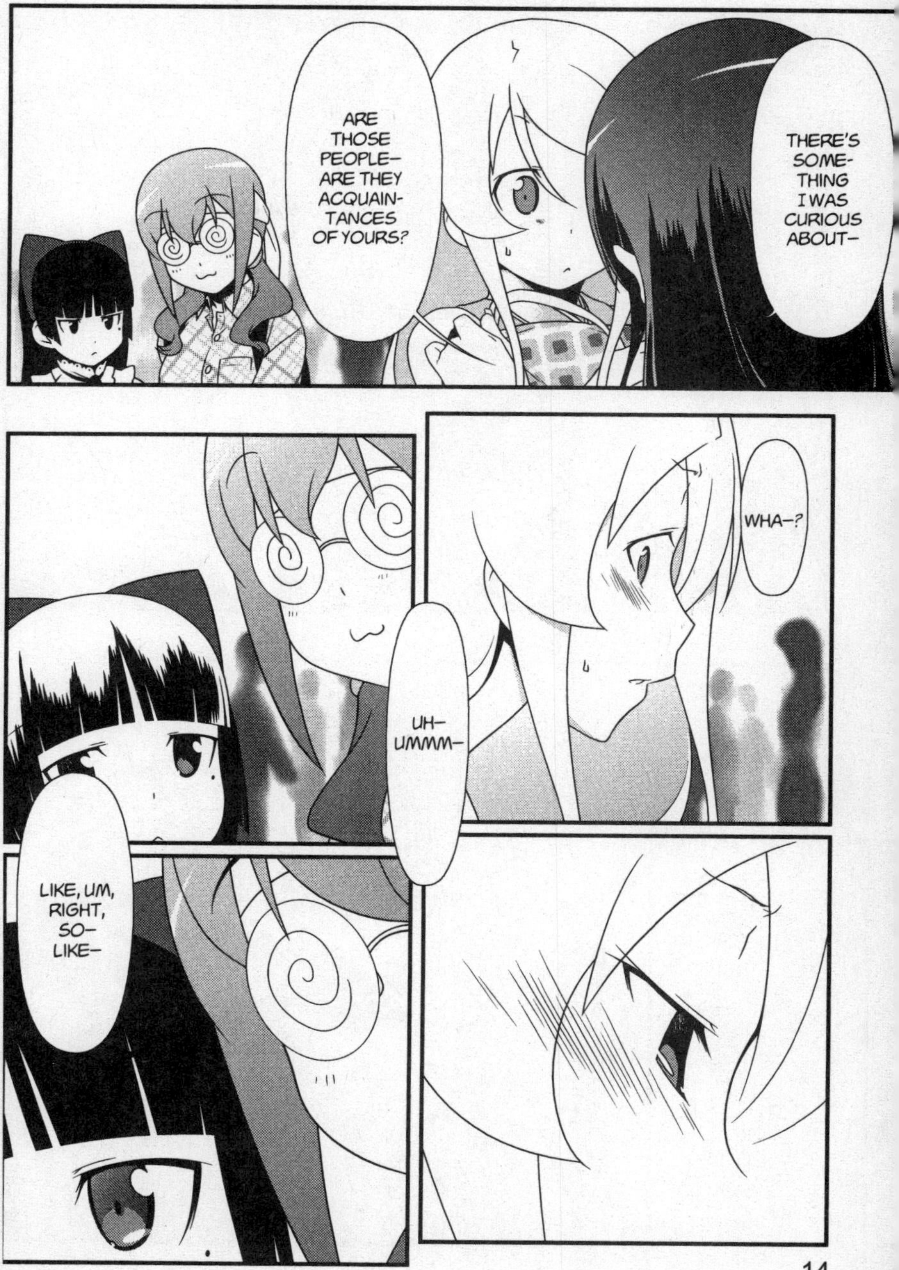
THERE'S SOME-THING I WAS CURIOUS ABOUT—
ARE THOSE PEOPLE— ARE THEY ACQUAIN-TANCES OF YOURS?
WHA—?
UH— UMMM—
LIKE, UM, RIGHT, SO— LIKE—

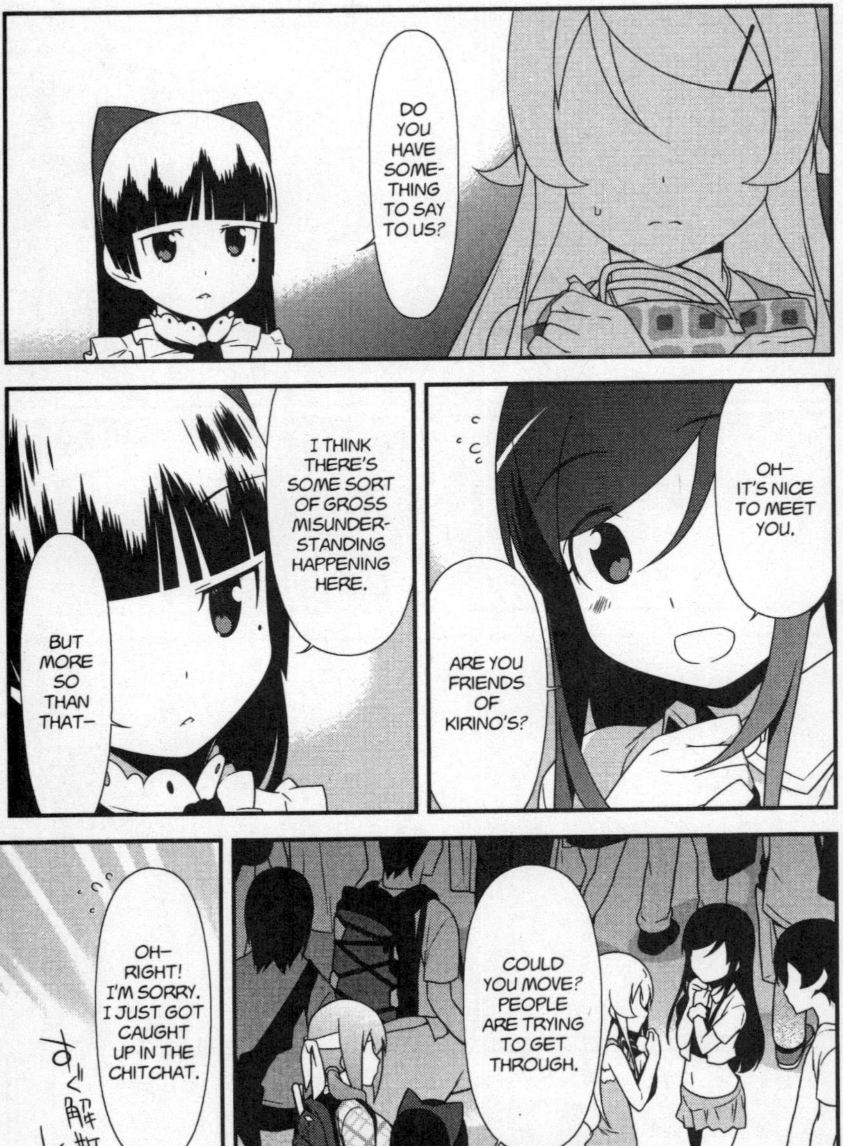
DO YOU HAVE SOME-THING TO SAY TO US?
OH— IT'S NICE TO MEET YOU.
ARE YOU FRIENDS OF KIRINO'S?
I THINK THERE'S SOME SORT OF GROSS MISUNDER-STANDING HAPPENING HERE.
BUT MORE SO THAN THAT—
COULD YOU MOVE? PEOPLE ARE TRYING TO GET THROUGH.
OH— RIGHT! I'M SORRY. I JUST GOT CAUGHT UP IN THE CHITCHAT.
すぐ解散します
I'll just be on my way...

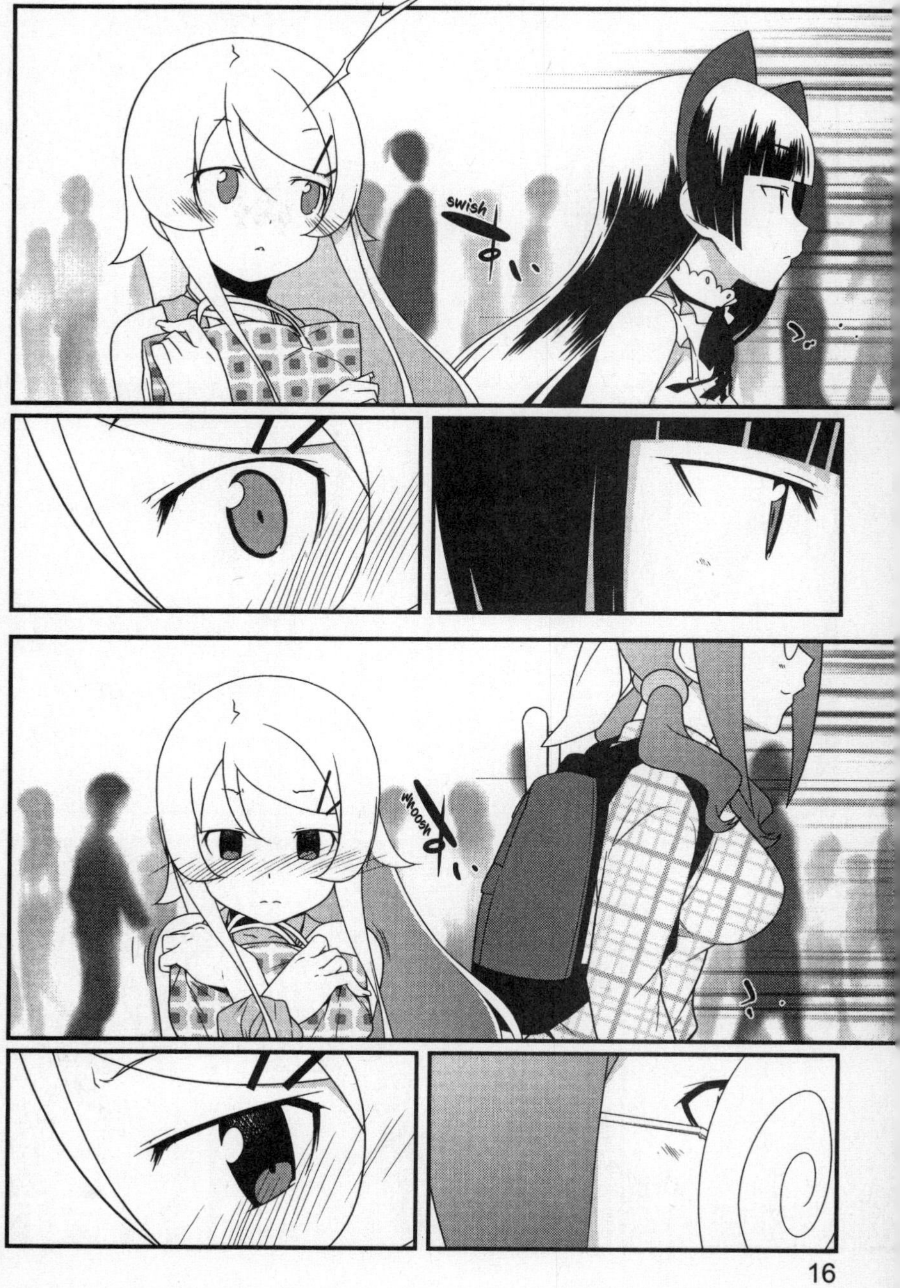
swish
whoosh

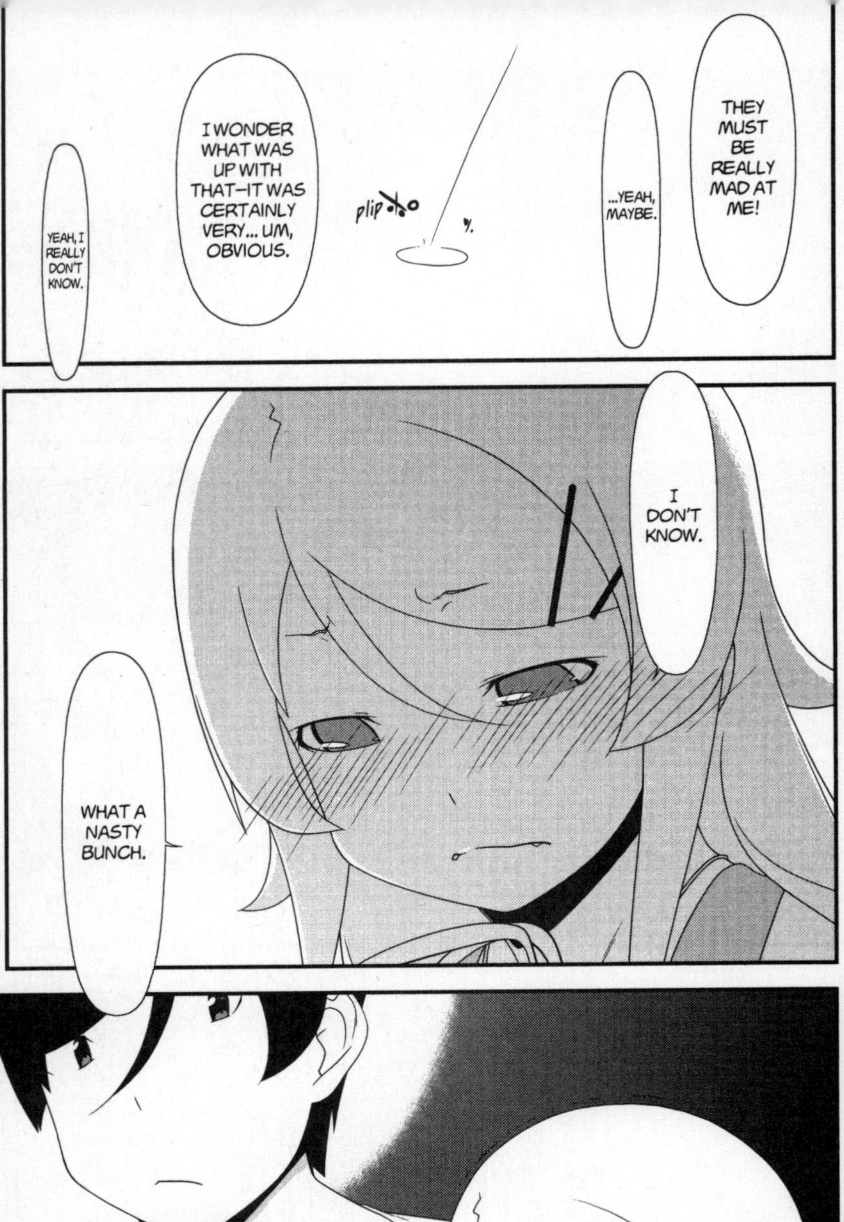
THEY MUST BE REALLY MAD AT ME!
...YEAH, MAYBE.
plip
I WONDER WHAT WAS UP WITH THAT—IT WAS CERTAINLY VERY... UM, OBVIOUS.
YEAH, I REALLY DON'T KNOW.
I DON'T KNOW.
WHAT A NASTY BUNCH.

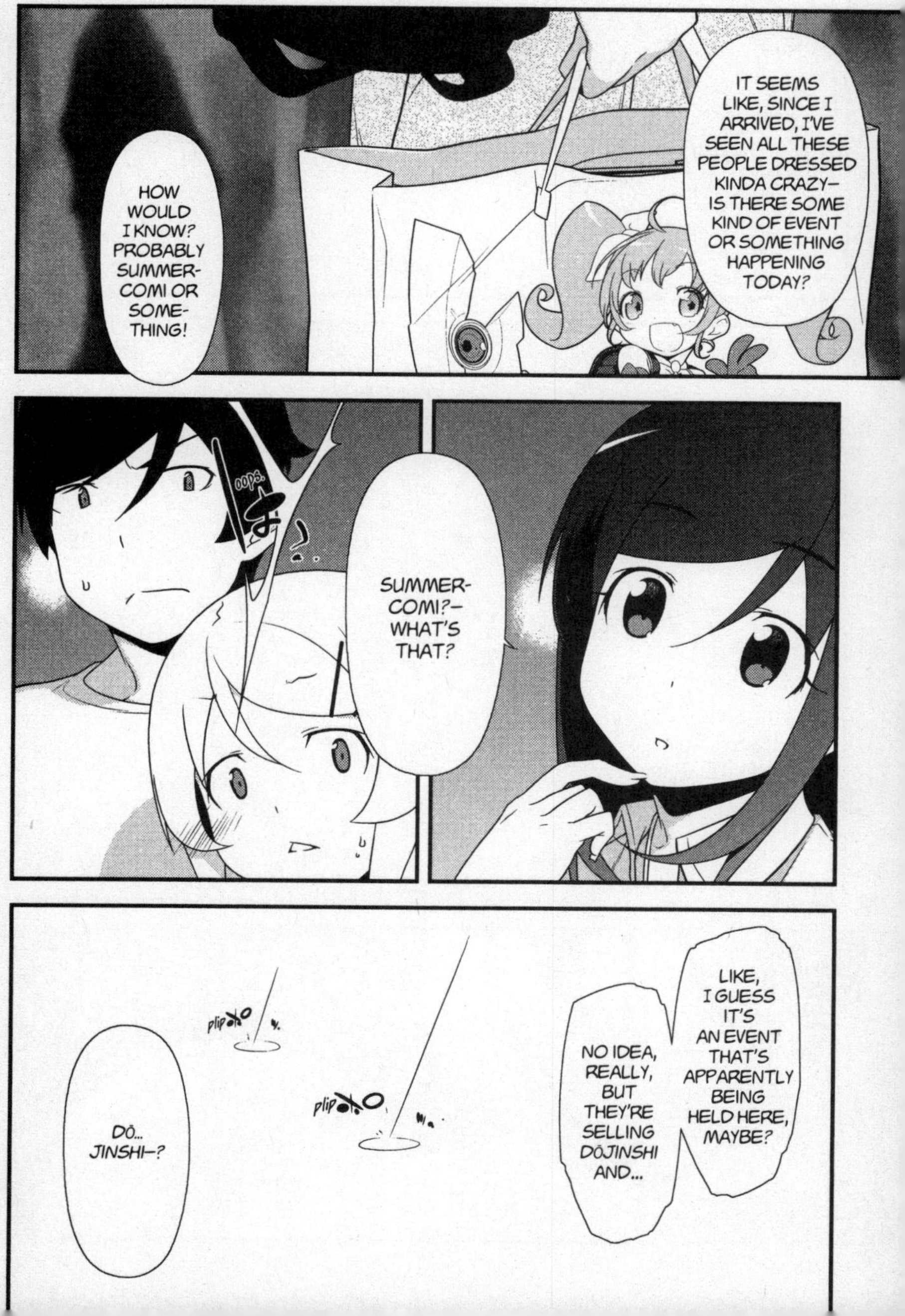
IT SEEMS LIKE, SINCE I ARRIVED, I'VE SEEN ALL THESE PEOPLE DRESSED KINDA CRAZY— IS THERE SOME KIND OF EVENT OR SOMETHING HAPPENING TODAY?
HOW WOULD I KNOW? PROBABLY SUMMER-COMI OR SOME-THING!
SUMMER-COMI?— WHAT'S THAT?
oops.
LIKE, I GUESS IT'S AN EVENT THAT'S APPARENTLY BEING HELD HERE, MAYBE?
NO IDEA, REALLY, BUT THEY'RE SELLING DŌJINSHI AND...
plip
plip
DŌ... JINSHI—?

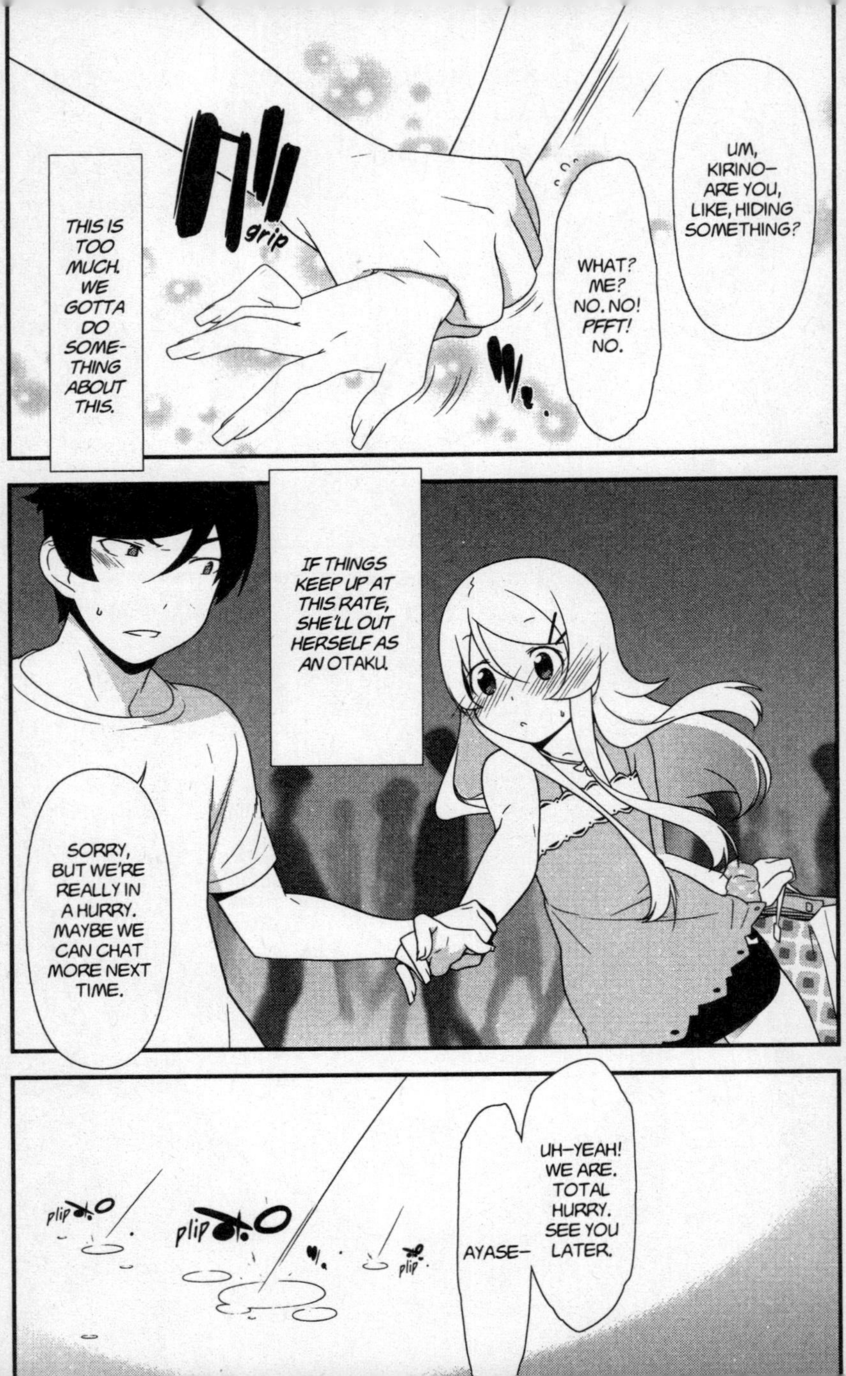
UM, KIRINO— ARE YOU, LIKE, HIDING SOMETHING?
WHAT? ME? NO. NO! PFFT! NO.
grip
THIS IS TOO MUCH. WE GOTTA DO SOME-THING ABOUT THIS.
IF THINGS KEEP UP AT THIS RATE, SHE'LL OUT HERSELF AS AN OTAKU.
SORRY, BUT WE'RE REALLY IN A HURRY. MAYBE WE CAN CHAT MORE NEXT TIME.
UH—YEAH! WE ARE. TOTAL HURRY. SEE YOU LATER.
AYASE—
plip
plip
plip

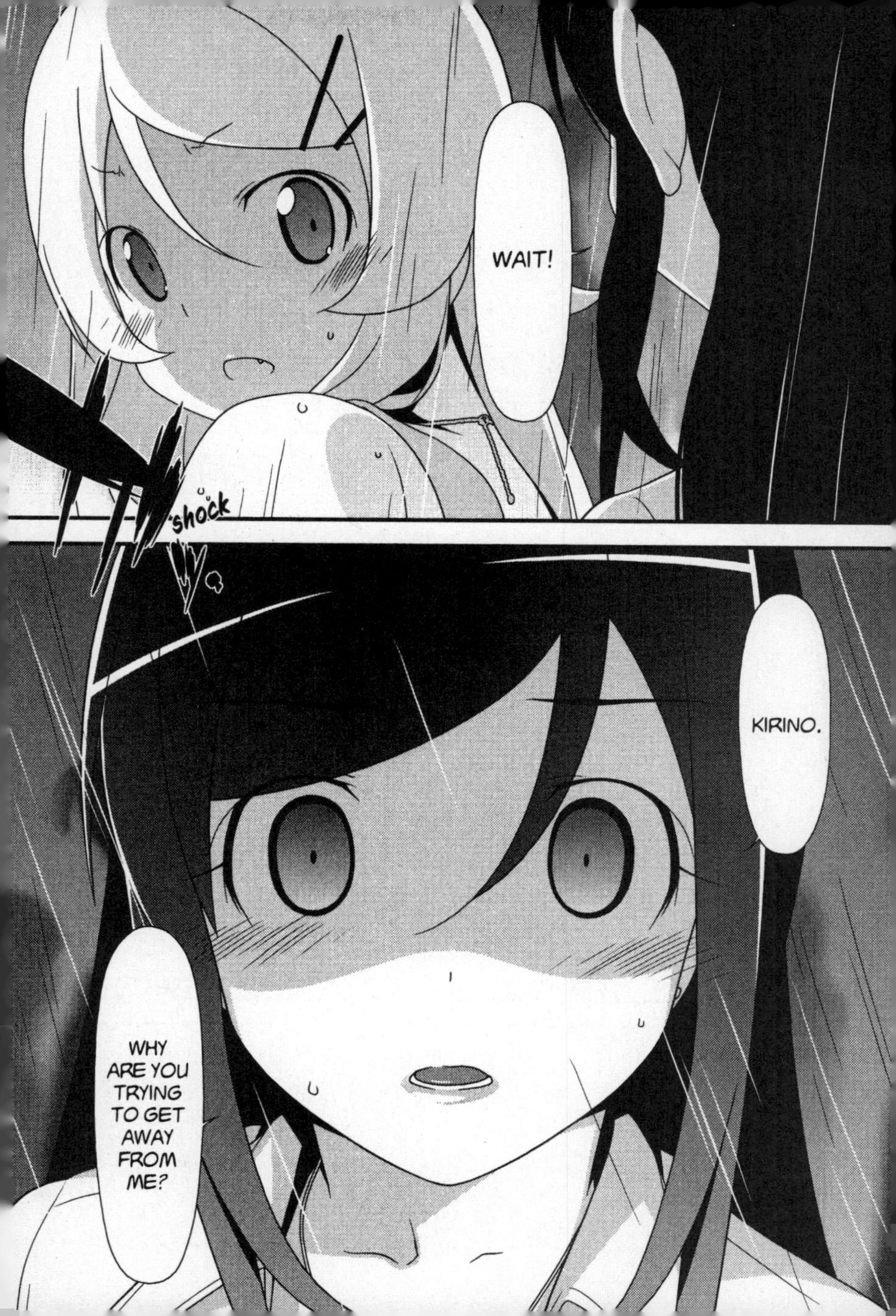
WAIT!
shock
KIRINO.
WHY ARE YOU TRYING TO GET AWAY FROM ME?

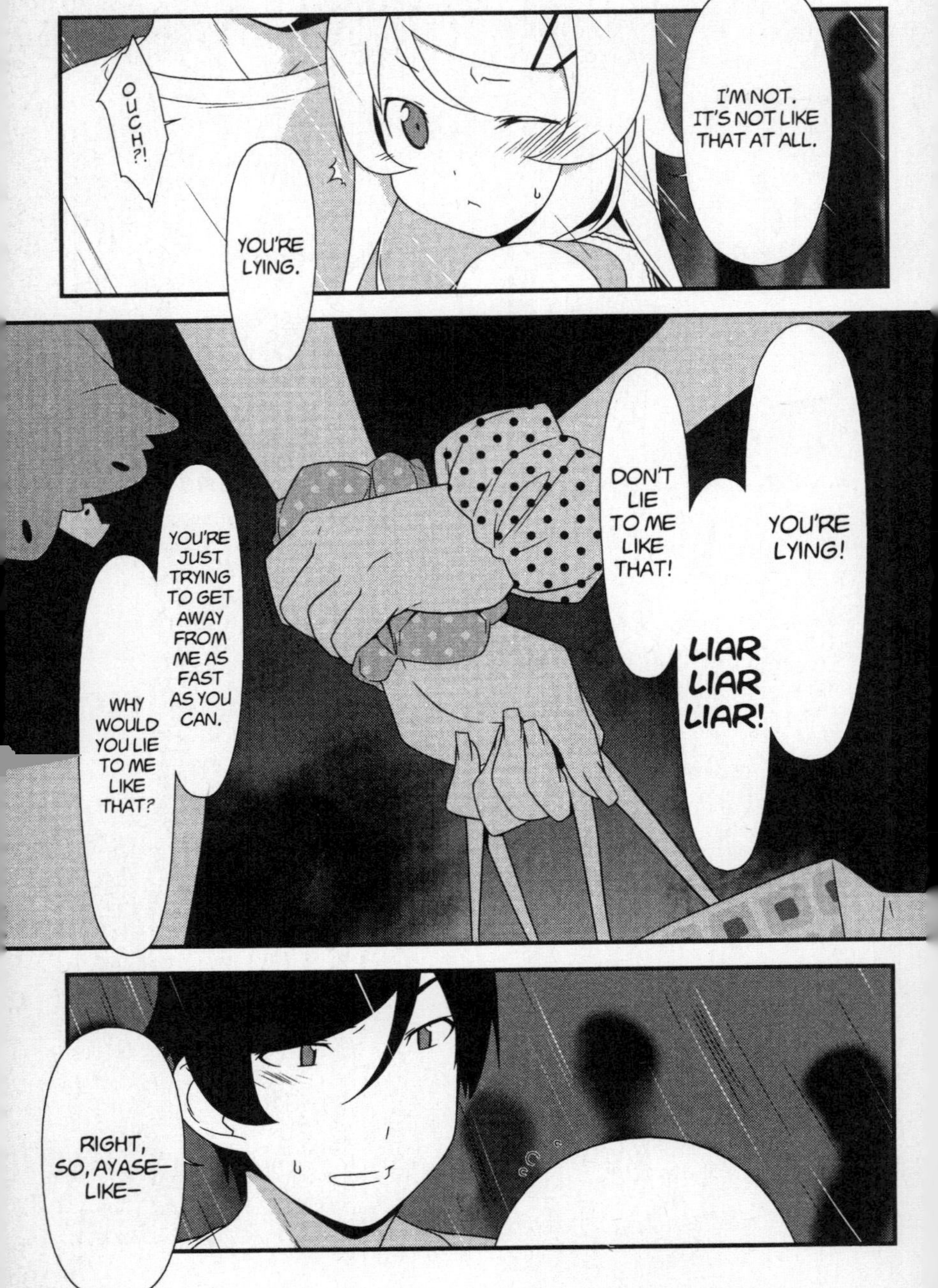
I'M NOT. IT'S NOT LIKE THAT AT ALL.
YOU'RE LYING.
OUCH?!
YOU'RE LYING!
LIAR LIAR LIAR!
DON'T LIE TO ME LIKE THAT!
YOU'RE JUST TRYING TO GET AWAY FROM ME AS FAST AS YOU CAN.
WHY WOULD YOU LIE TO ME LIKE THAT?
RIGHT, SO, AYASE— LIKE—

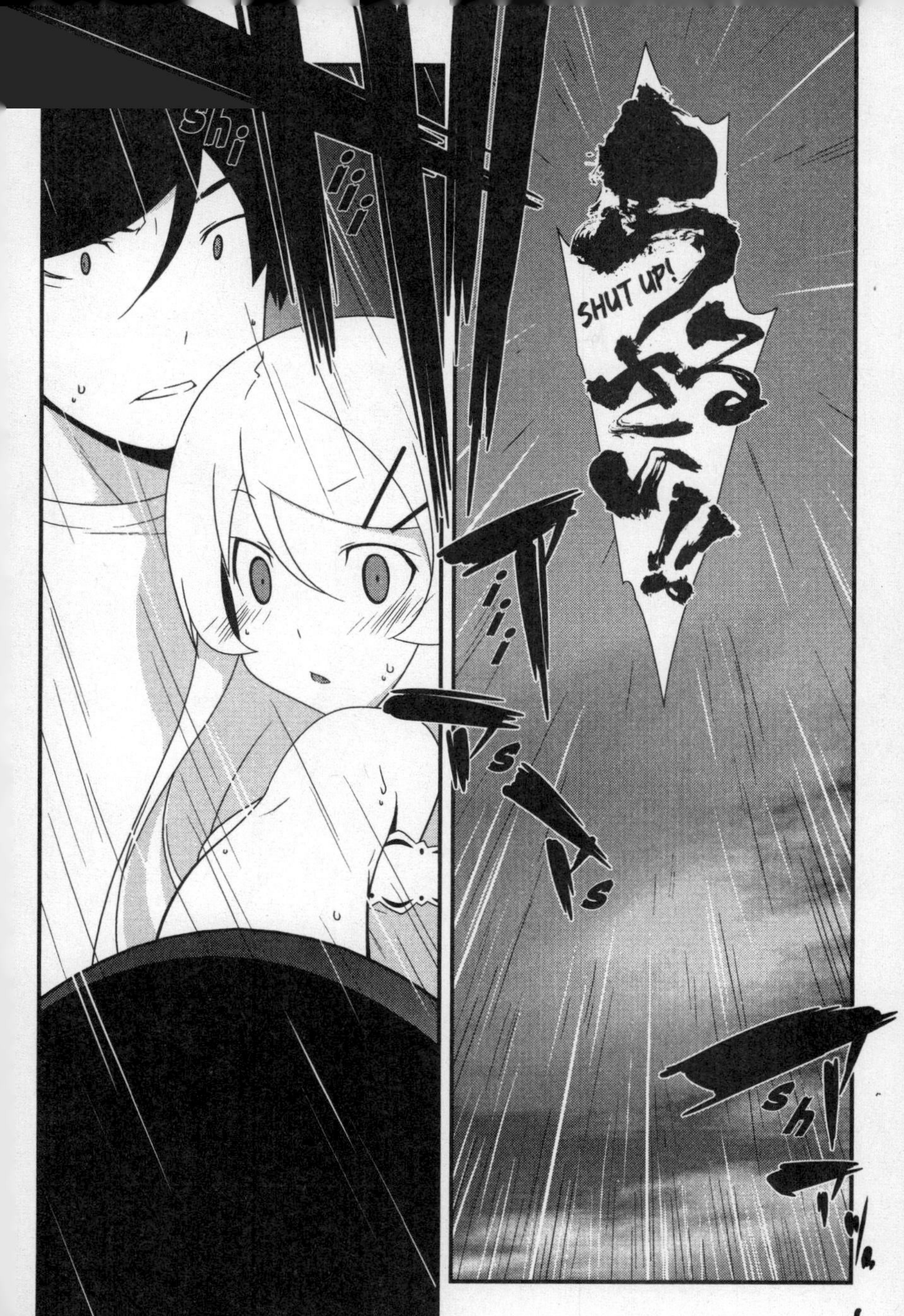
SHUT UP!
iiii
s
s
sh
shi
iii

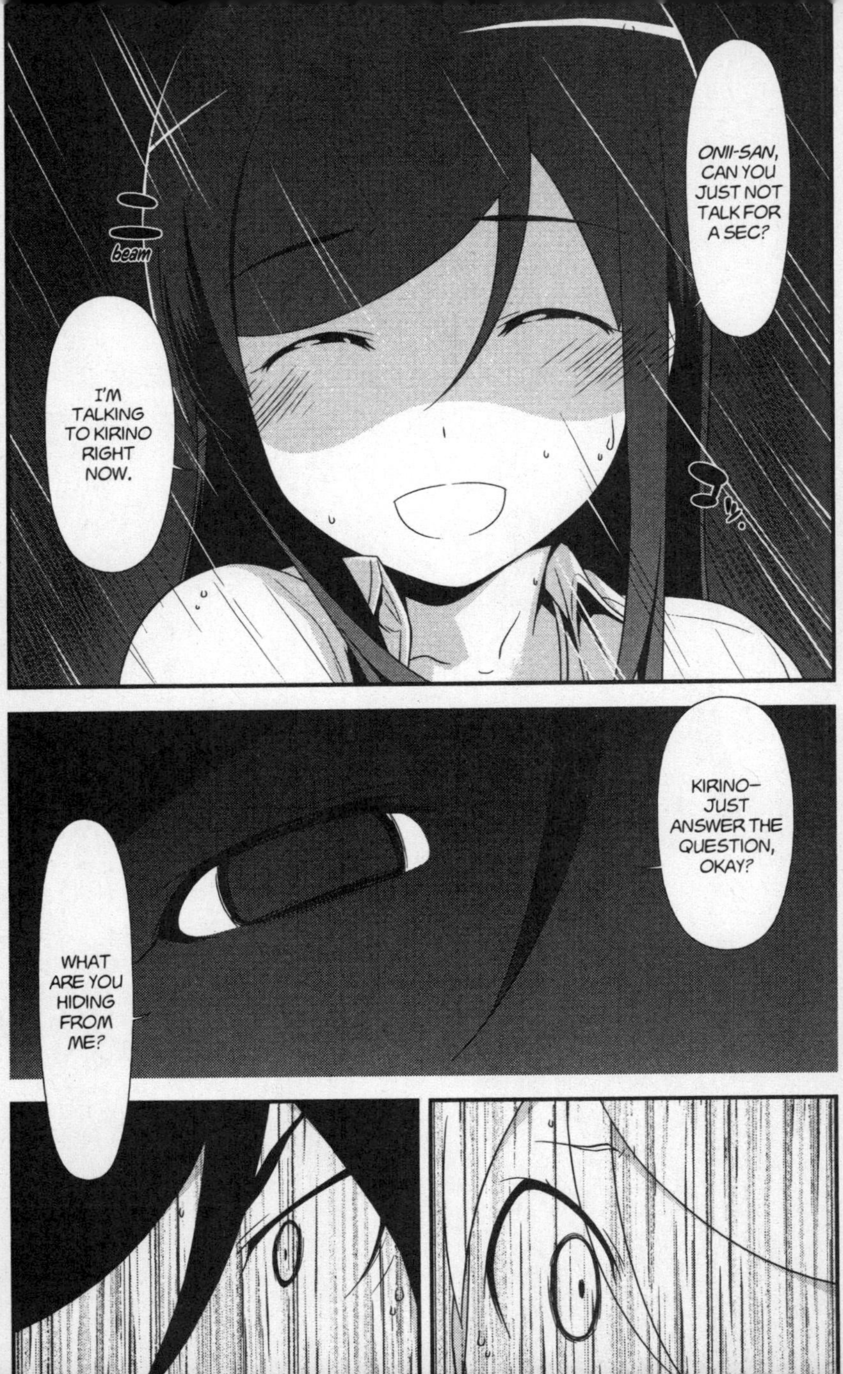
ONII-SAN, CAN YOU JUST NOT TALK FOR A SEC?
beam
I'M TALKING TO KIRINO RIGHT NOW.
KIRINO— JUST ANSWER THE QUESTION, OKAY?
WHAT ARE YOU HIDING FROM ME?

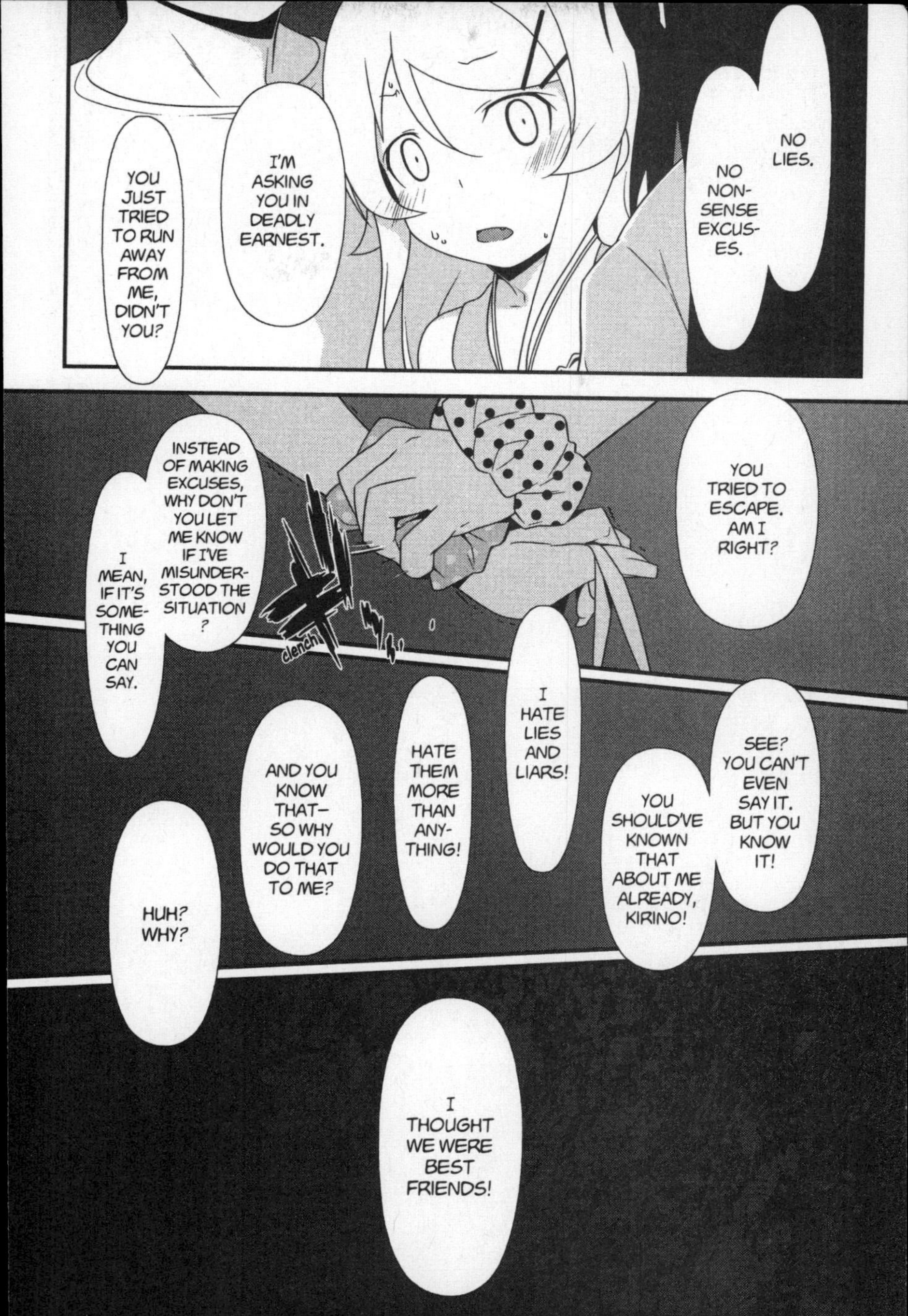
NO LIES.
NO NONSENSE EXCUSES.
I'M ASKING YOU IN DEADLY EARNEST.
YOU JUST TRIED TO RUN AWAY FROM ME, DIDN'T YOU?
YOU TRIED TO ESCAPE. AM I RIGHT?
INSTEAD OF MAKING EXCUSES, WHY DON'T YOU LET ME KNOW IF I'VE MISUNDERSTOOD THE SITUATION?
I MEAN, IF IT'S SOMETHING YOU CAN SAY.
clench!
SEE? YOU CAN'T EVEN SAY IT. BUT YOU KNOW IT!
YOU SHOULD'VE KNOWN THAT ABOUT ME ALREADY, KIRINO!
I HATE LIES AND LIARS!
HATE THEM MORE THAN ANYTHING!
AND YOU KNOW THAT— SO WHY WOULD YOU DO THAT TO ME?
HUH? WHY?
I THOUGHT WE WERE BEST FRIENDS!

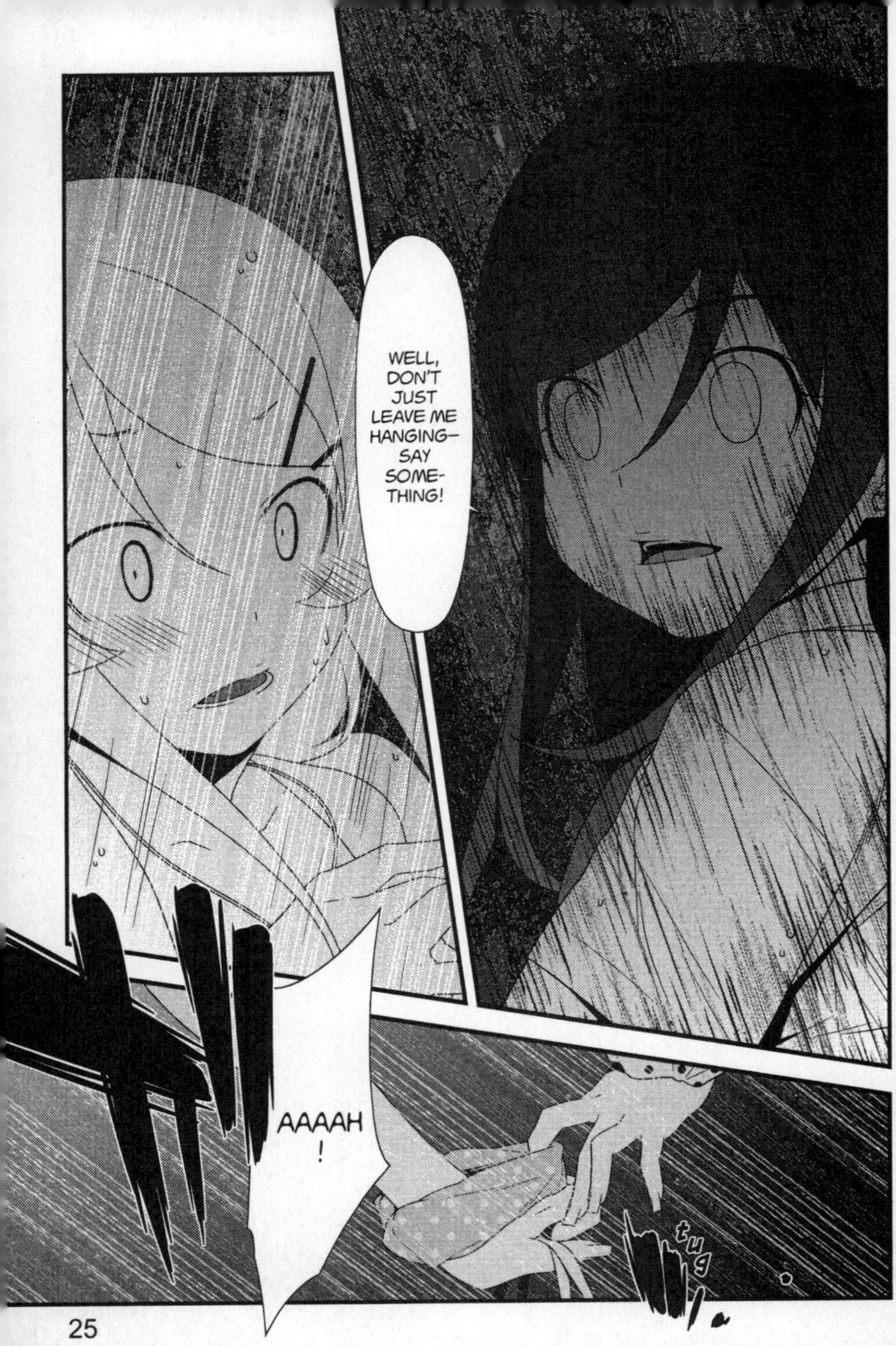
WELL, DON'T JUST LEAVE ME HANGING—SAY SOME-THING!
AAAAH!
tug

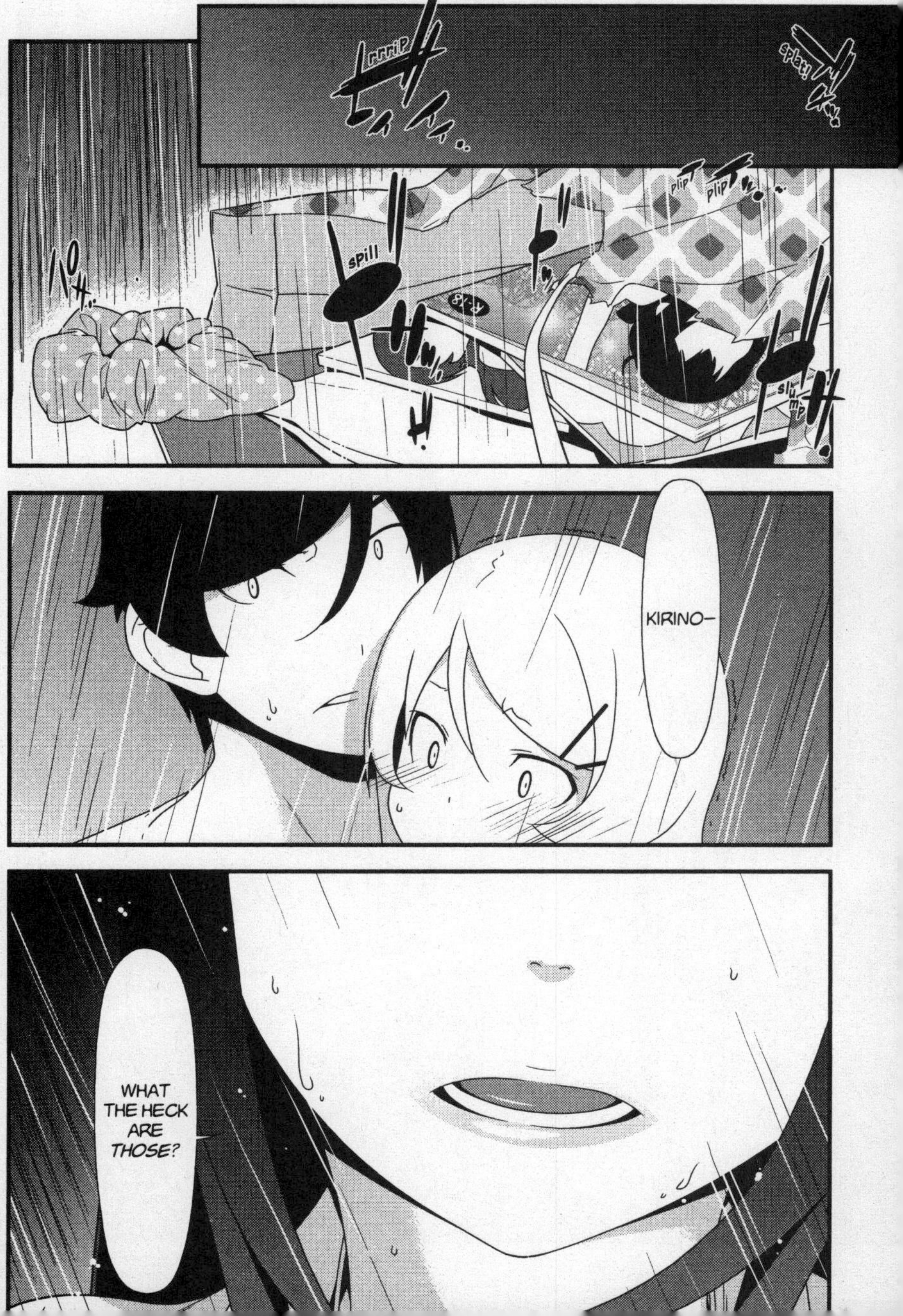
splat!
rrrip
plip
plip
slump
spill
KIRINO-
WHAT THE HECK ARE THOSE?

俺の妹が
こんなに
可愛いわけが
ない

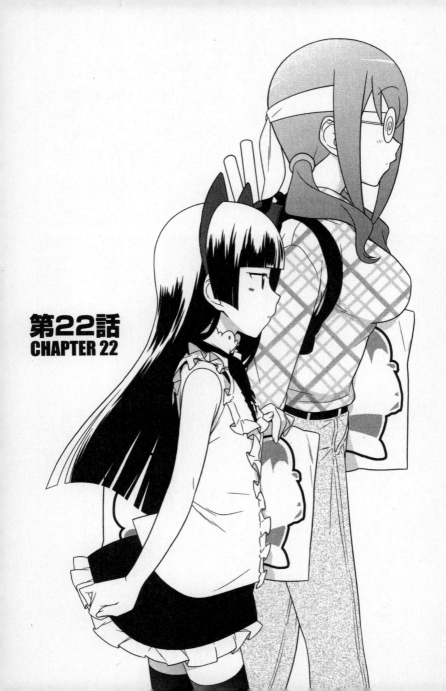

第22話
CHAPTER 22

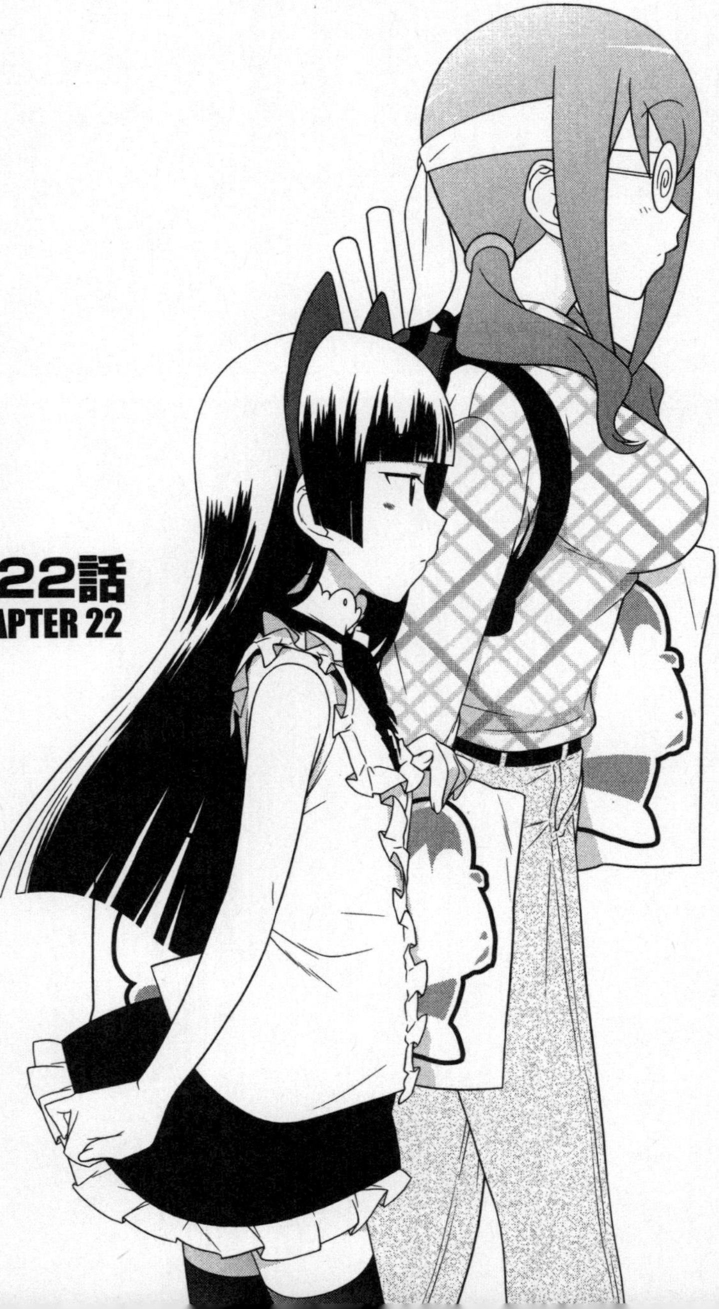

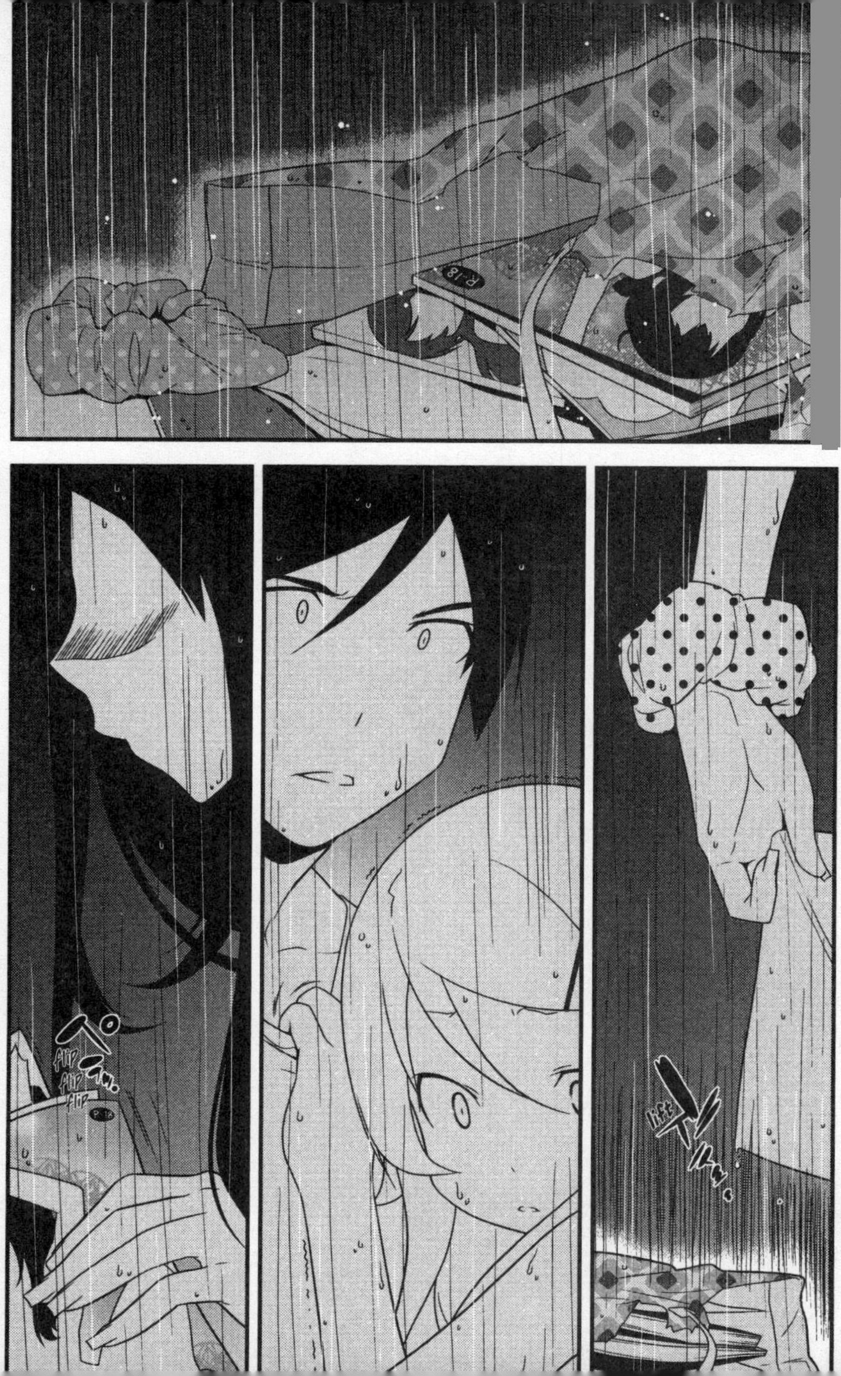
R-18
lift
flip flip flip

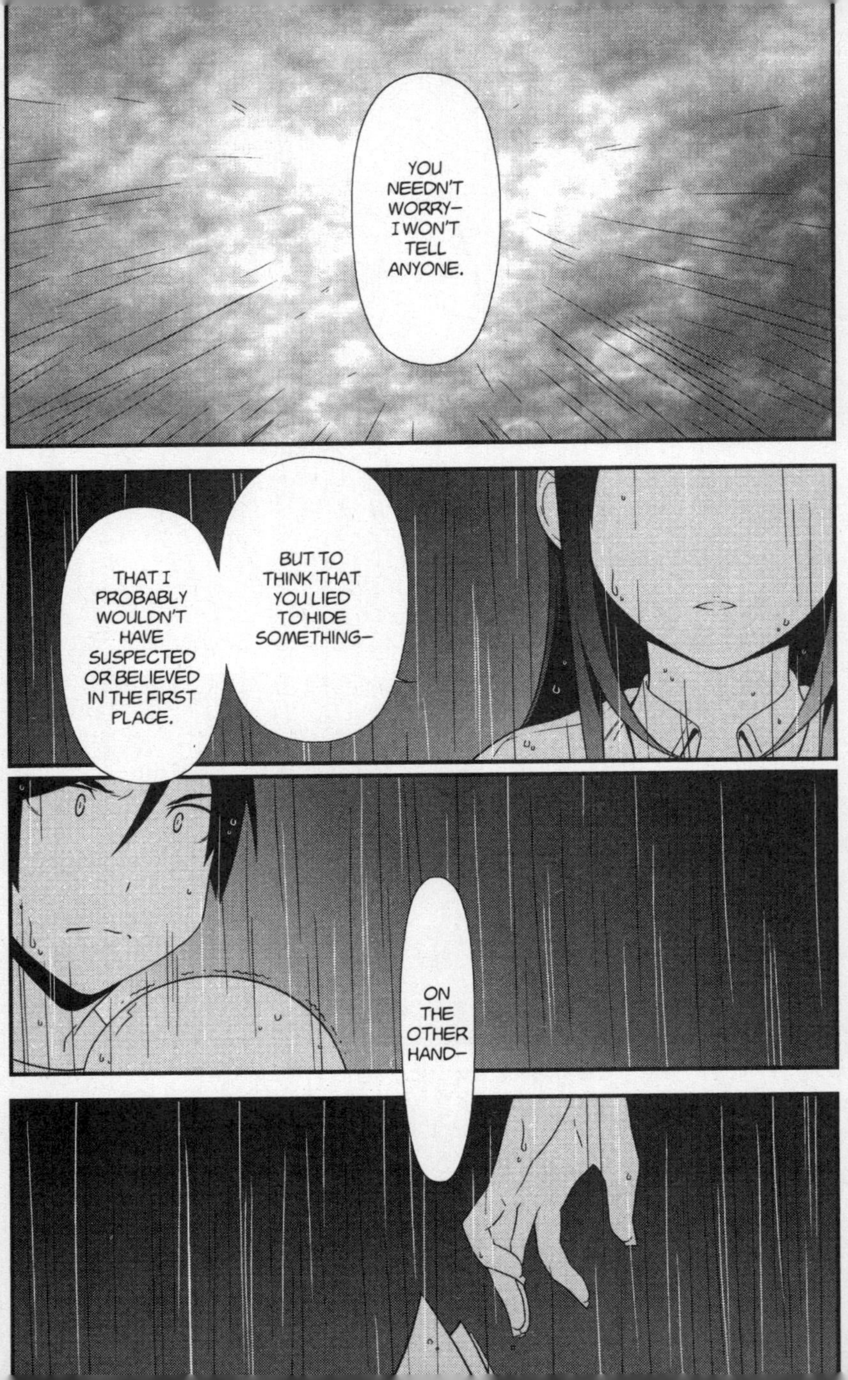
YOU NEEDN'T WORRY— I WON'T TELL ANYONE.
BUT TO THINK THAT YOU LIED TO HIDE SOMETHING—
THAT I PROBABLY WOULDN'T HAVE SUSPECTED OR BELIEVED IN THE FIRST PLACE.
ON THE OTHER HAND—

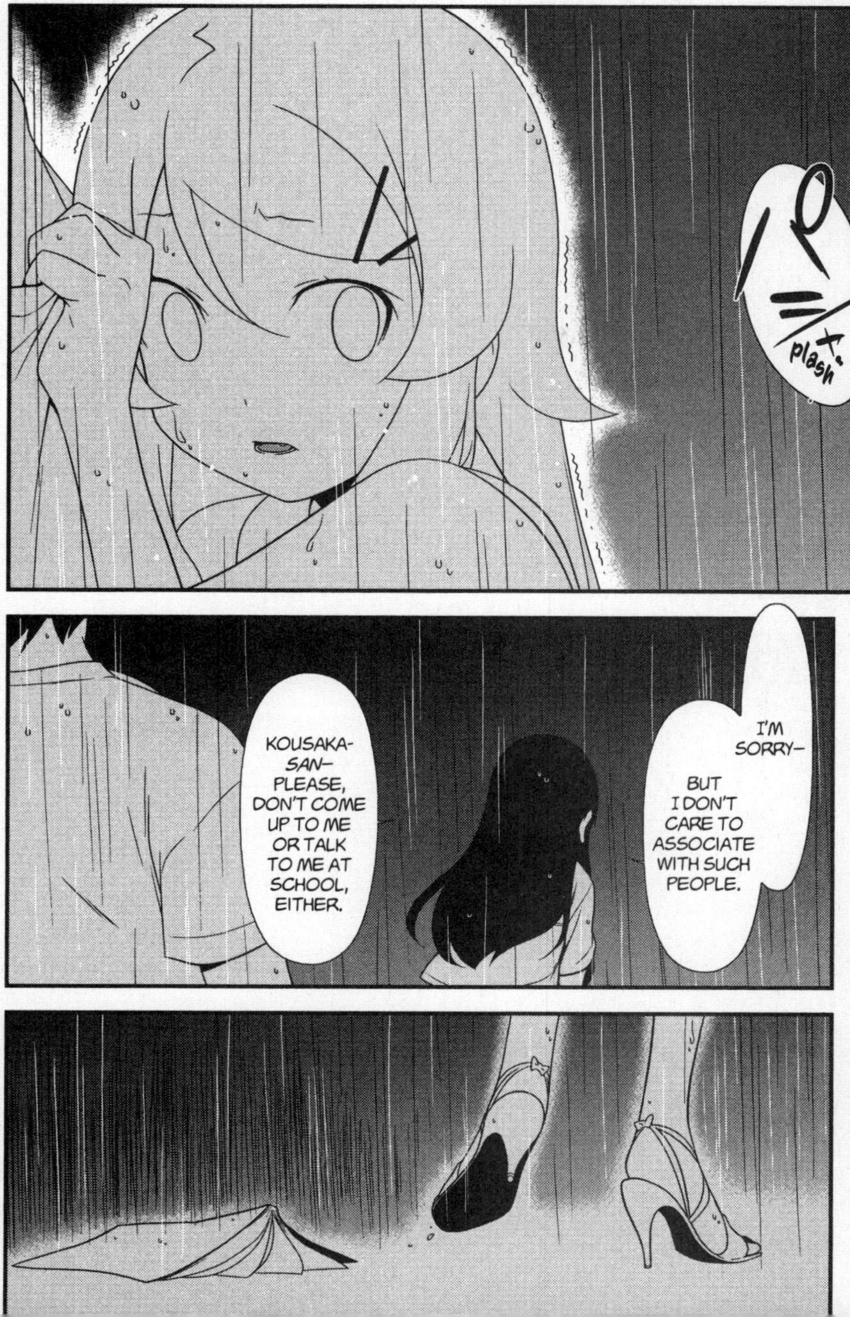
plash
I'M SORRY—
BUT I DON'T CARE TO ASSOCIATE WITH SUCH PEOPLE.
KOUSAKA-SAN—PLEASE, DON'T COME UP TO ME OR TALK TO ME AT SCHOOL, EITHER.

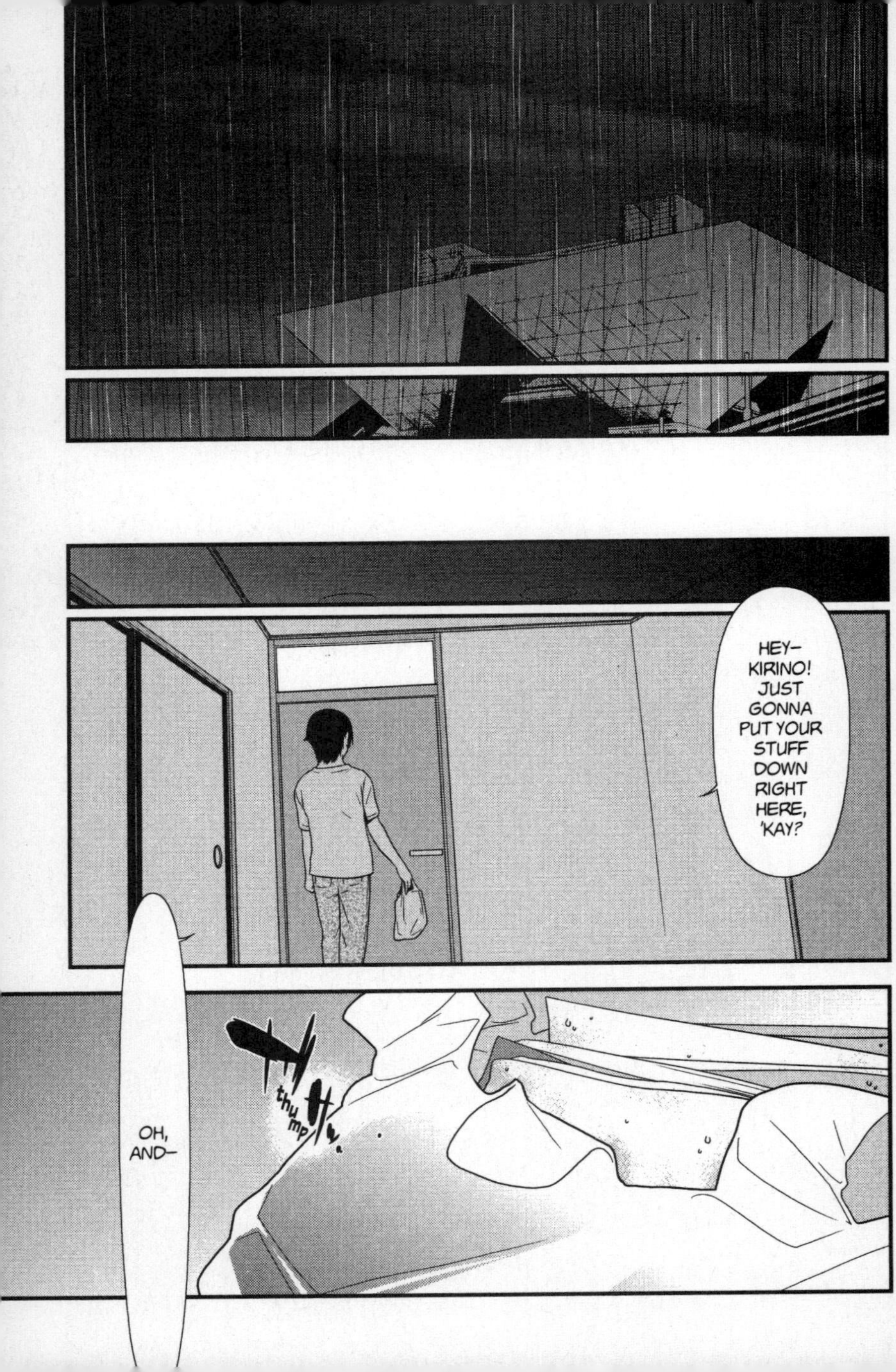
HEY– KIRINO! JUST GONNA PUT YOUR STUFF DOWN RIGHT HERE, 'KAY?
OH, AND–
thump

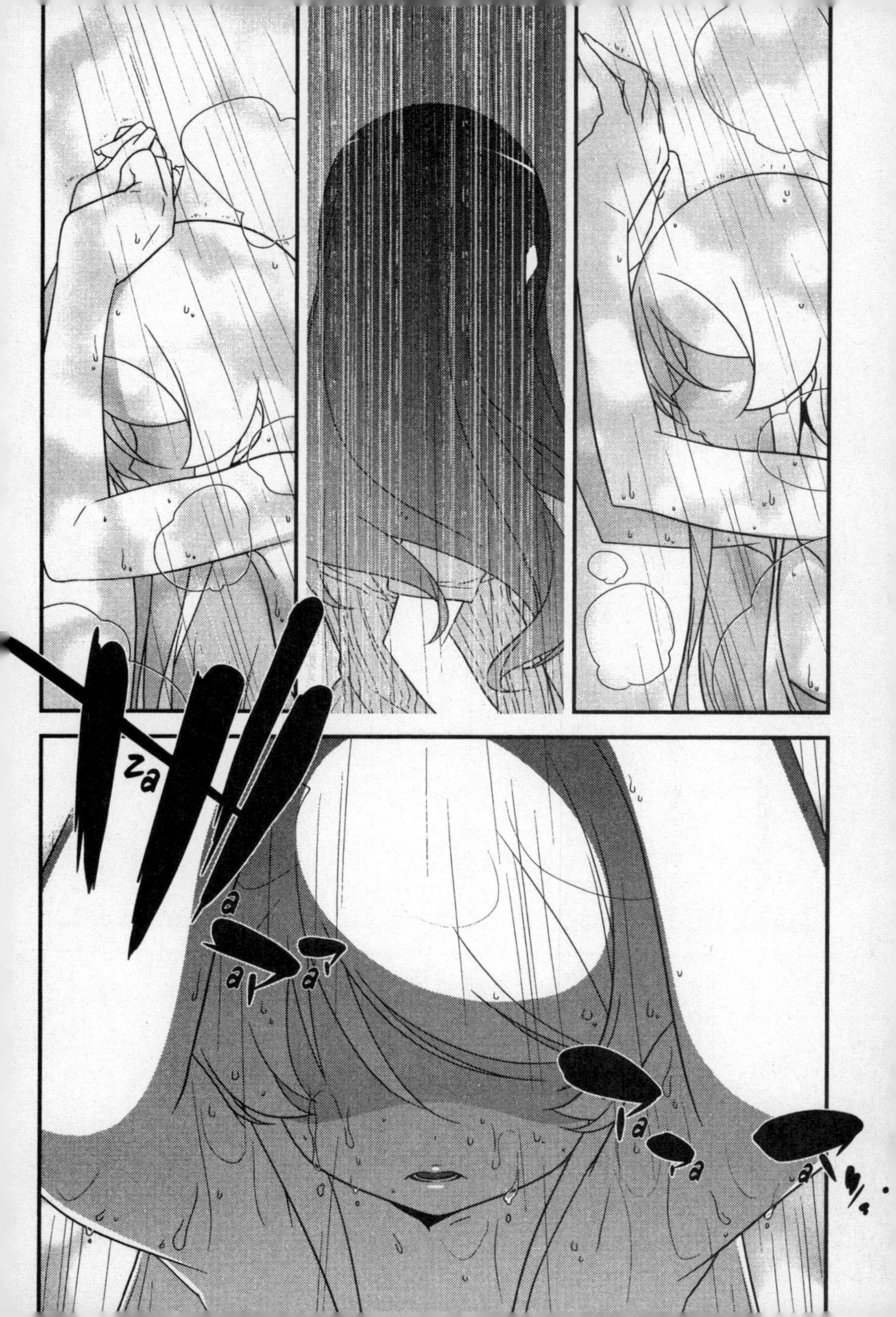
za
a
a
a
a
a
a

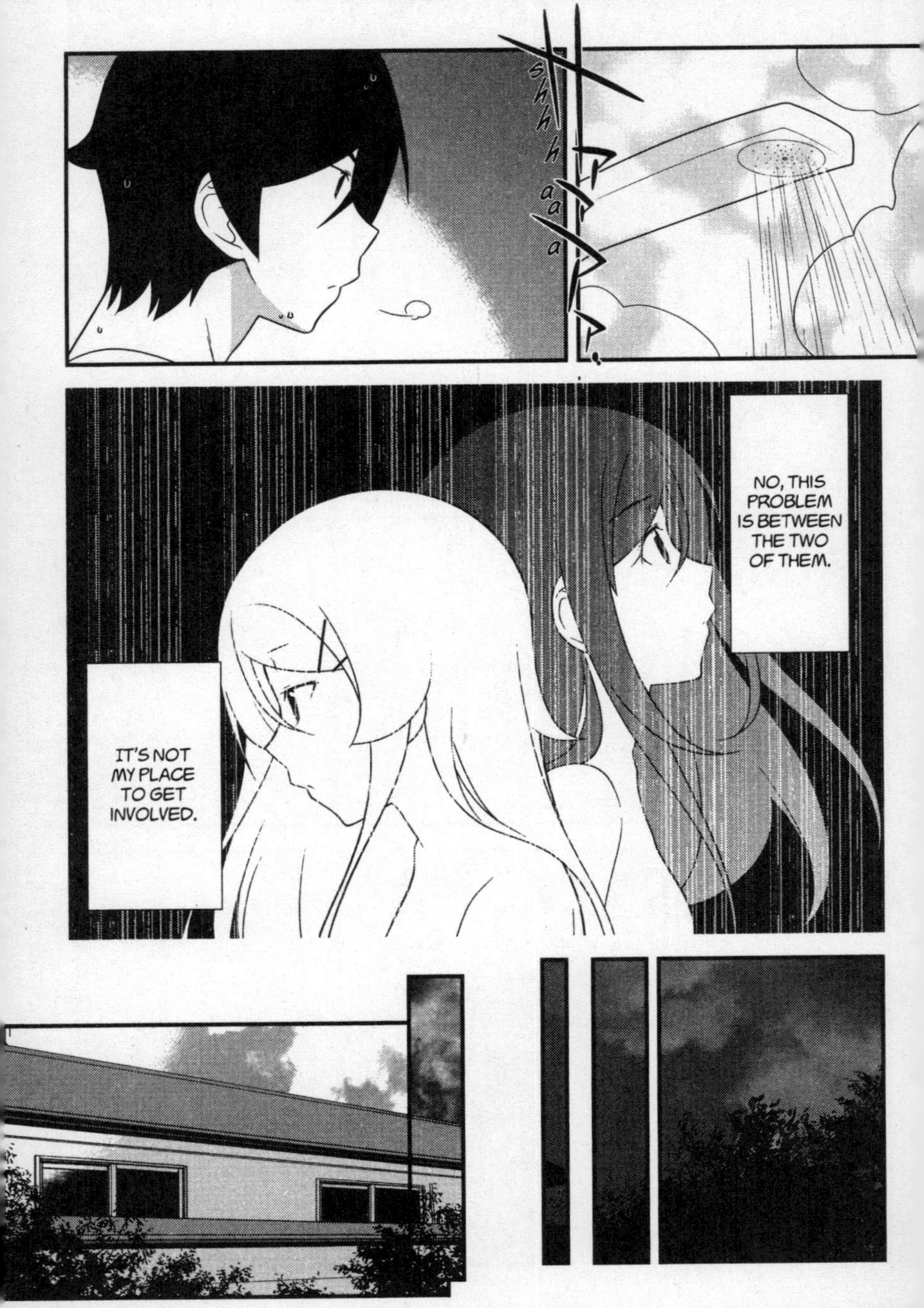
shhhaaa
NO, THIS PROBLEM IS BETWEEN THE TWO OF THEM.
IT'S NOT MY PLACE TO GET INVOLVED.

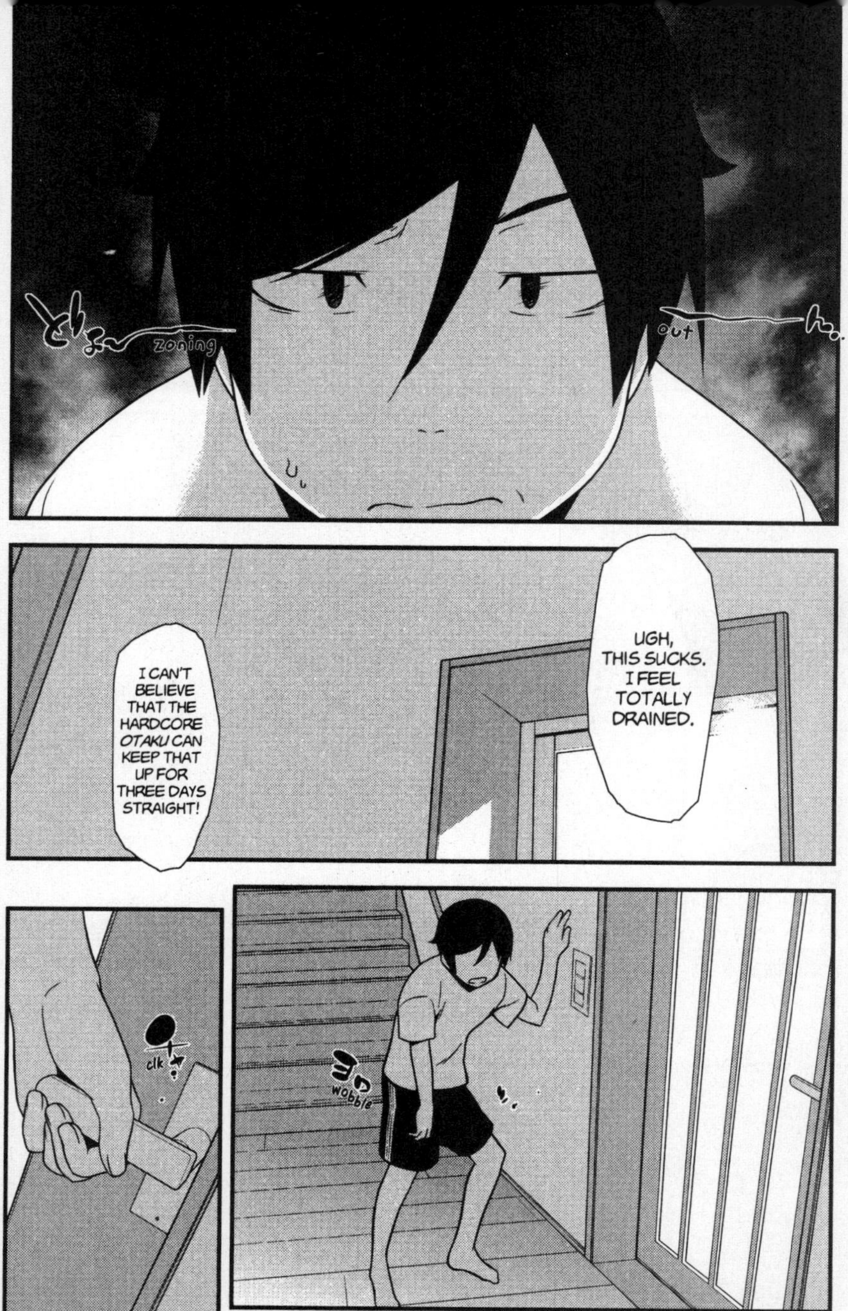
とりょ~ zoning out ~ん。
UGH, THIS SUCKS. I FEEL TOTALLY DRAINED.
I CAN'T BELIEVE THAT THE HARDCORE OTAKU CAN KEEP THAT UP FOR THREE DAYS STRAIGHT!
ヨロ wobble
clk

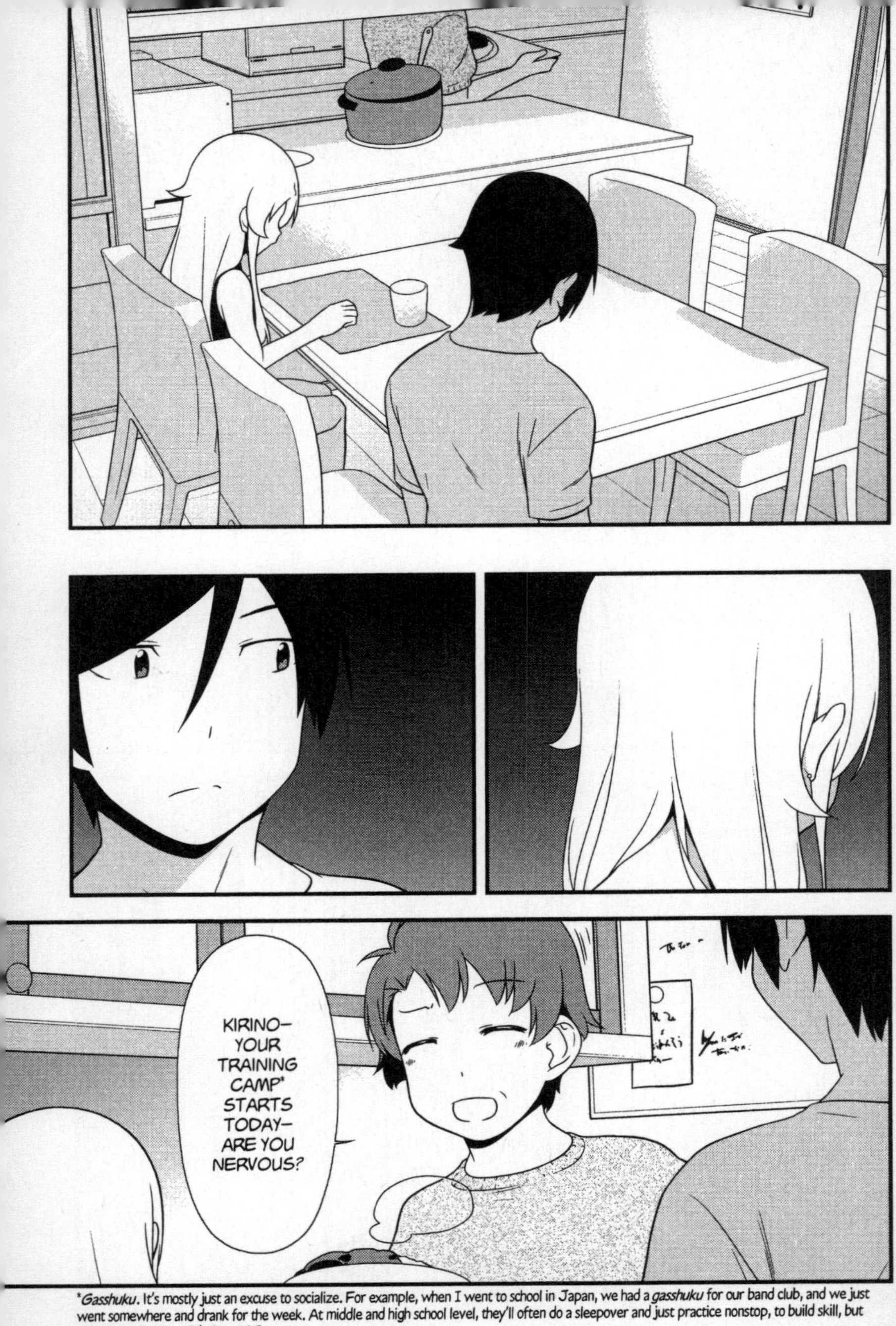
KIRINO— YOUR TRAINING CAMP* STARTS TODAY— ARE YOU NERVOUS?

*_Gasshuku_. It's mostly just an excuse to socialize. For example, when I went to school in Japan, we had a _gasshuku_ for our band club, and we just went somewhere and drank for the week. At middle and high school level, they'll often do a sleepover and just practice nonstop, to build skill, but more importantly, solidarity.—MG.

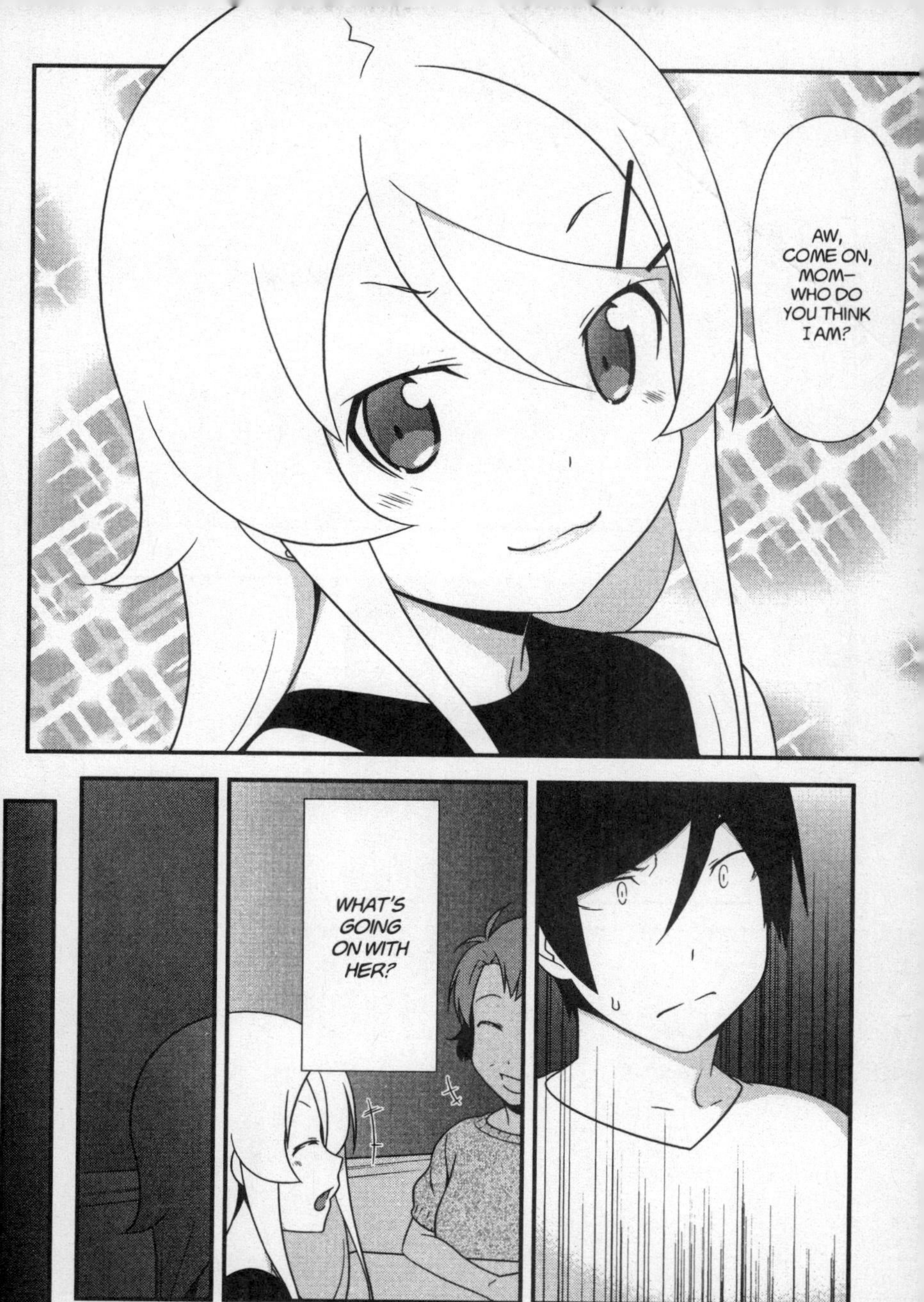

AW, COME ON, MOM— WHO DO YOU THINK I AM?
WHAT'S GOING ON WITH HER?

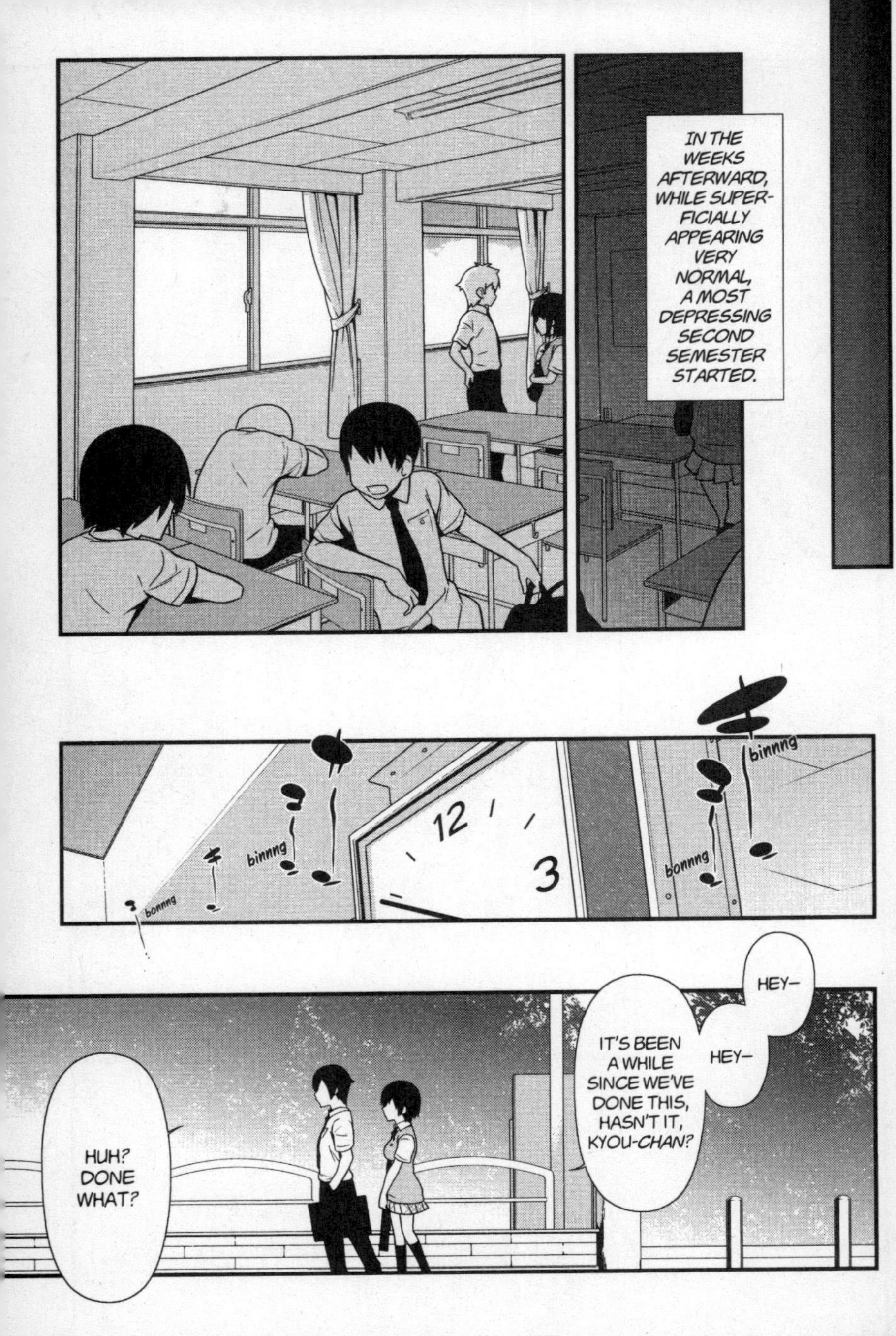
IN THE WEEKS AFTERWARD, WHILE SUPER-FICIALLY APPEARING VERY NORMAL, A MOST DEPRESSING SECOND SEMESTER STARTED.
binnng
bonnng
12
3
binnng
bonnng
HEY–
HEY–
IT'S BEEN A WHILE SINCE WE'VE DONE THIS, HASN'T IT, KYOU-CHAN?
HUH? DONE WHAT?

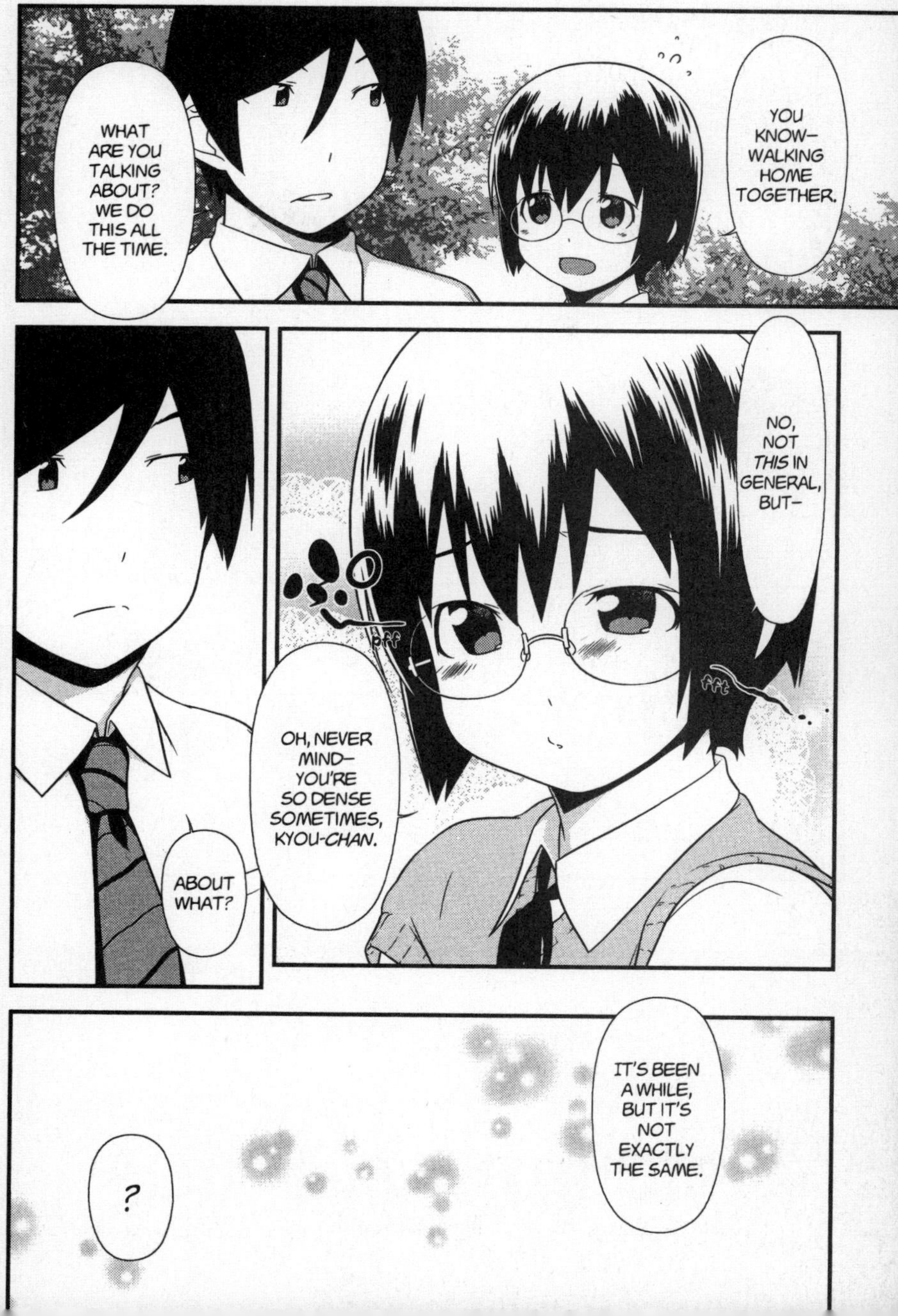
YOU KNOW— WALKING HOME TOGETHER.
WHAT ARE YOU TALKING ABOUT? WE DO THIS ALL THE TIME.
NO, NOT *THIS* IN GENERAL, BUT—
fft
pff
OH, NEVER MIND— YOU'RE SO DENSE SOMETIMES, KYOU-*CHAN*.
ABOUT WHAT?
IT'S BEEN A WHILE, BUT IT'S NOT EXACTLY THE SAME.
?

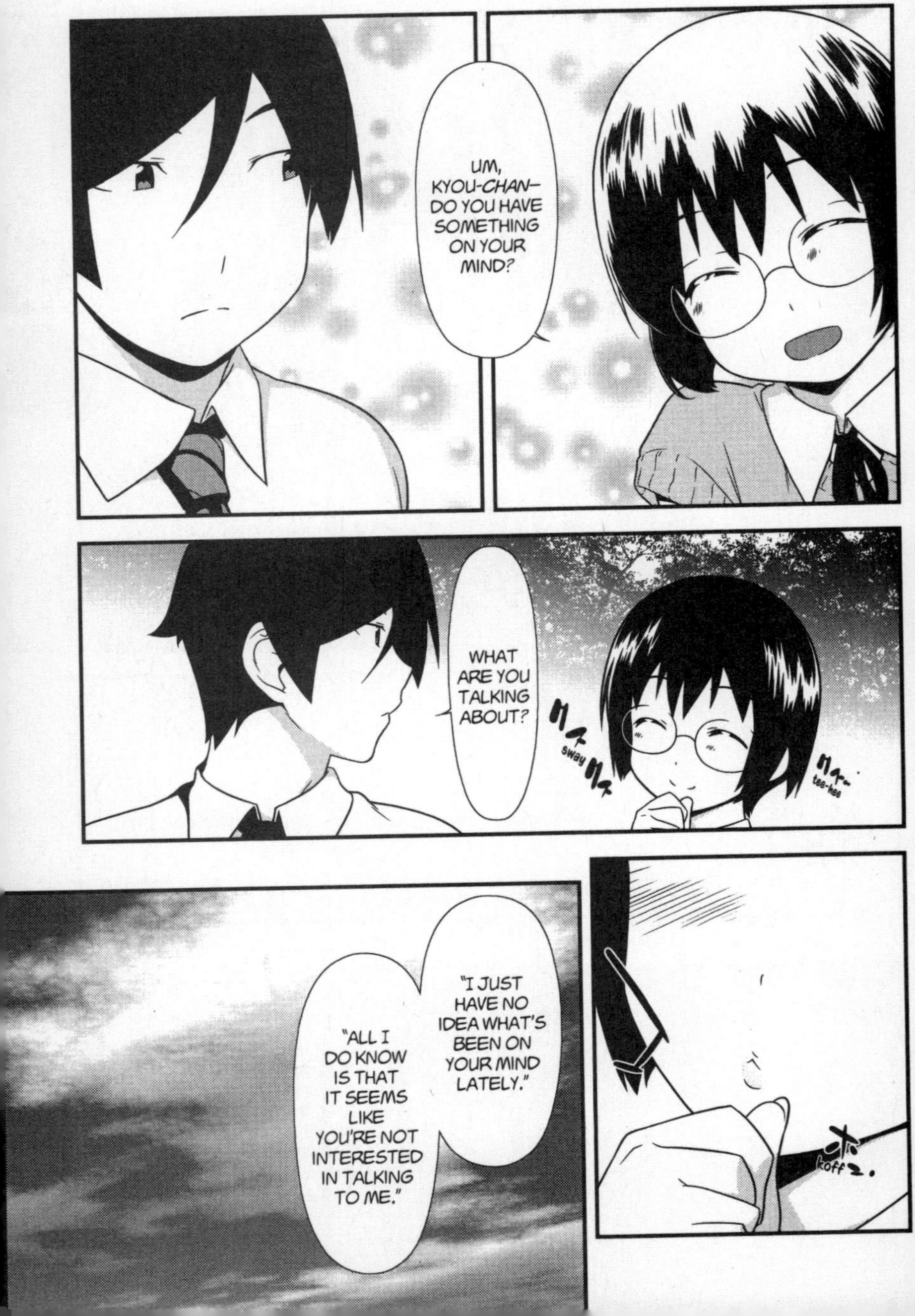
UM, KYOU-CHAN— DO YOU HAVE SOMETHING ON YOUR MIND?
WHAT ARE YOU TALKING ABOUT?
sway
tee-hee
koff
"I JUST HAVE NO IDEA WHAT'S BEEN ON YOUR MIND LATELY."
"ALL I DO KNOW IS THAT IT SEEMS LIKE YOU'RE NOT INTERESTED IN TALKING TO ME."

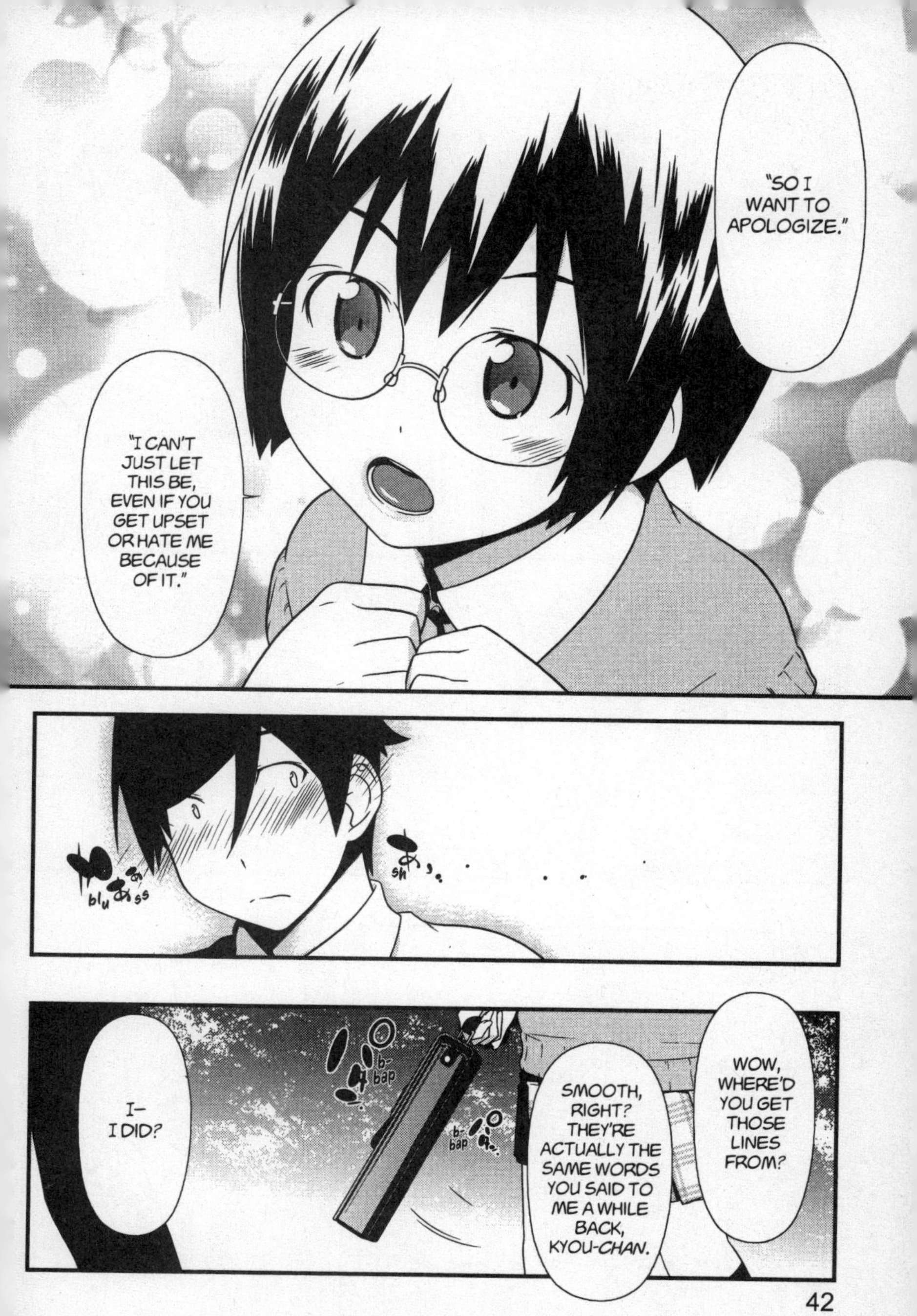
"SO I WANT TO APOLOGIZE."
"I CAN'T JUST LET THIS BE, EVEN IF YOU GET UPSET OR HATE ME BECAUSE OF IT."
sh
. . . . . .
WOW, WHERE'D YOU GET THOSE LINES FROM?
SMOOTH, RIGHT? THEY'RE ACTUALLY THE SAME WORDS YOU SAID TO ME A WHILE BACK, KYOU-CHAN.
b-bap
b-bap
I— I DID?

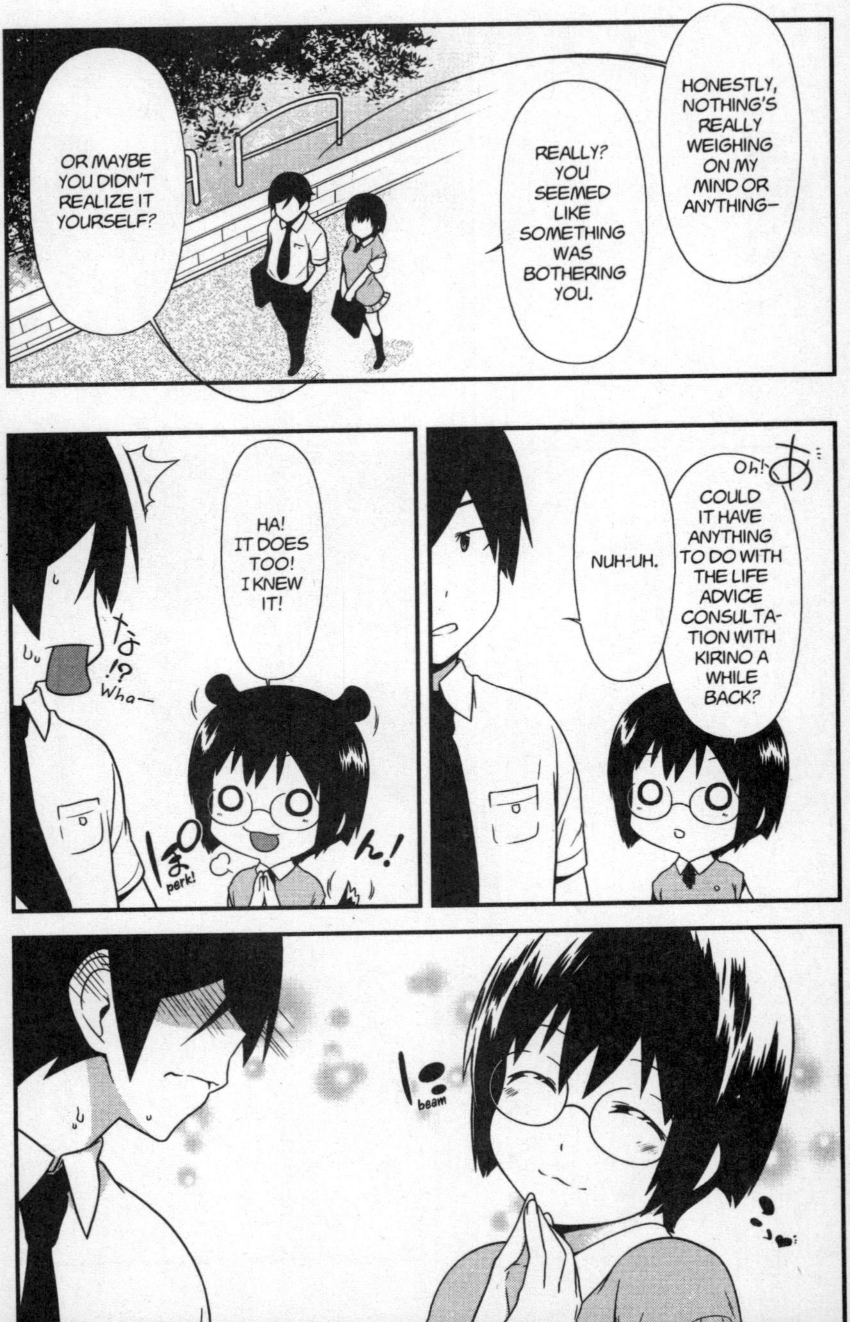
HONESTLY, NOTHING'S REALLY WEIGHING ON MY MIND OR ANYTHING—
REALLY? YOU SEEMED LIKE SOMETHING WAS BOTHERING YOU.
OR MAYBE YOU DIDN'T REALIZE IT YOURSELF?
Oh!
COULD IT HAVE ANYTHING TO DO WITH THE LIFE ADVICE CONSULTA-TION WITH KIRINO A WHILE BACK?
NUH-UH.
HA! IT DOES TOO! I KNEW IT!
Wha—
perk!
beam

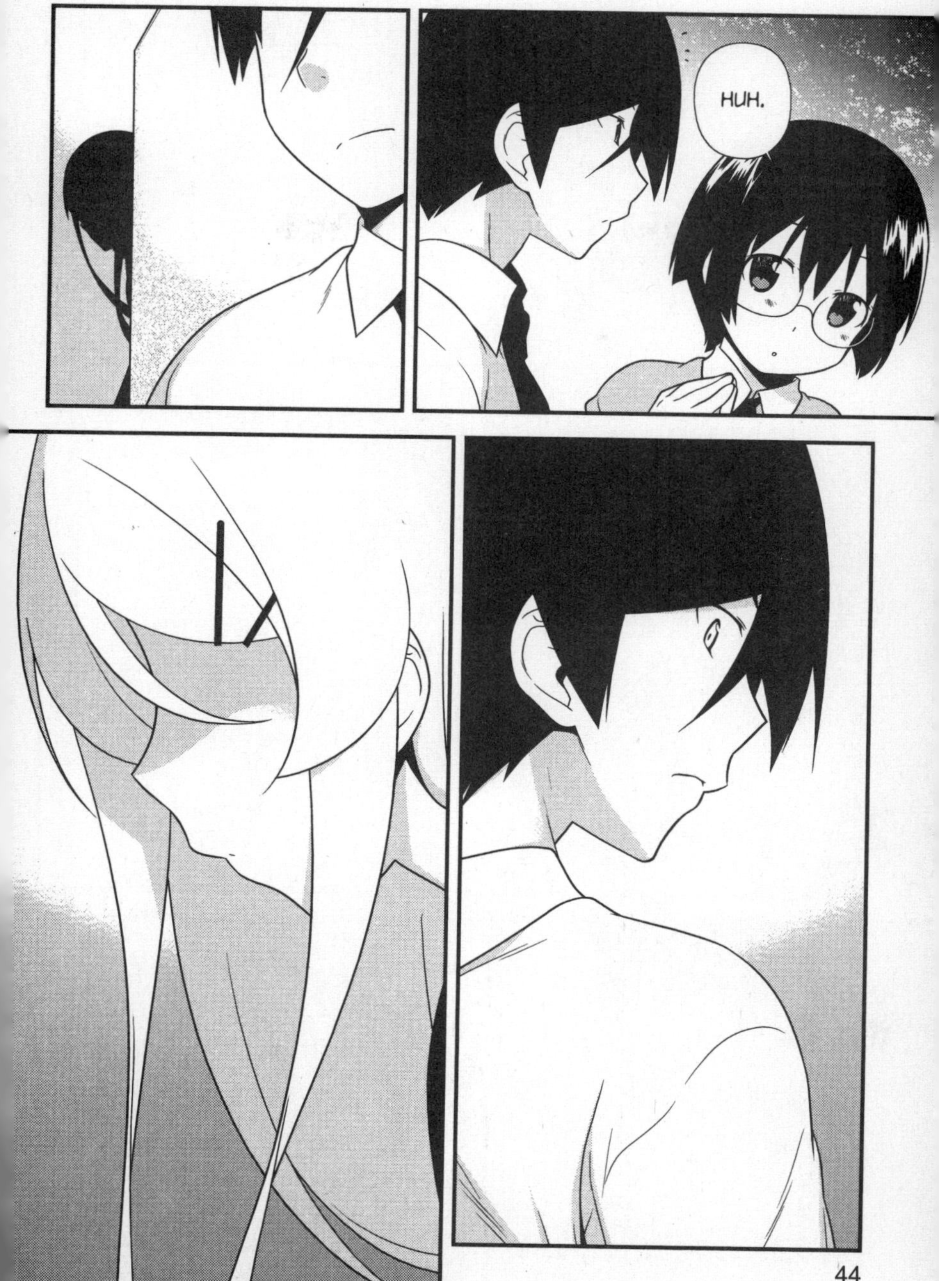
HUH.

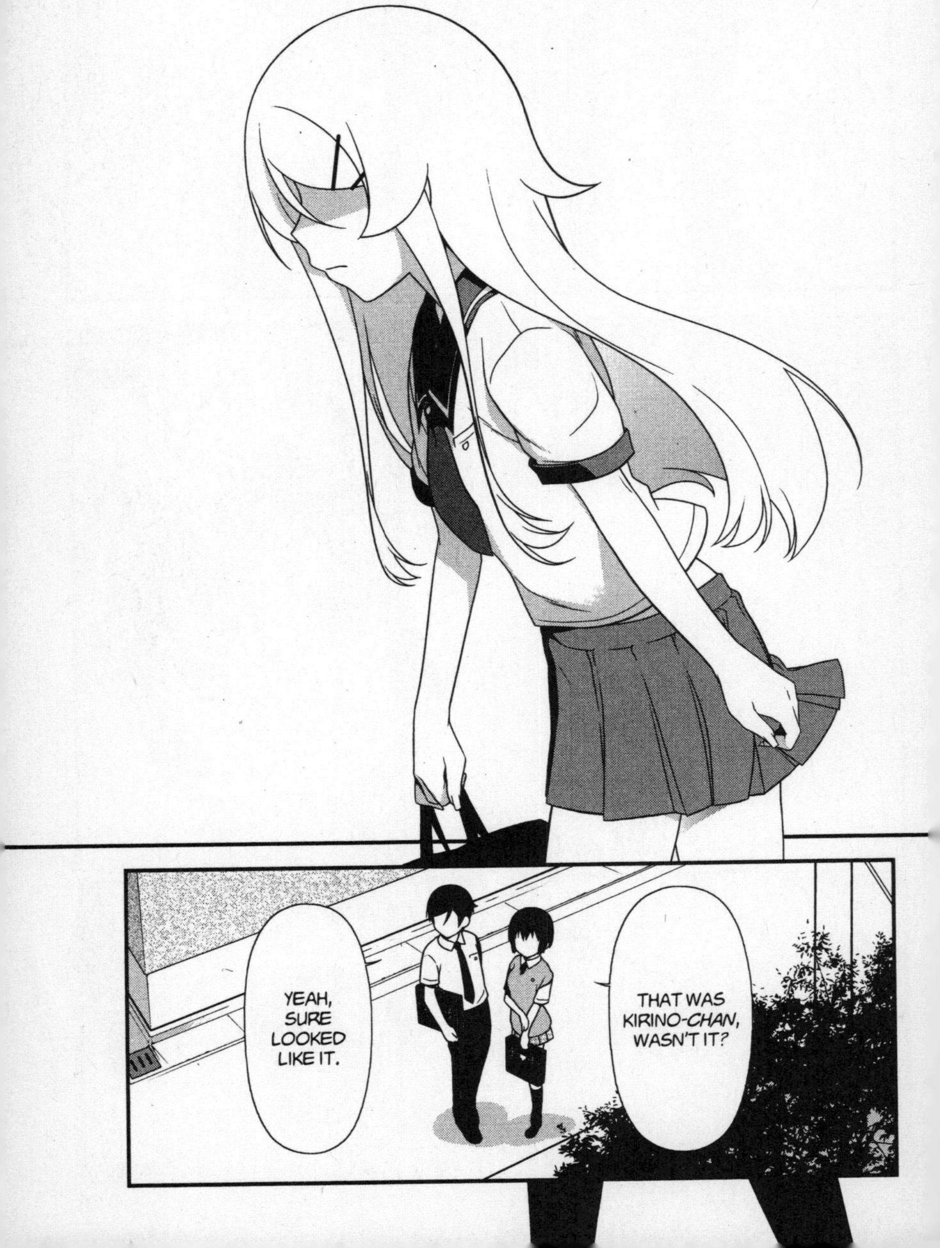
THAT WAS KIRINO-*CHAN*, WASN'T IT?
YEAH, SURE LOOKED LIKE IT.

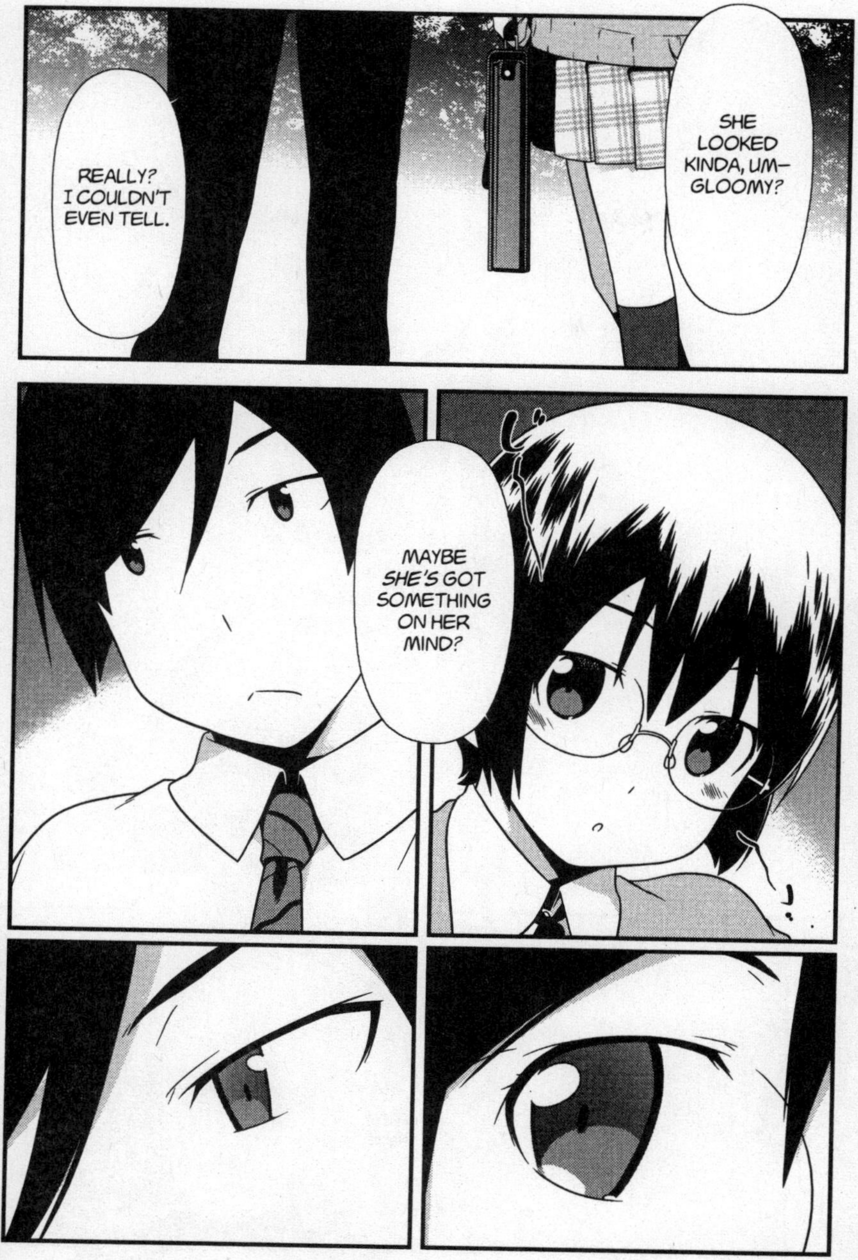
SHE LOOKED KINDA, UM— GLOOMY?
REALLY? I COULDN'T EVEN TELL.
MAYBE SHE'S GOT SOMETHING ON HER MIND?

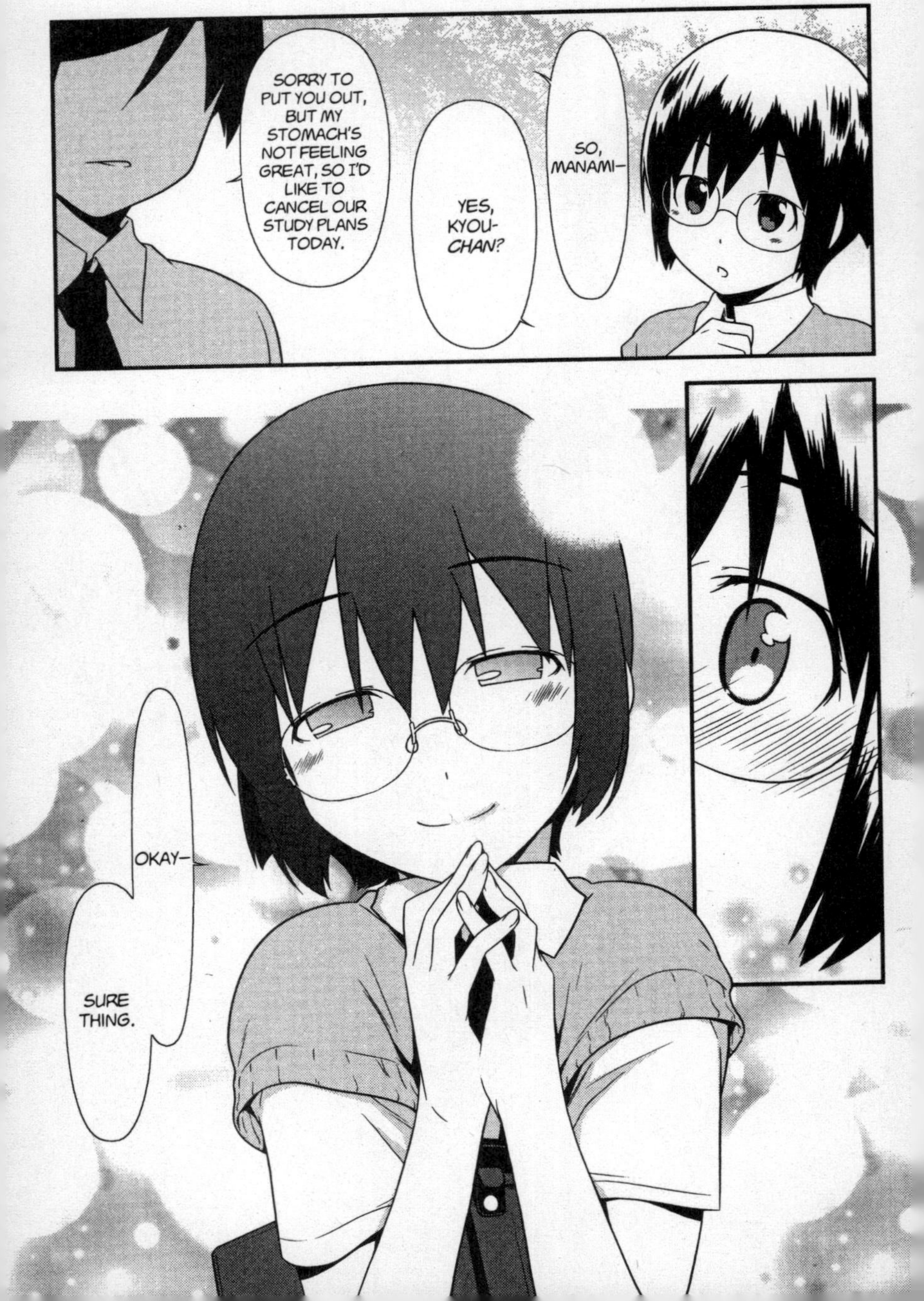
SO, MANAMI—
YES, KYOU-CHAN?
SORRY TO PUT YOU OUT, BUT MY STOMACH'S NOT FEELING GREAT, SO I'D LIKE TO CANCEL OUR STUDY PLANS TODAY.
OKAY—
SURE THING.

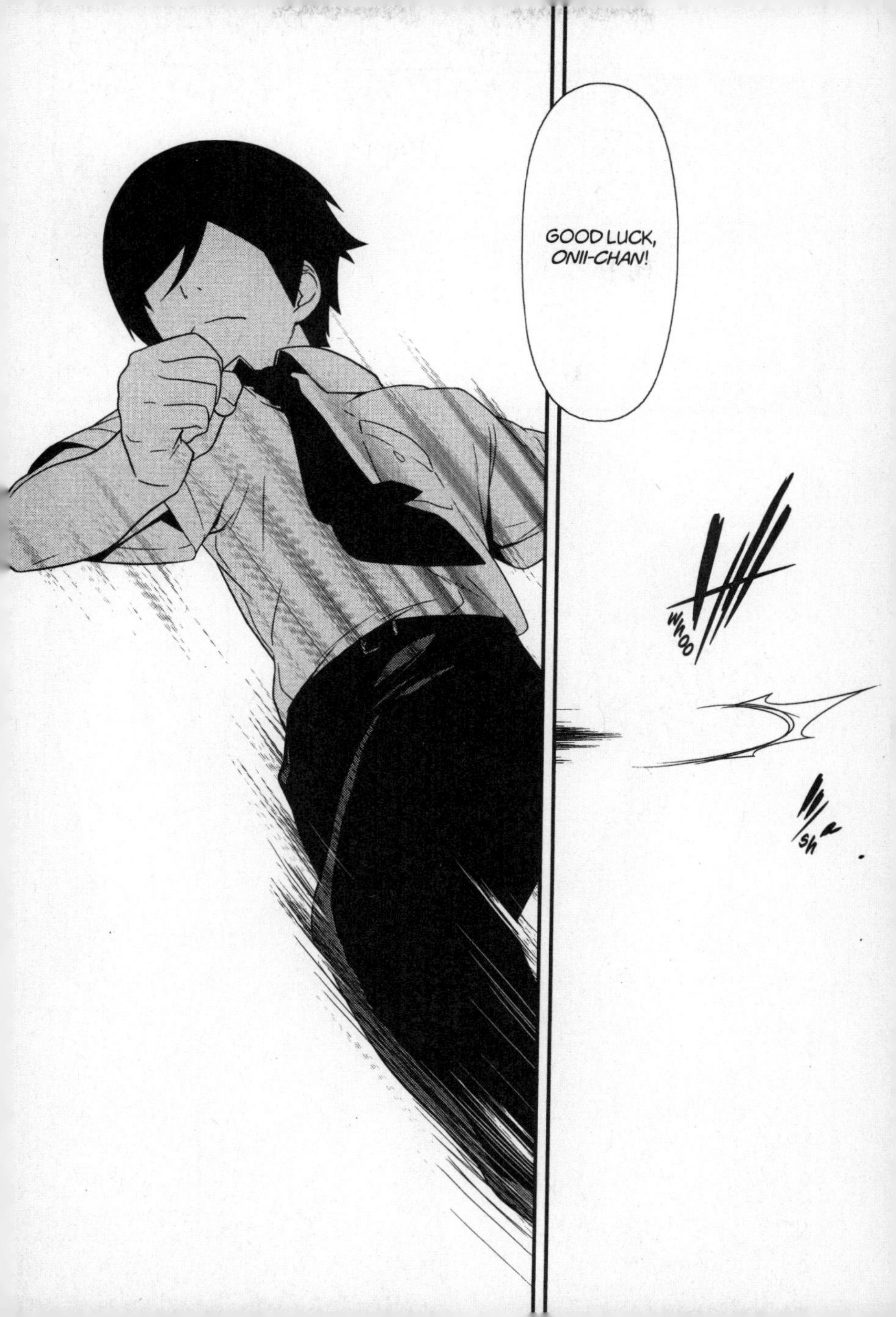
GOOD LUCK, ONII-CHAN!
WHOO
SH

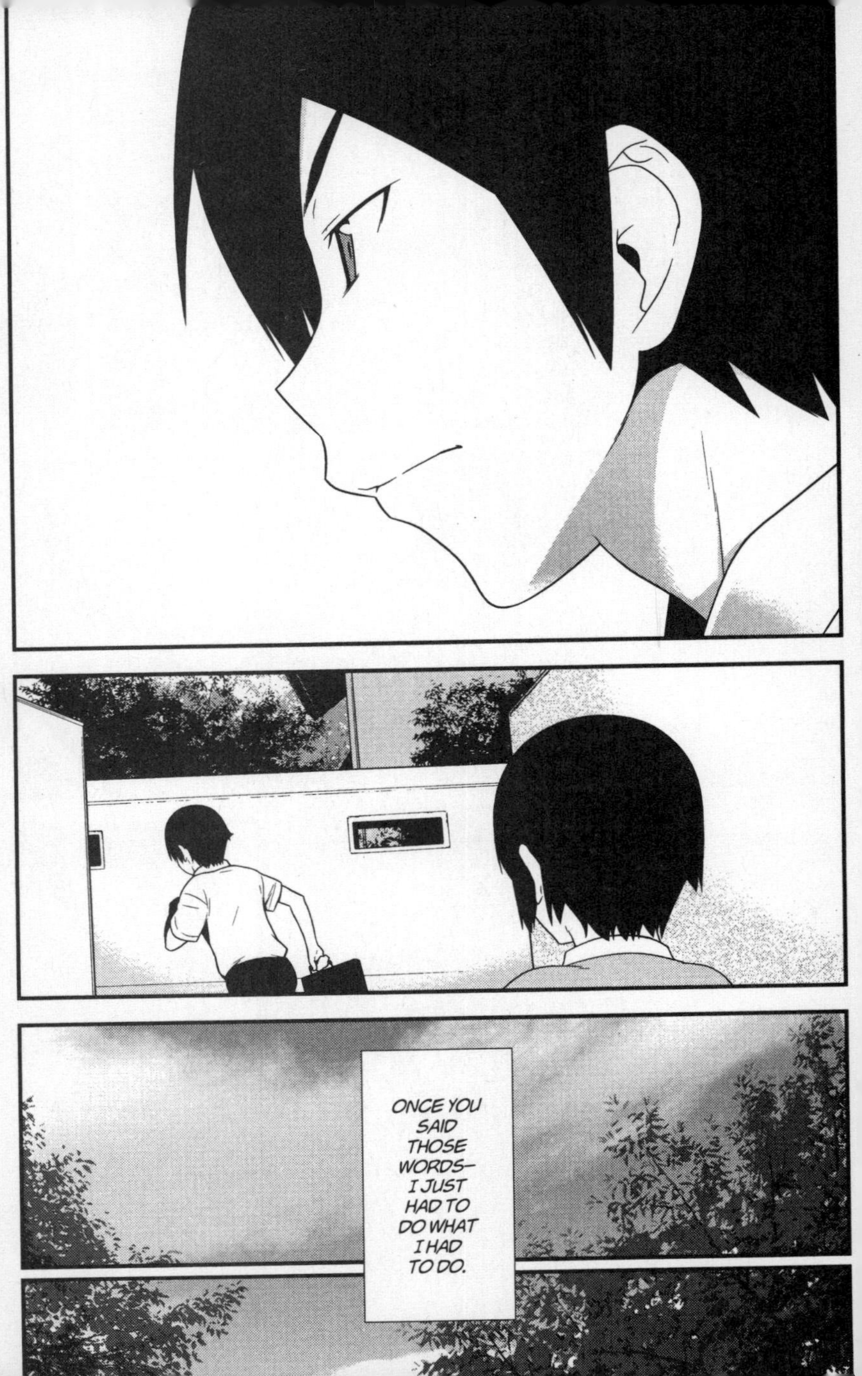
ONCE YOU SAID THOSE WORDS- I JUST HAD TO DO WHAT I HAD TO DO.

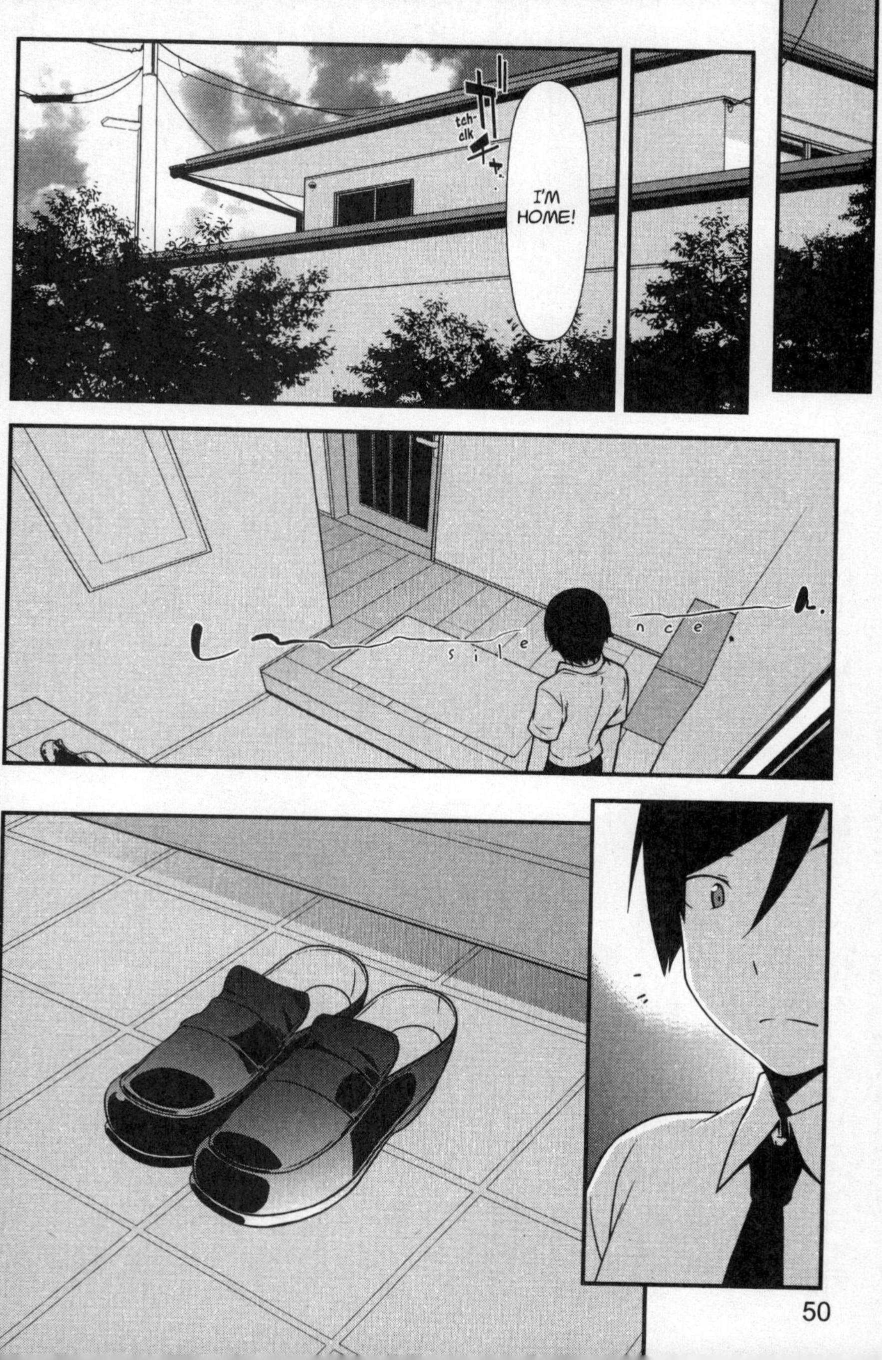
tch-clk
I'M HOME!
silence

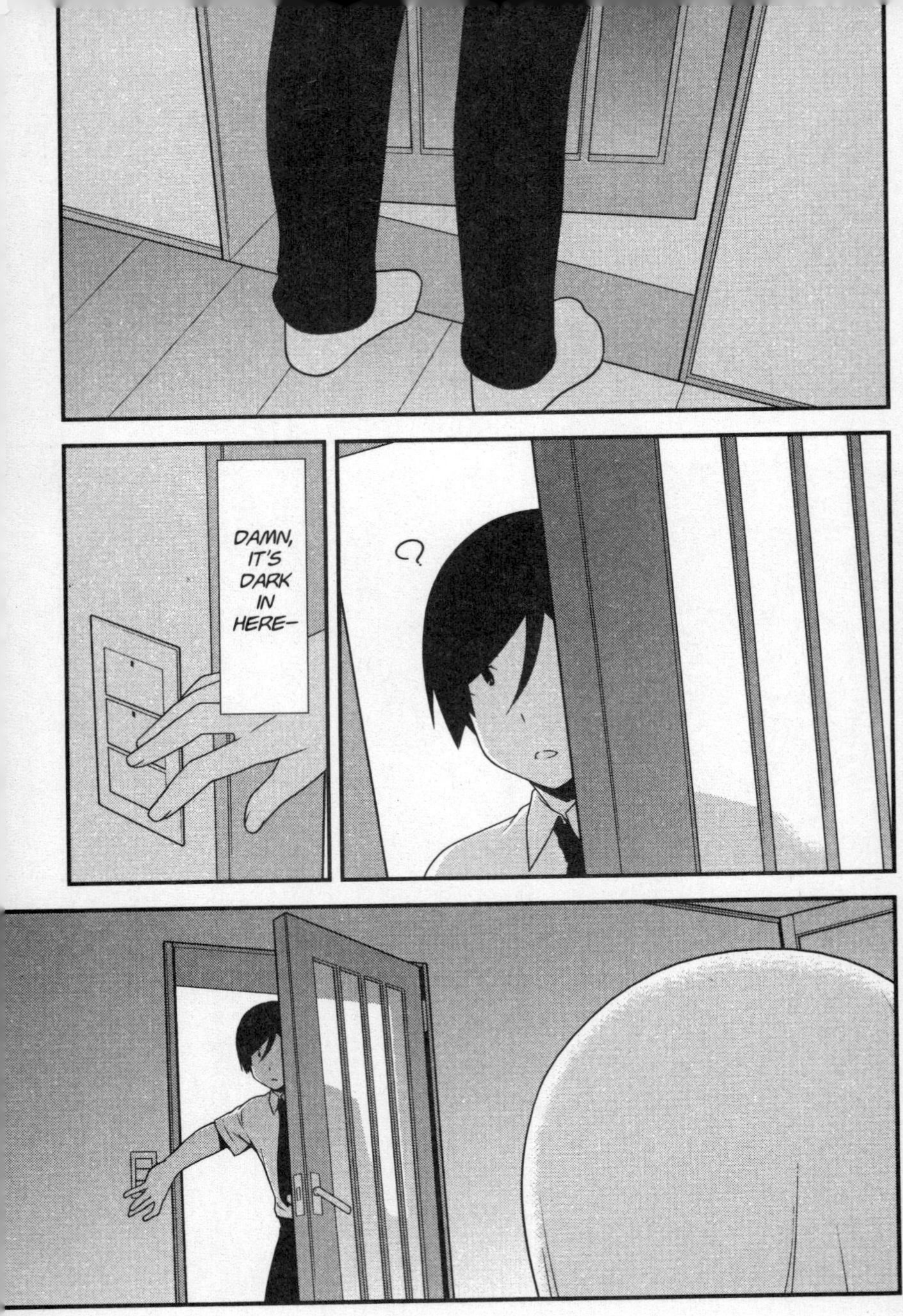
?
DAMN, IT'S DARK IN HERE–

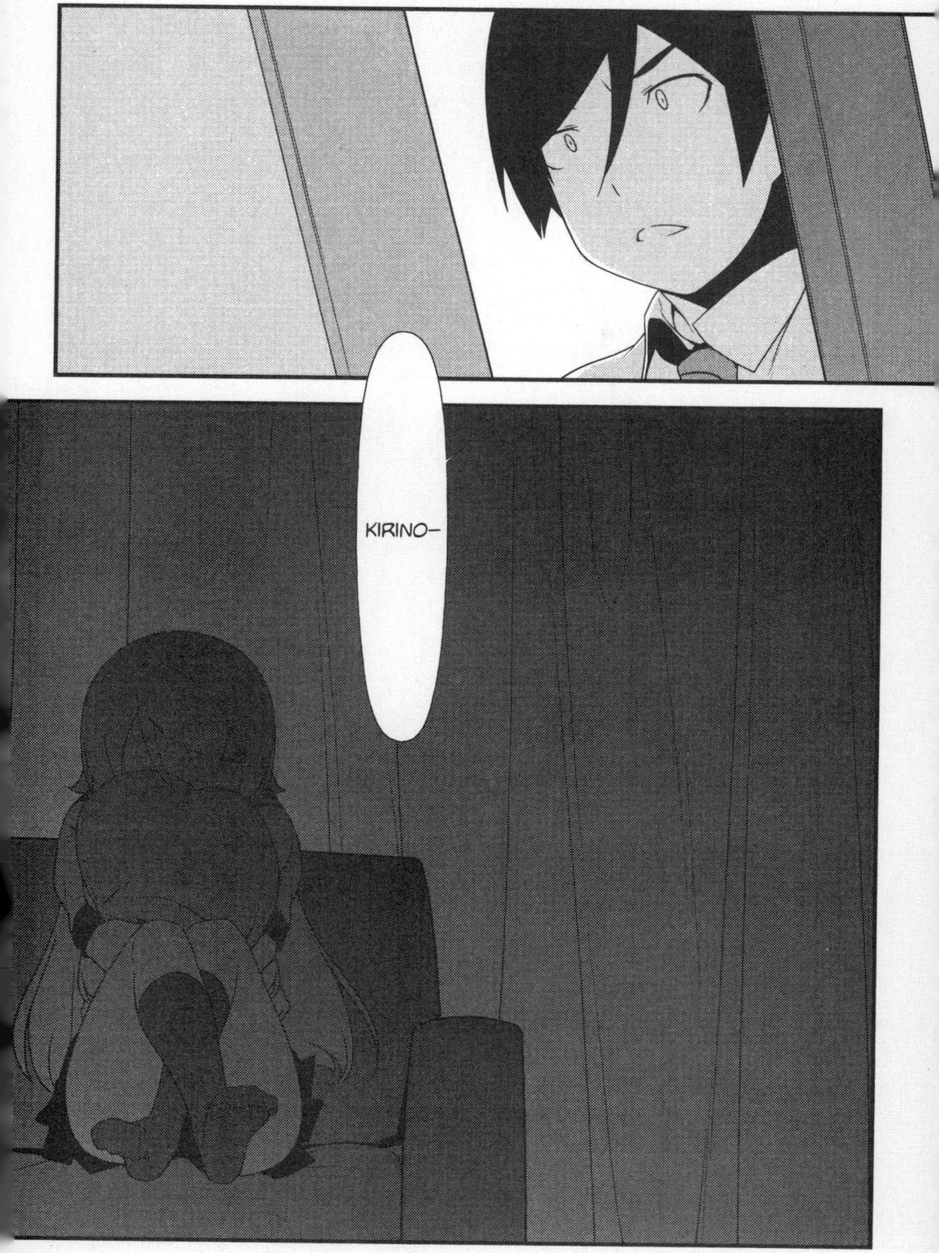
KIRINO—

俺の妹が
こんなに
可愛いわけが
ない

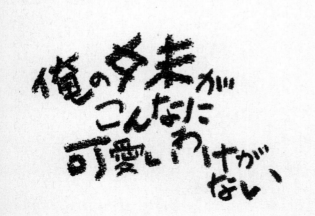

第23話
CHAPTER 23

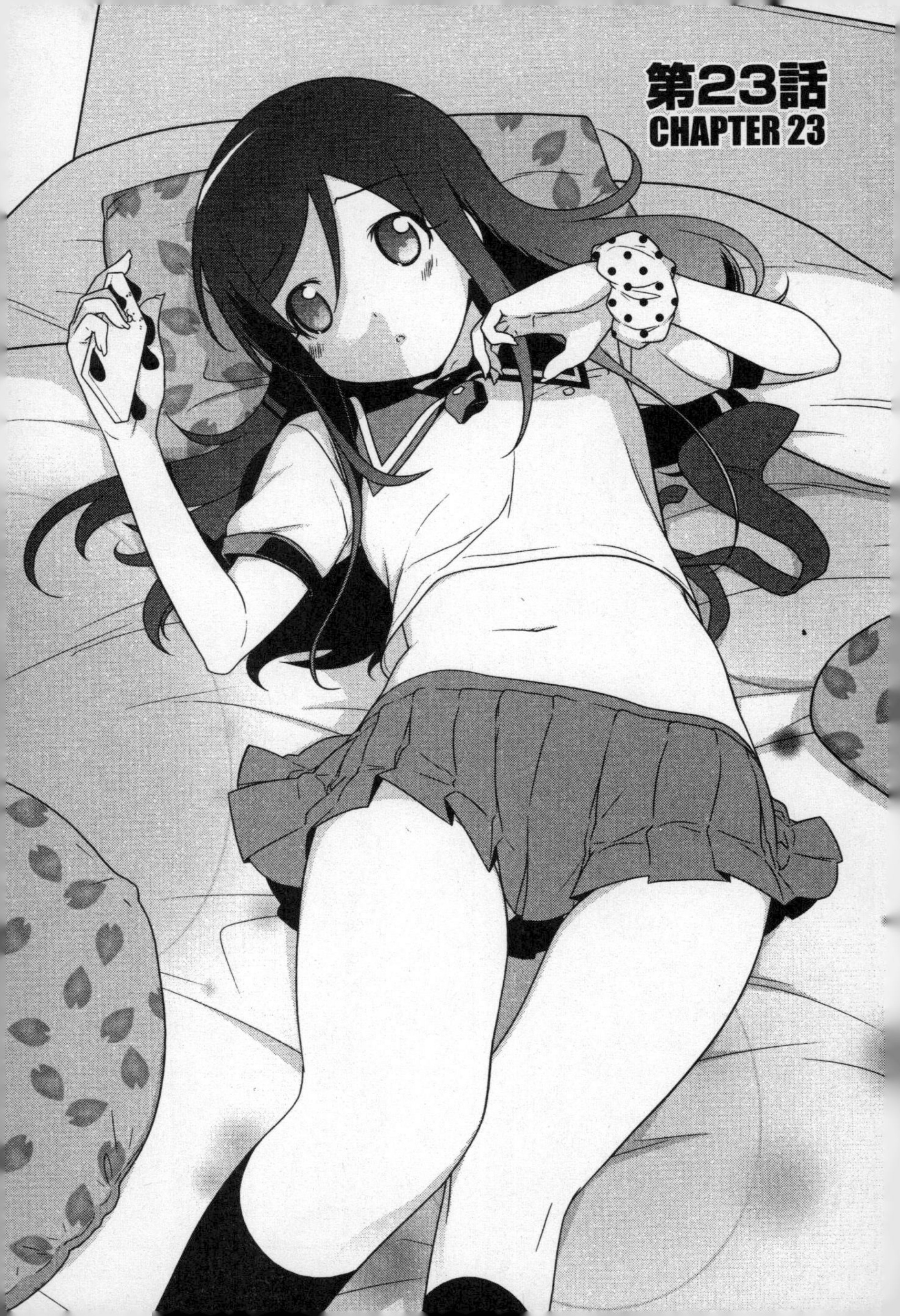

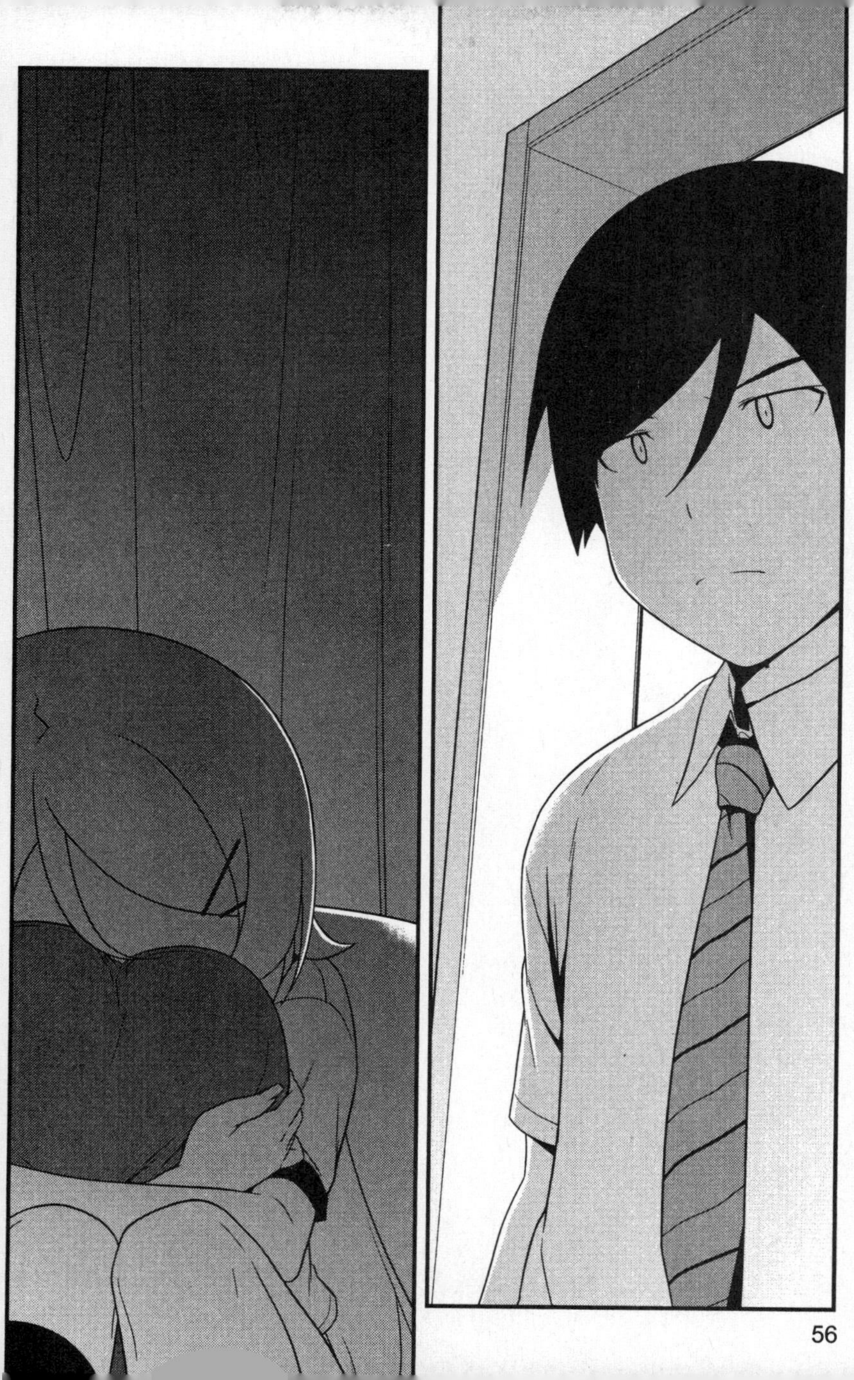

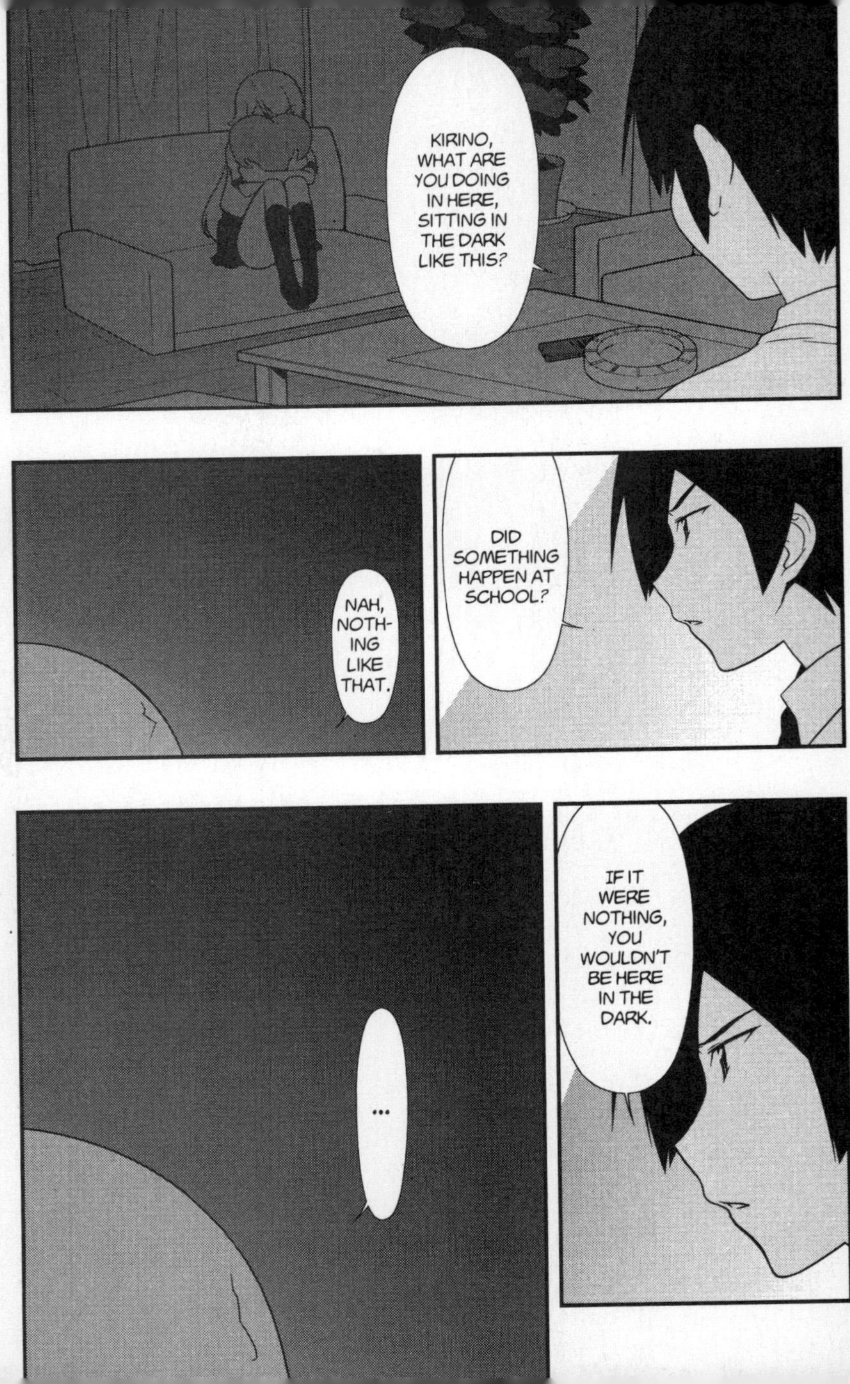
KIRINO, WHAT ARE YOU DOING IN HERE, SITTING IN THE DARK LIKE THIS?
DID SOMETHING HAPPEN AT SCHOOL?
NAH, NOTHING LIKE THAT.
IF IT WERE NOTHING, YOU WOULDN'T BE HERE IN THE DARK.
...

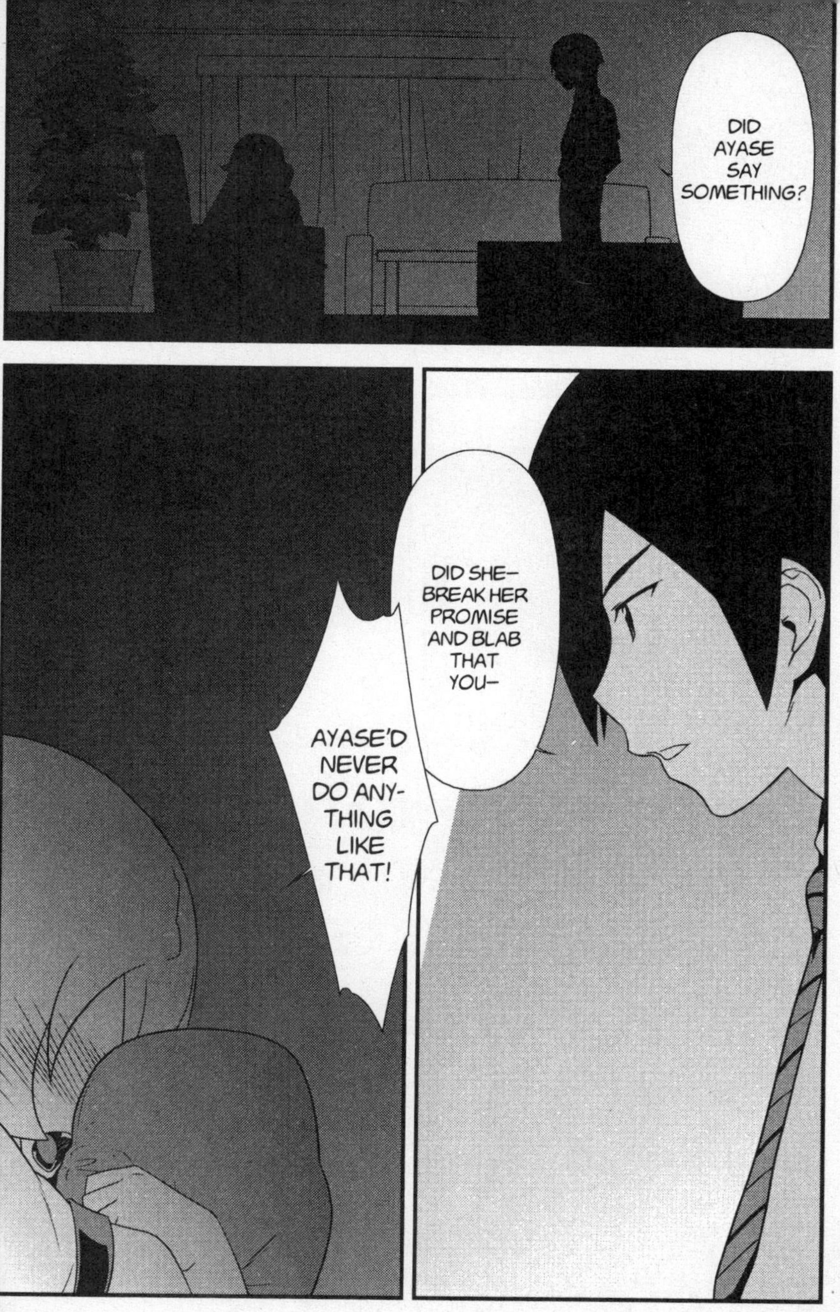
DID AYASE SAY SOMETHING?
DID SHE— BREAK HER PROMISE AND BLAB THAT YOU—
AYASE'D NEVER DO ANY-THING LIKE THAT!

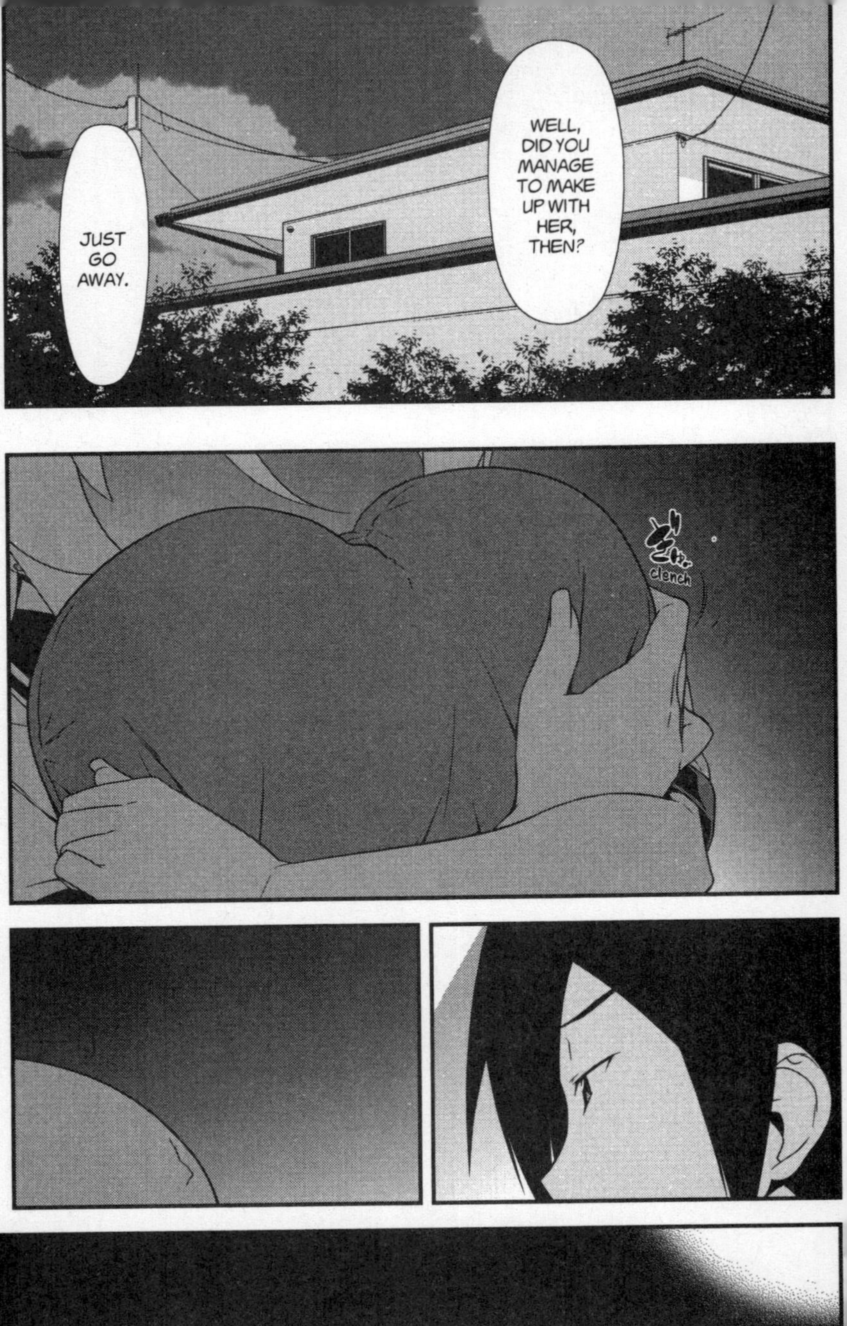
WELL, DID YOU MANAGE TO MAKE UP WITH HER, THEN?
JUST GO AWAY.
clench

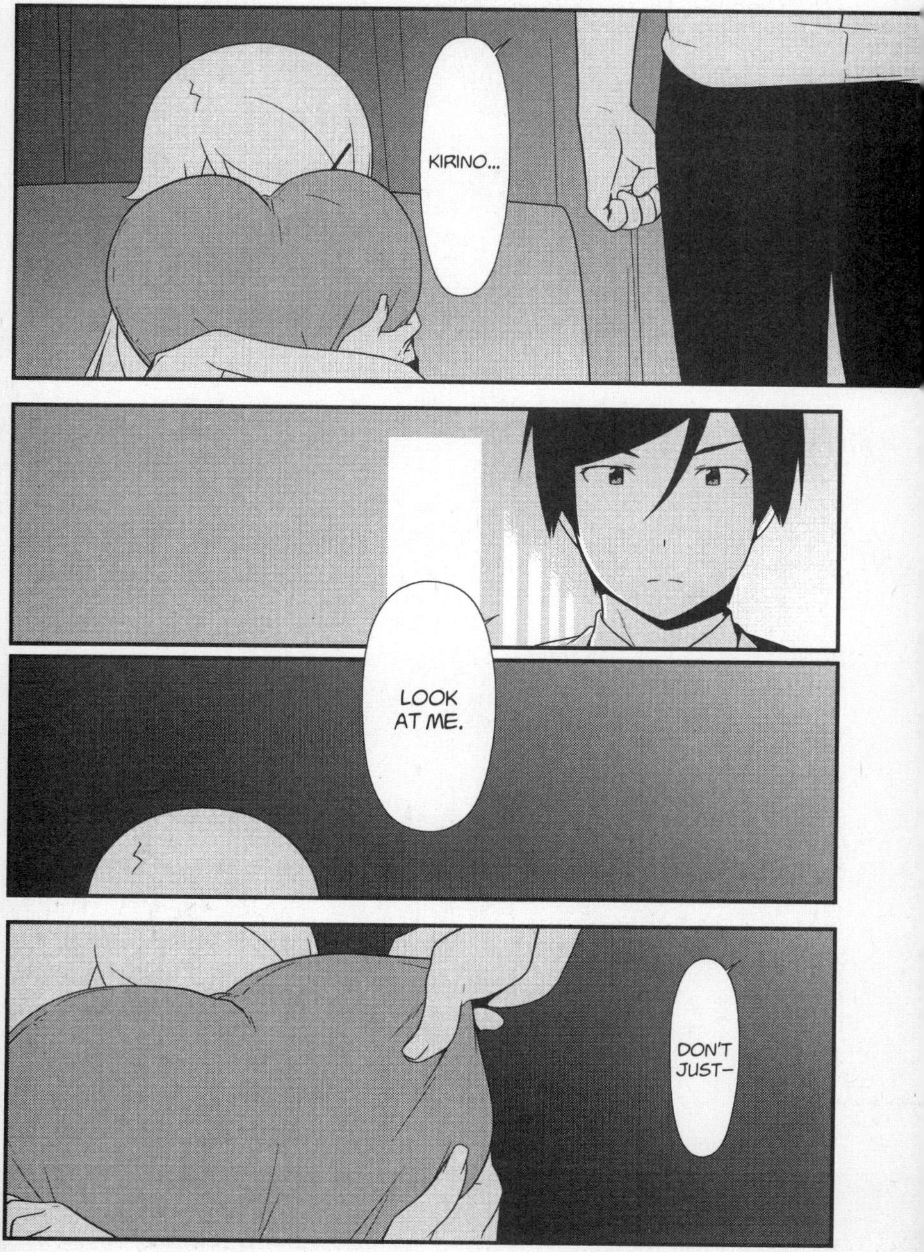
KIRINO...
LOOK AT ME.
DON'T JUST-

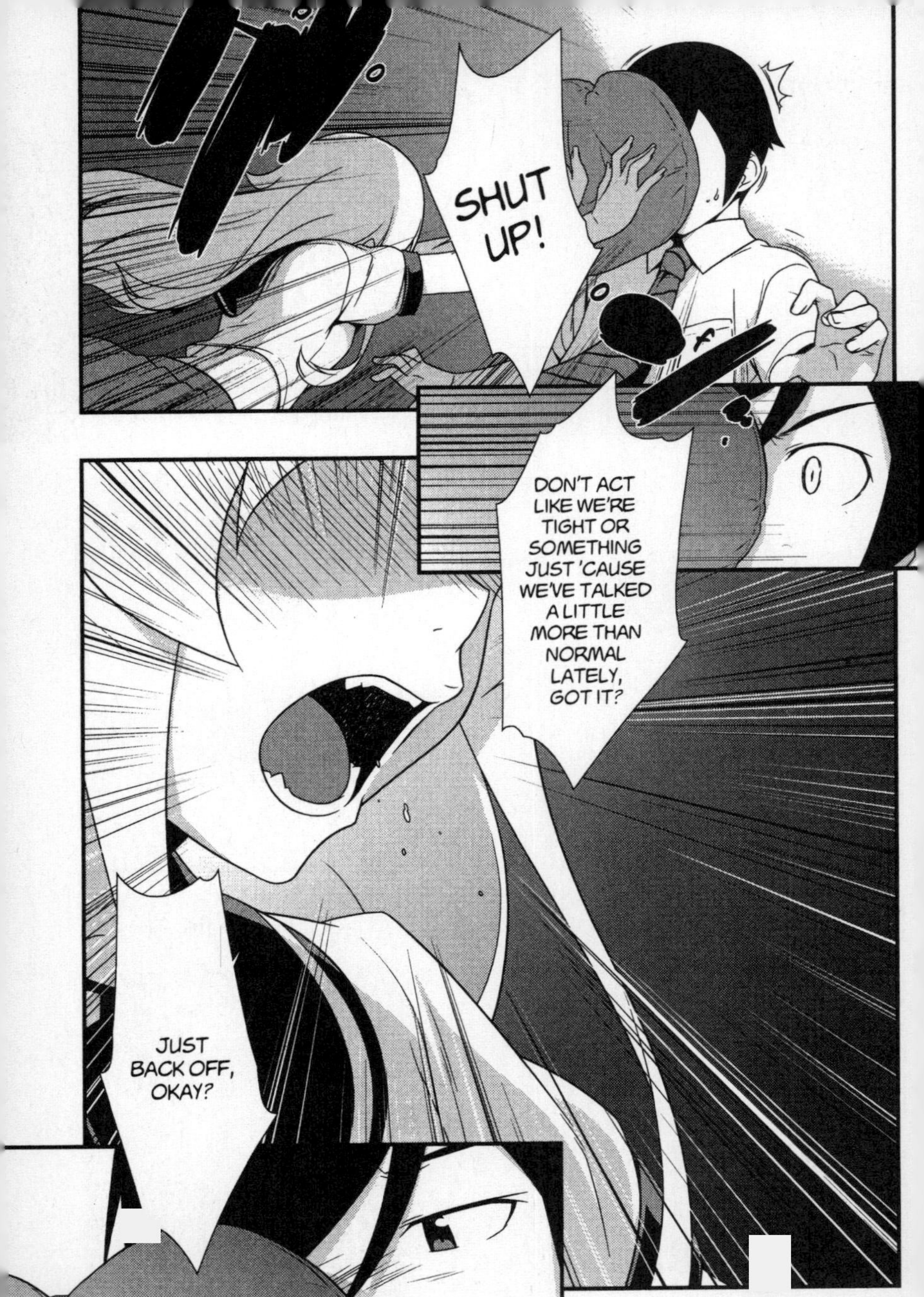
SHUT UP!
DON'T ACT LIKE WE'RE TIGHT OR SOMETHING JUST 'CAUSE WE'VE TALKED A LITTLE MORE THAN NORMAL LATELY, GOT IT?
JUST BACK OFF, OKAY?

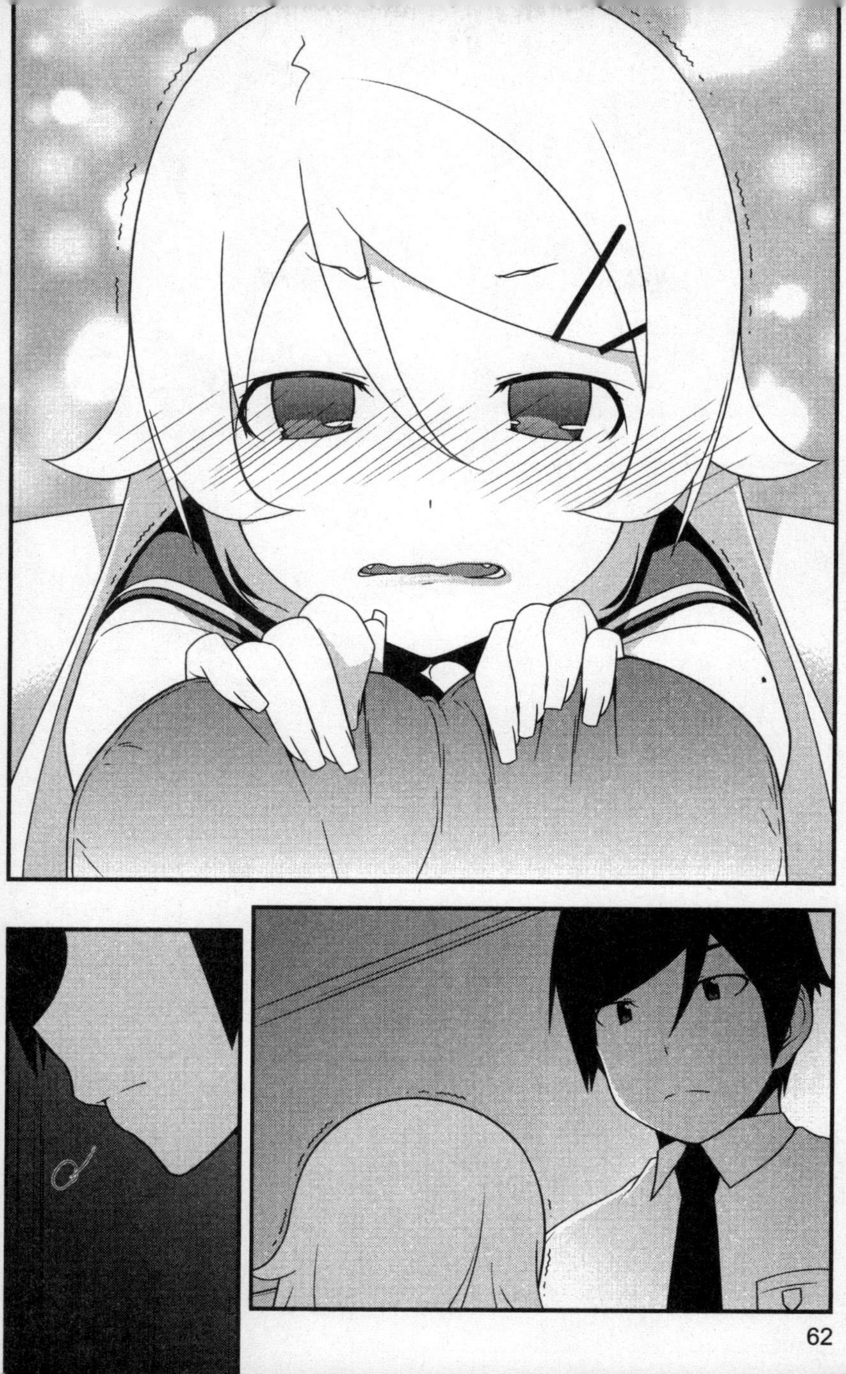

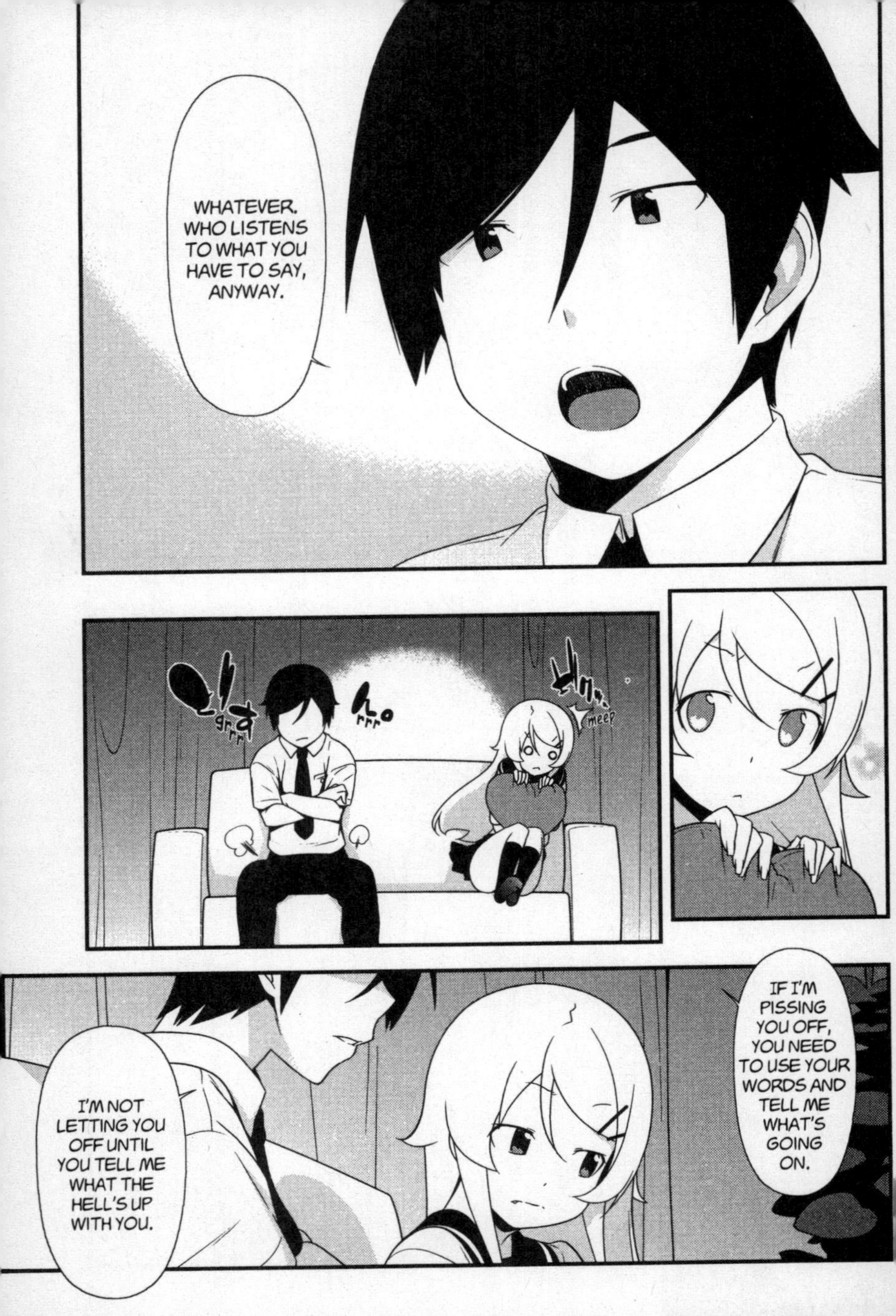
WHATEVER. WHO LISTENS TO WHAT YOU HAVE TO SAY, ANYWAY.
meep
rrr
grrr
IF I'M PISSING YOU OFF, YOU NEED TO USE YOUR WORDS AND TELL ME WHAT'S GOING ON.
I'M NOT LETTING YOU OFF UNTIL YOU TELL ME WHAT THE HELL'S UP WITH YOU.

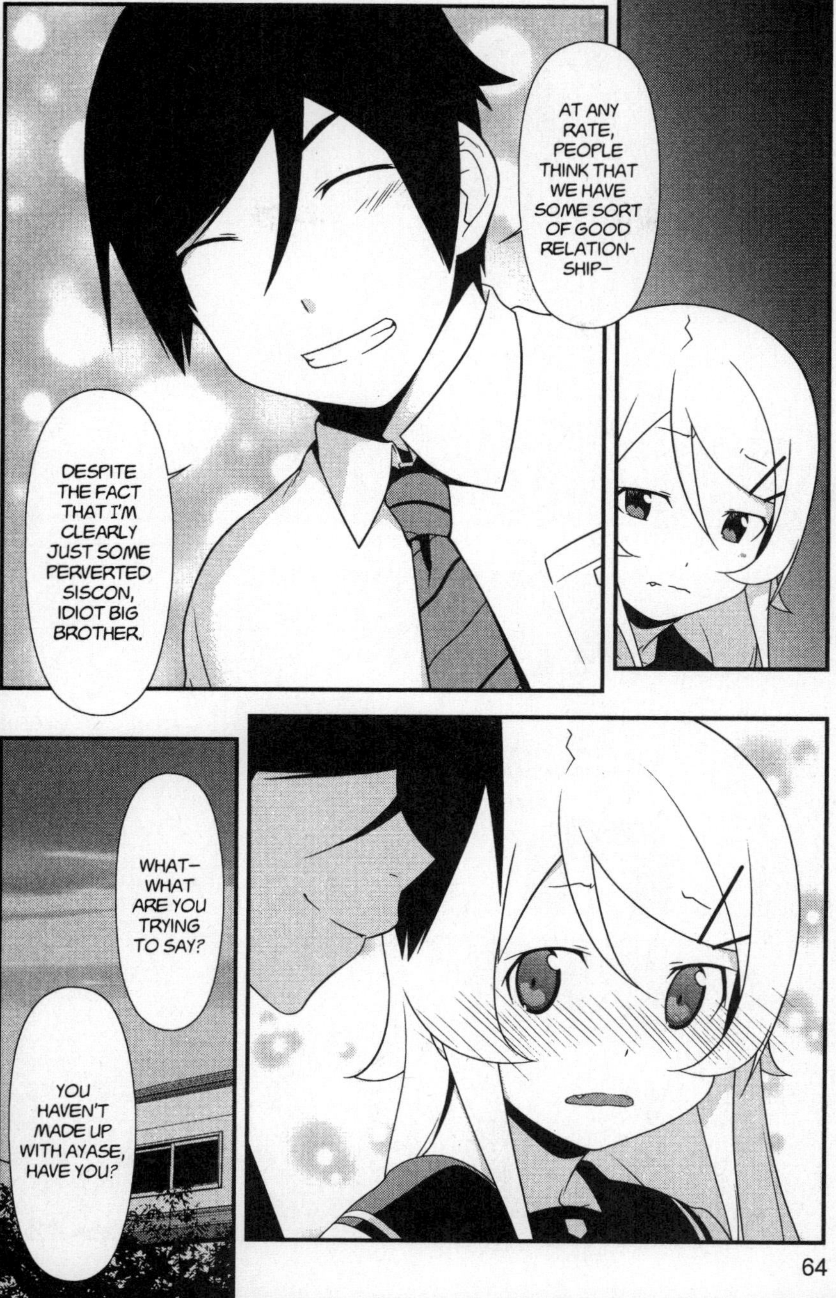
AT ANY RATE, PEOPLE THINK THAT WE HAVE SOME SORT OF GOOD RELATION-SHIP–
DESPITE THE FACT THAT I'M CLEARLY JUST SOME PERVERTED SISCON, IDIOT BIG BROTHER.
WHAT– WHAT ARE YOU TRYING TO SAY?
YOU HAVEN'T MADE UP WITH AYASE, HAVE YOU?

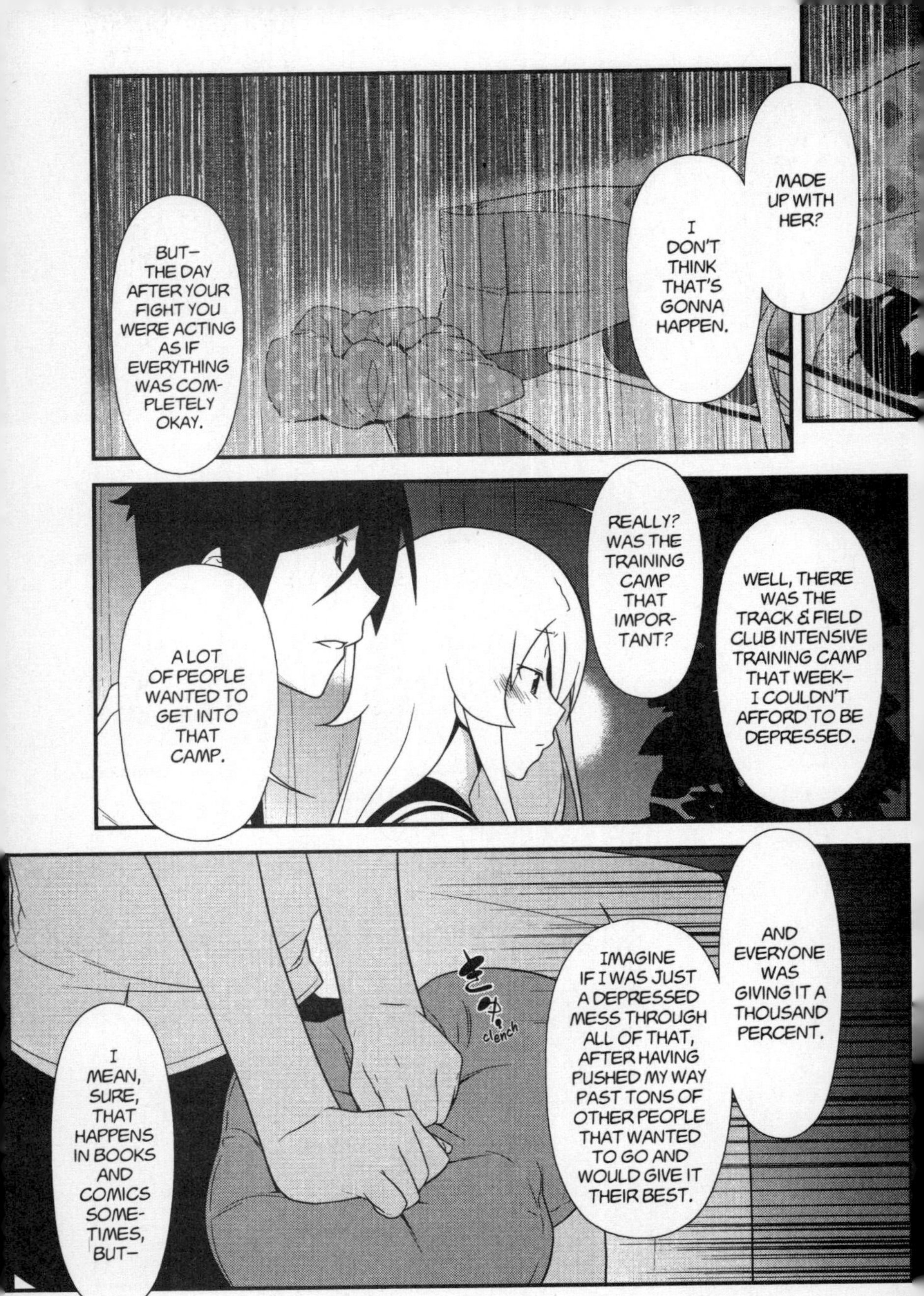
MADE UP WITH HER?
I DON'T THINK THAT'S GONNA HAPPEN.
BUT— THE DAY AFTER YOUR FIGHT YOU WERE ACTING AS IF EVERYTHING WAS COMPLETELY OKAY.
WELL, THERE WAS THE TRACK & FIELD CLUB INTENSIVE TRAINING CAMP THAT WEEK— I COULDN'T AFFORD TO BE DEPRESSED.
REALLY? WAS THE TRAINING CAMP THAT IMPORTANT?
A LOT OF PEOPLE WANTED TO GET INTO THAT CAMP.
AND EVERYONE WAS GIVING IT A THOUSAND PERCENT.
IMAGINE IF I WAS JUST A DEPRESSED MESS THROUGH ALL OF THAT, AFTER HAVING PUSHED MY WAY PAST TONS OF OTHER PEOPLE THAT WANTED TO GO AND WOULD GIVE IT THEIR BEST.
clench
I MEAN, SURE, THAT HAPPENS IN BOOKS AND COMICS SOMETIMES, BUT—

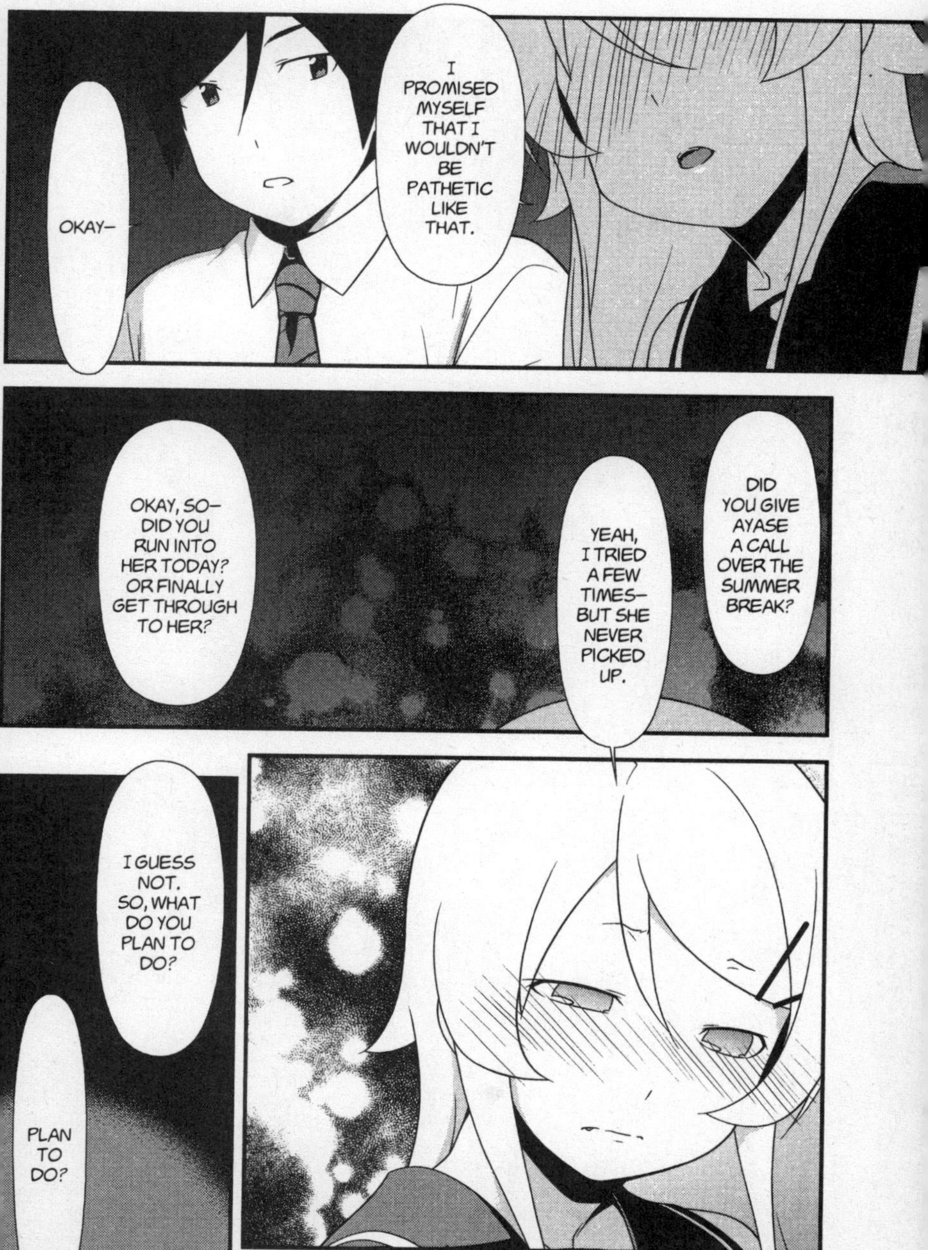
I PROMISED MYSELF THAT I WOULDN'T BE PATHETIC LIKE THAT.
OKAY—
DID YOU GIVE AYASE A CALL OVER THE SUMMER BREAK?
YEAH, I TRIED A FEW TIMES— BUT SHE NEVER PICKED UP.
OKAY, SO— DID YOU RUN INTO HER TODAY? OR FINALLY GET THROUGH TO HER?
I GUESS NOT. SO, WHAT DO YOU PLAN TO DO?
PLAN TO DO?

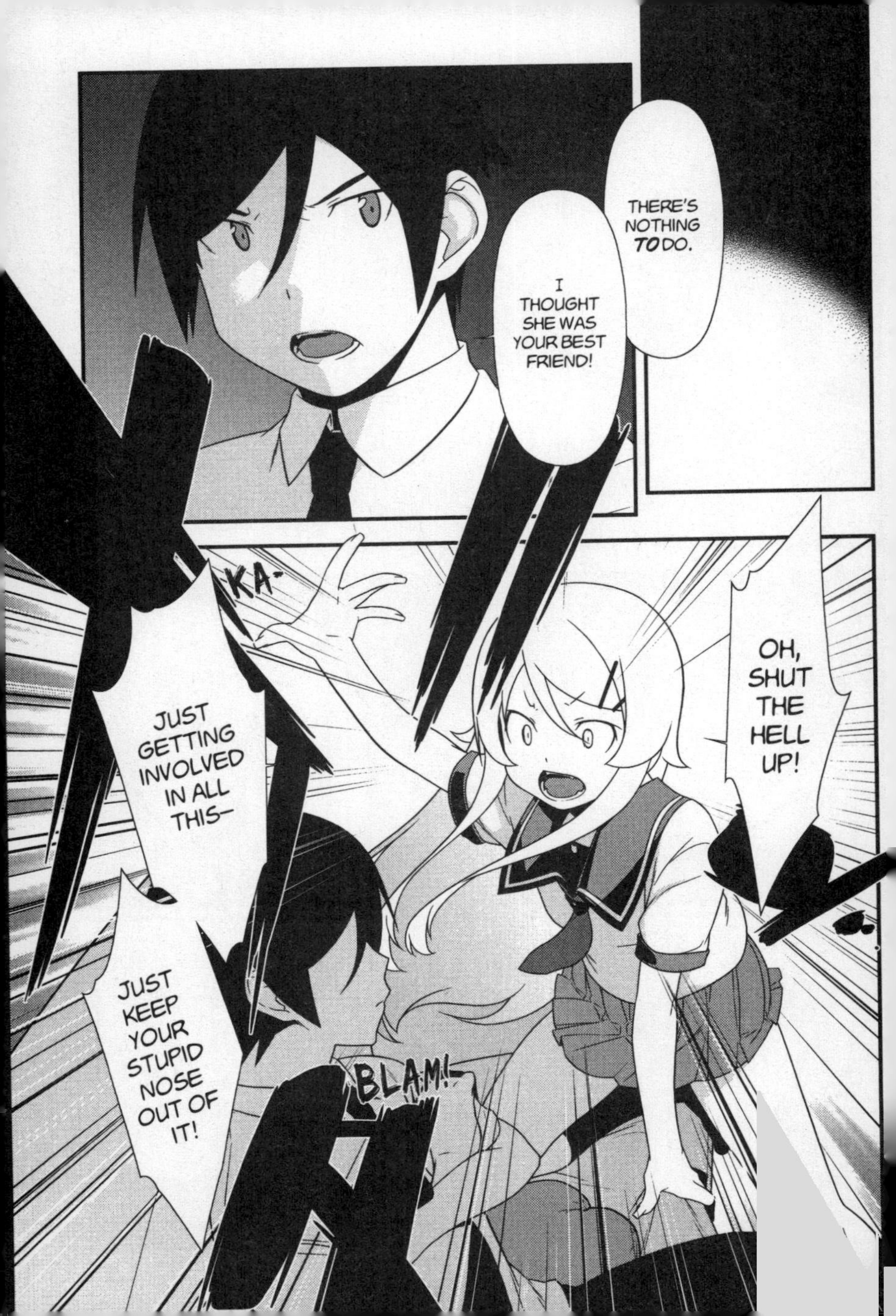
THERE'S NOTHING TO DO.
I THOUGHT SHE WAS YOUR BEST FRIEND!
OH, SHUT THE HELL UP!
KA-
JUST GETTING INVOLVED IN ALL THIS-
BLAM!
JUST KEEP YOUR STUPID NOSE OUT OF IT!

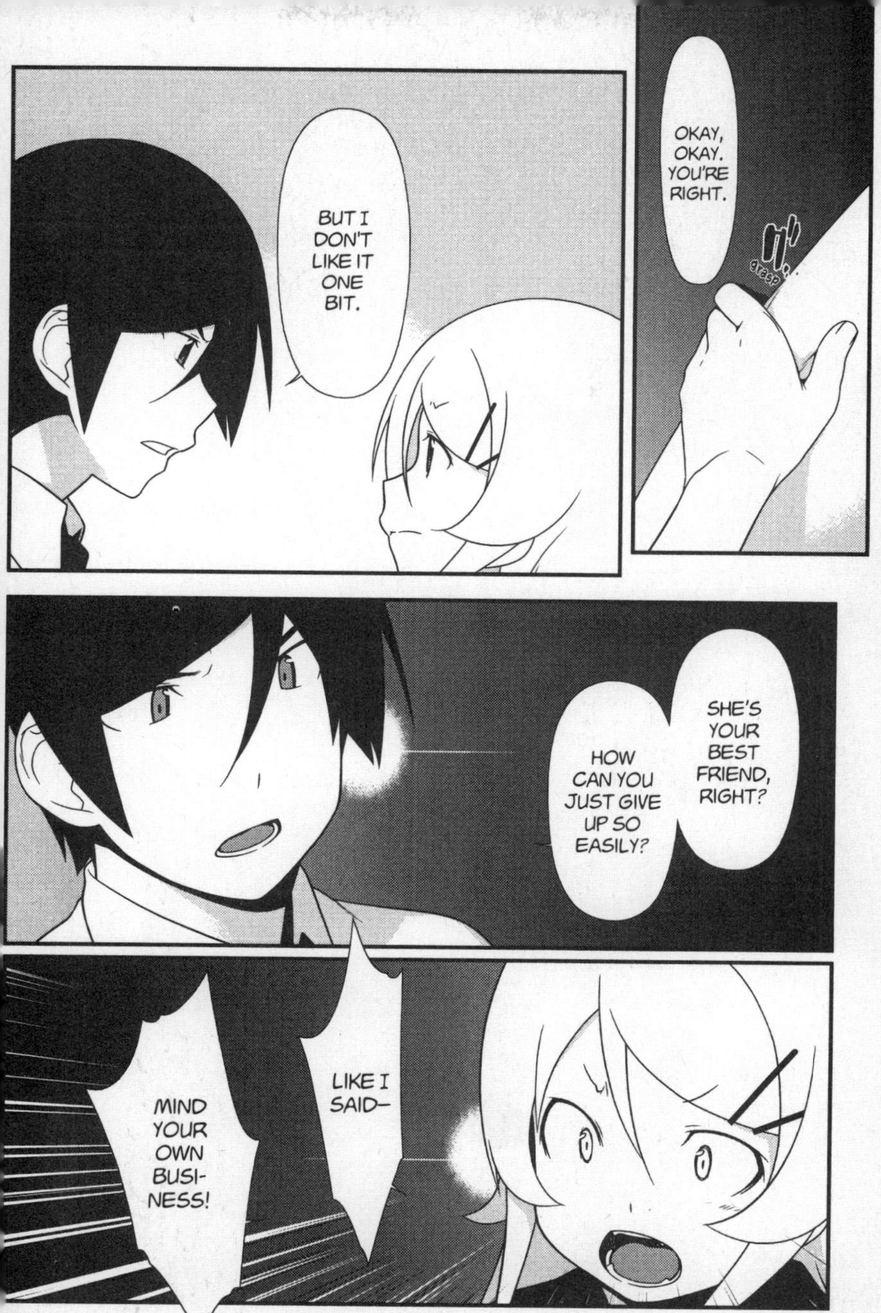
OKAY, OKAY. YOU'RE RIGHT.
grasp
BUT I DON'T LIKE IT ONE BIT.
SHE'S YOUR BEST FRIEND, RIGHT?
HOW CAN YOU JUST GIVE UP SO EASILY?
LIKE I SAID—
MIND YOUR OWN BUSI-NESS!

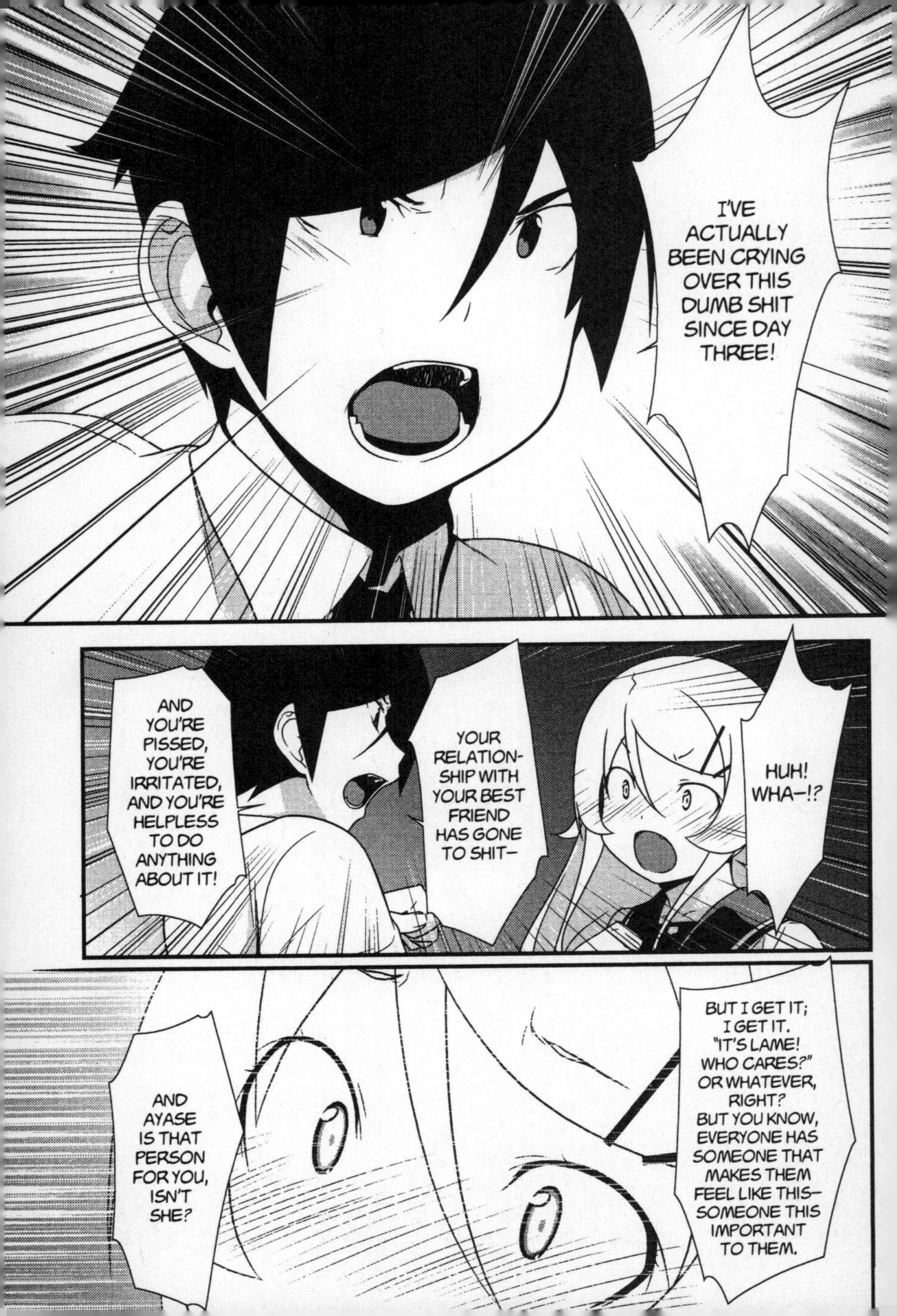
I'VE ACTUALLY BEEN CRYING OVER THIS DUMB SHIT SINCE DAY THREE!
HUH! WHA—!?
YOUR RELATIONSHIP WITH YOUR BEST FRIEND HAS GONE TO SHIT—
AND YOU'RE PISSED, YOU'RE IRRITATED, AND YOU'RE HELPLESS TO DO ANYTHING ABOUT IT!
BUT I GET IT; I GET IT. "IT'S LAME! WHO CARES?" OR WHATEVER, RIGHT? BUT YOU KNOW, EVERYONE HAS SOMEONE THAT MAKES THEM FEEL LIKE THIS— SOMEONE THIS IMPORTANT TO THEM.
AND AYASE IS THAT PERSON FOR YOU, ISN'T SHE?

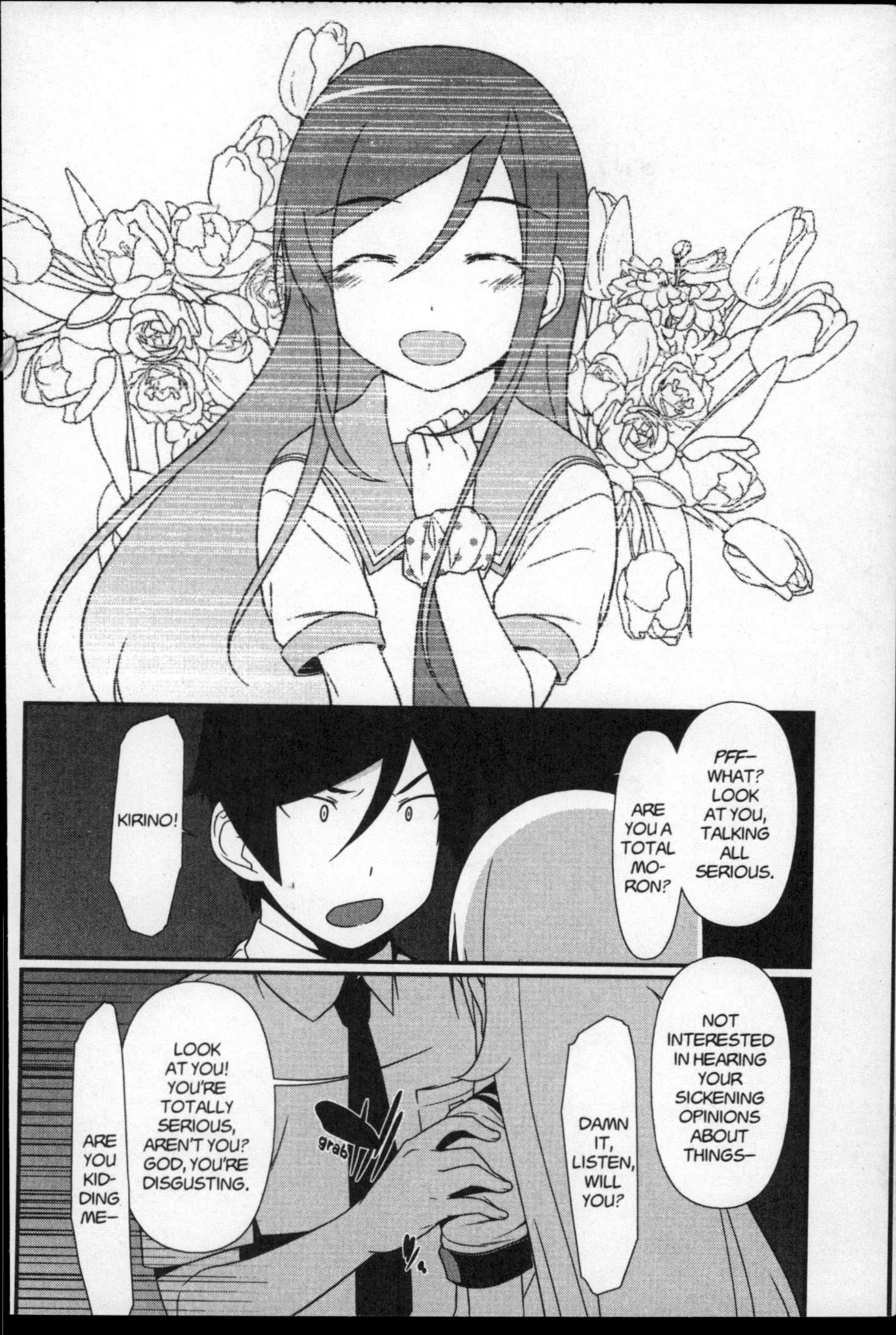
PFF— WHAT? LOOK AT YOU, TALKING ALL SERIOUS.
ARE YOU A TOTAL MO-RON?
KIRINO!
NOT INTERESTED IN HEARING YOUR SICKENING OPINIONS ABOUT THINGS—
DAMN IT, LISTEN, WILL YOU?
grab
LOOK AT YOU! YOU'RE TOTALLY SERIOUS, AREN'T YOU? GOD, YOU'RE DISGUSTING.
ARE YOU KIDDING ME—

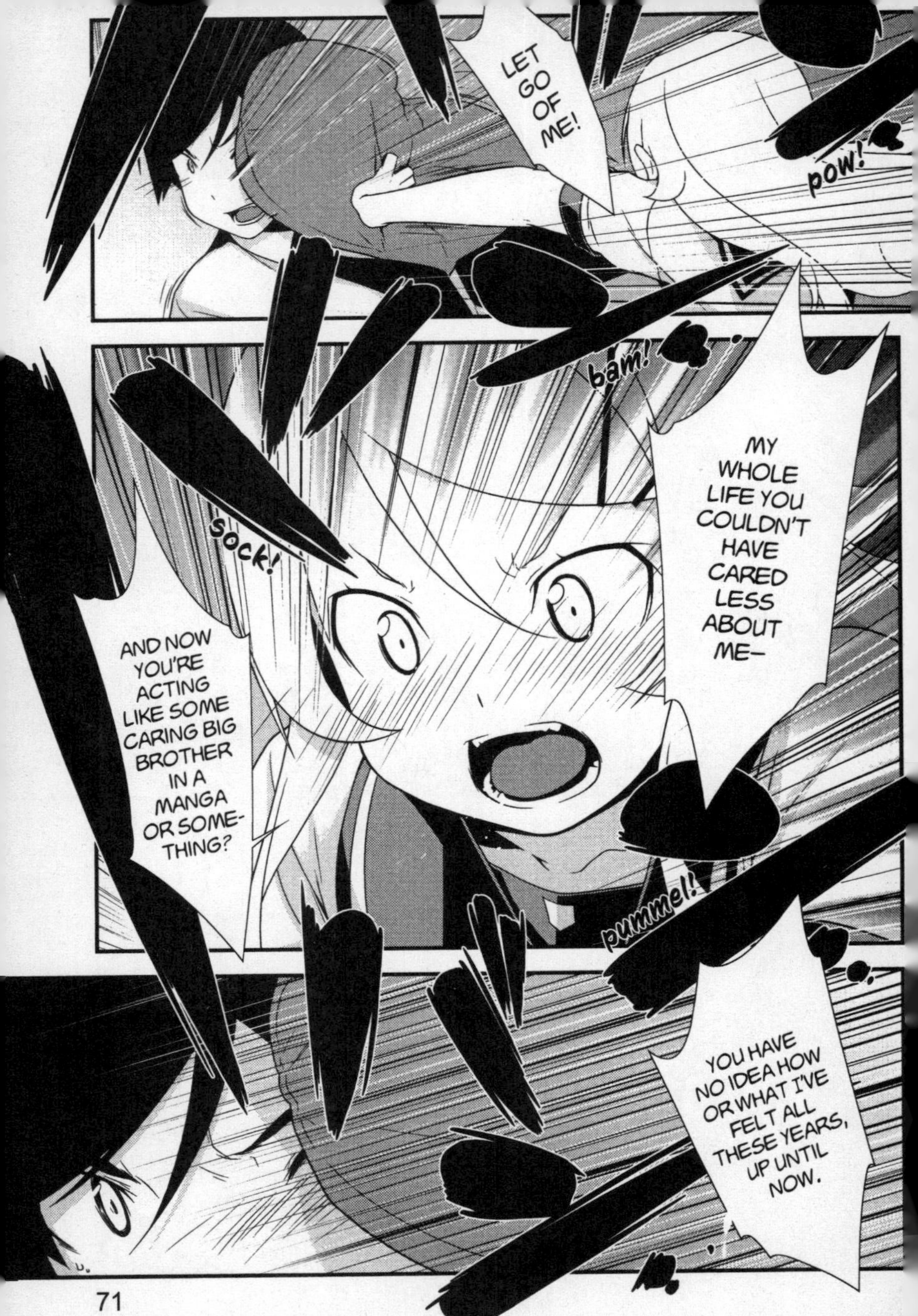
LET GO OF ME!
pow!
bam!
MY WHOLE LIFE YOU COULDN'T HAVE CARED LESS ABOUT ME–
sock!
AND NOW YOU'RE ACTING LIKE SOME CARING BIG BROTHER IN A MANGA OR SOME-THING?
pummel!
YOU HAVE NO IDEA HOW OR WHAT I'VE FELT ALL THESE YEARS, UP UNTIL NOW.

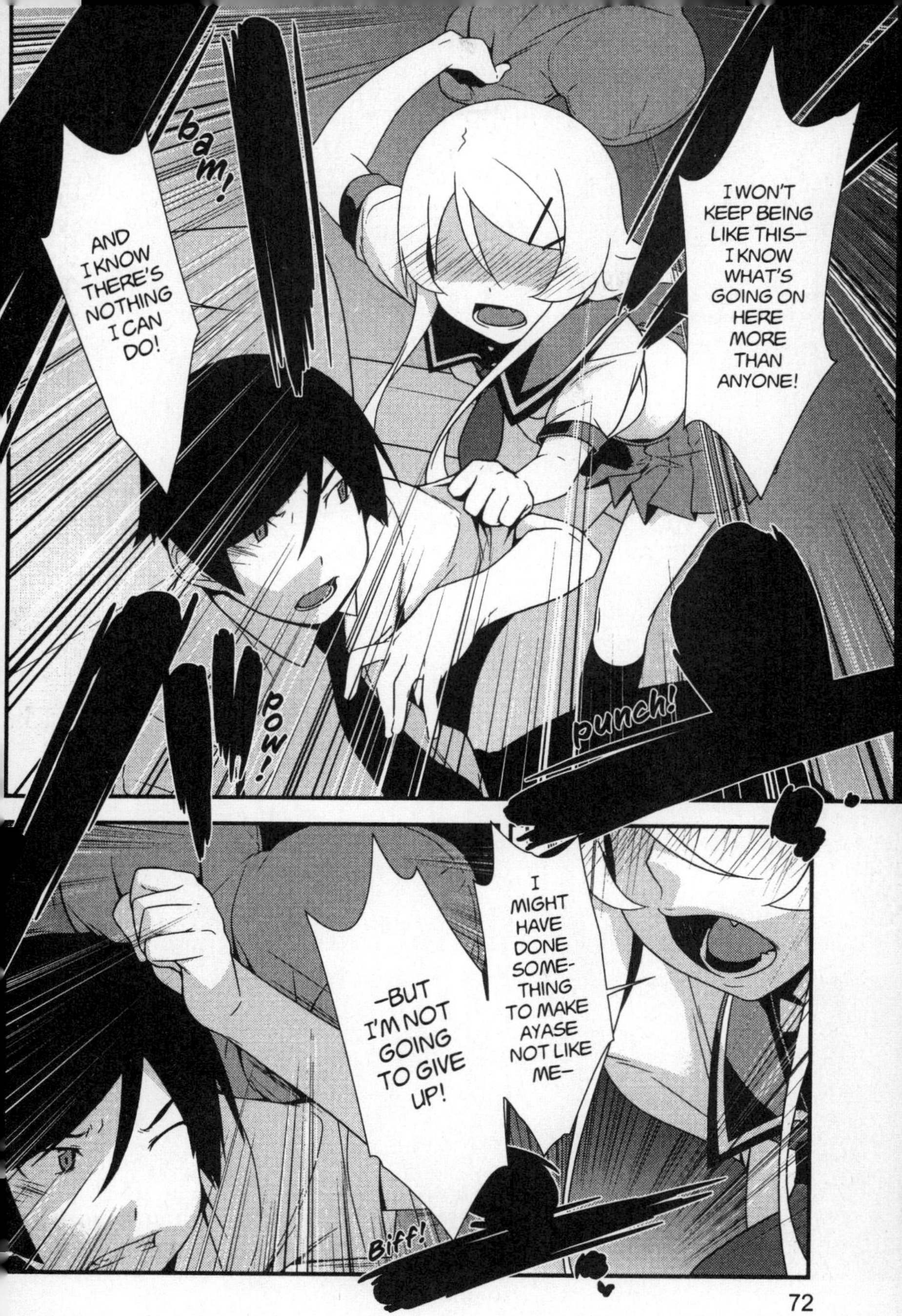
I WON'T KEEP BEING LIKE THIS— I KNOW WHAT'S GOING ON HERE MORE THAN ANYONE!
bam!
AND I KNOW THERE'S NOTHING I CAN DO!
punch!
POW!
I MIGHT HAVE DONE SOME-THING TO MAKE AYASE NOT LIKE ME—
—BUT I'M NOT GOING TO GIVE UP!
Biff!

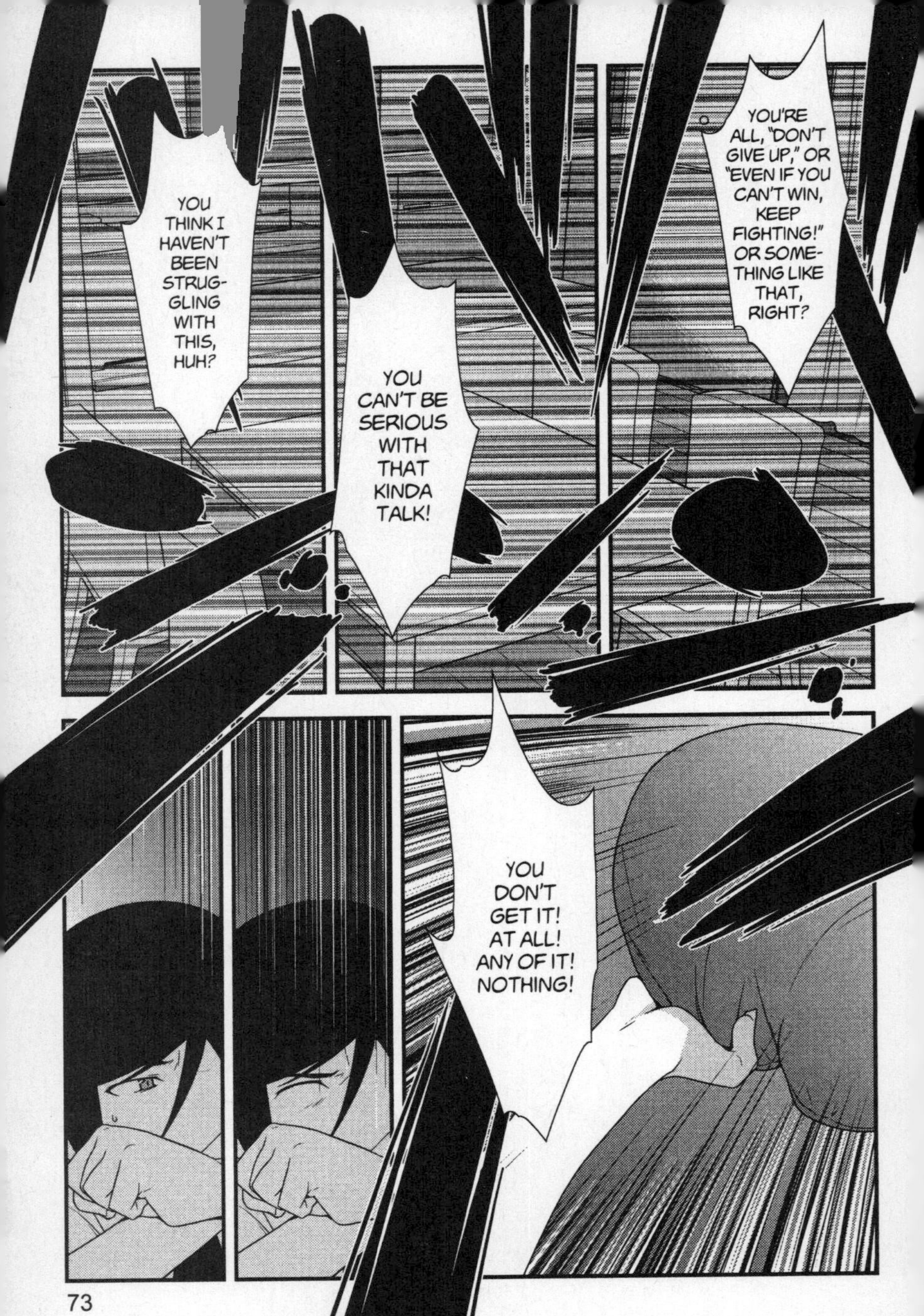
YOU'RE ALL, "DON'T GIVE UP," OR "EVEN IF YOU CAN'T WIN, KEEP FIGHTING!" OR SOME-THING LIKE THAT, RIGHT?
YOU CAN'T BE SERIOUS WITH THAT KINDA TALK!
YOU THINK I HAVEN'T BEEN STRUG-GLING WITH THIS, HUH?
YOU DON'T GET IT! AT ALL! ANY OF IT! NOTHING!

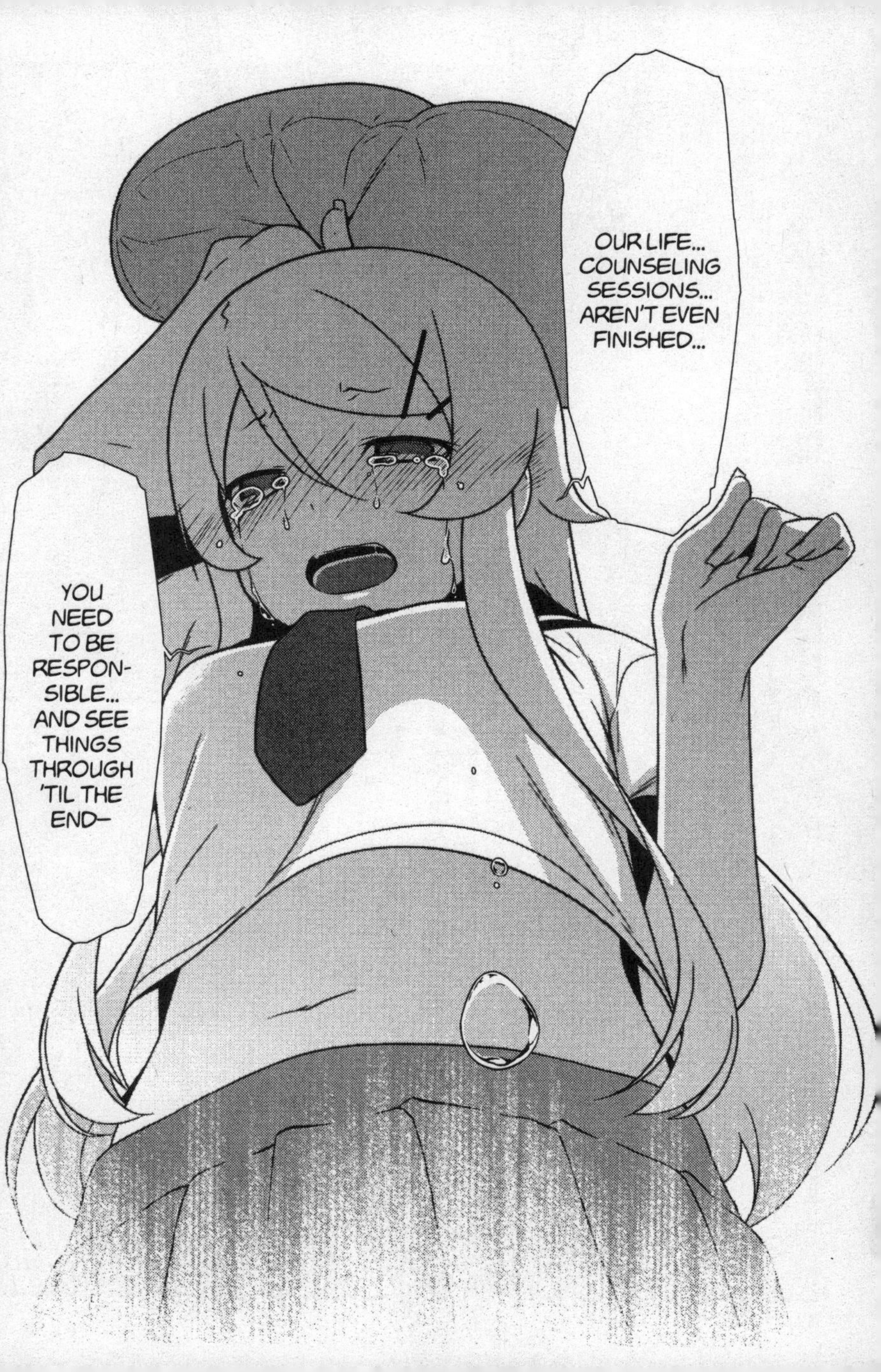
OUR LIFE... COUNSELING SESSIONS... AREN'T EVEN FINISHED...
YOU NEED TO BE RESPON-SIBLE... AND SEE THINGS THROUGH 'TIL THE END-

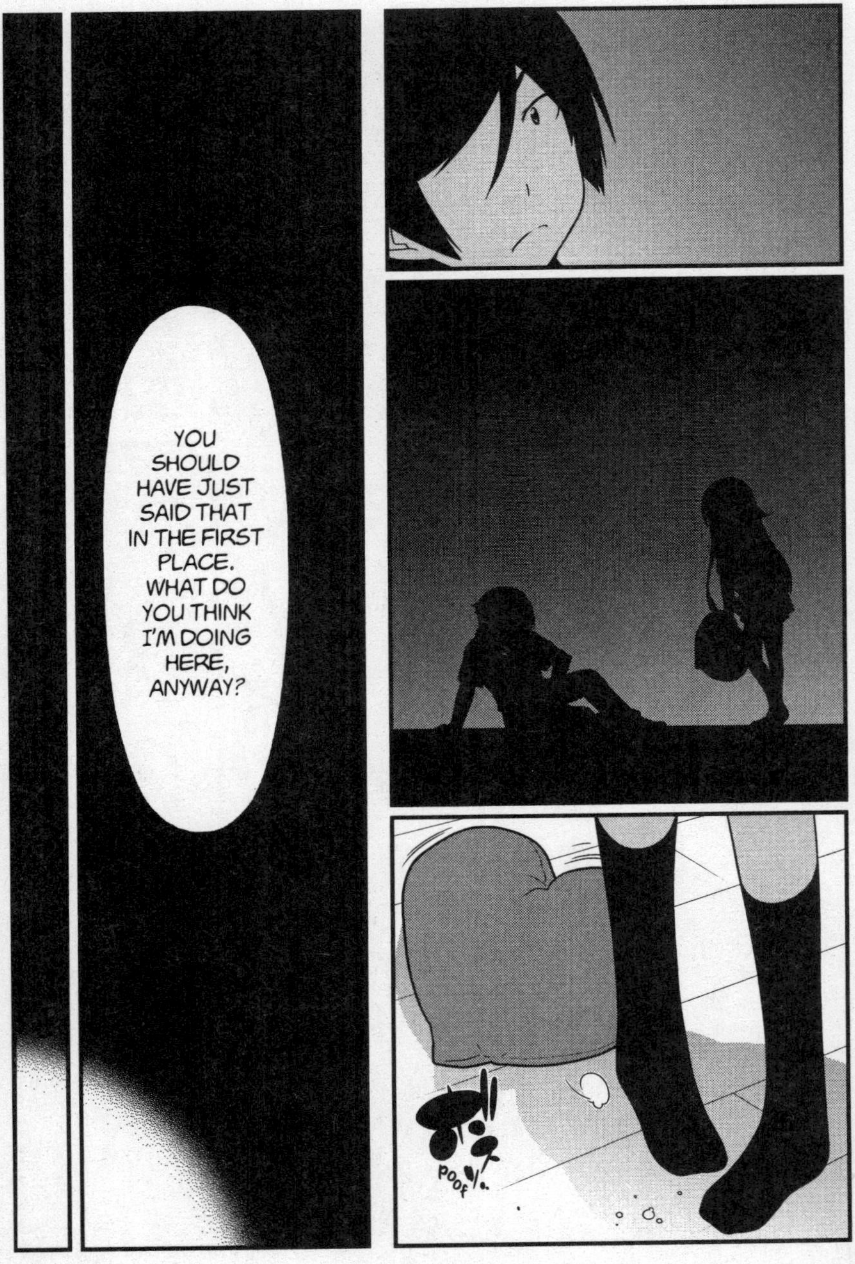
POOF
YOU SHOULD HAVE JUST SAID THAT IN THE FIRST PLACE. WHAT DO YOU THINK I'M DOING HERE, ANYWAY?

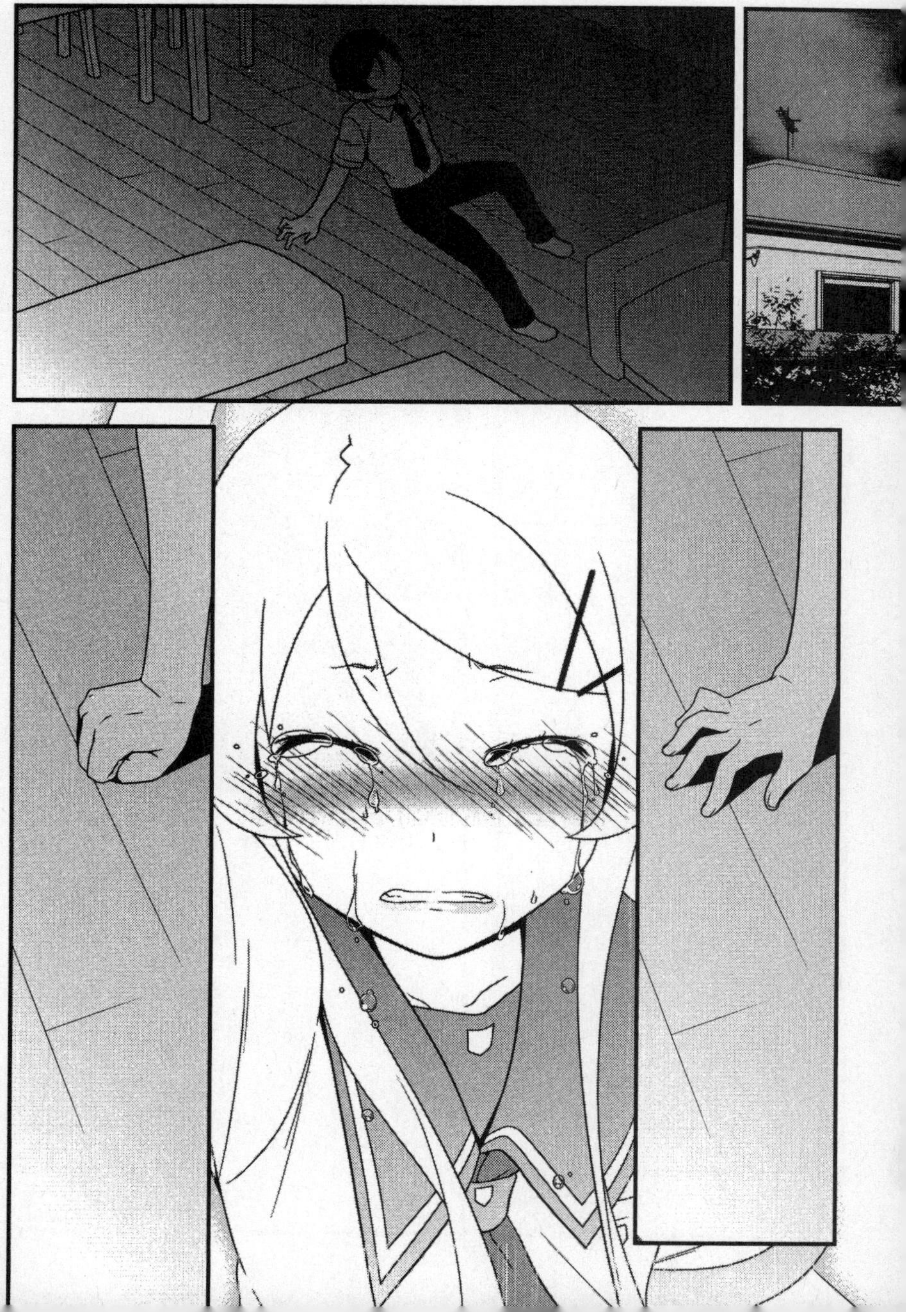

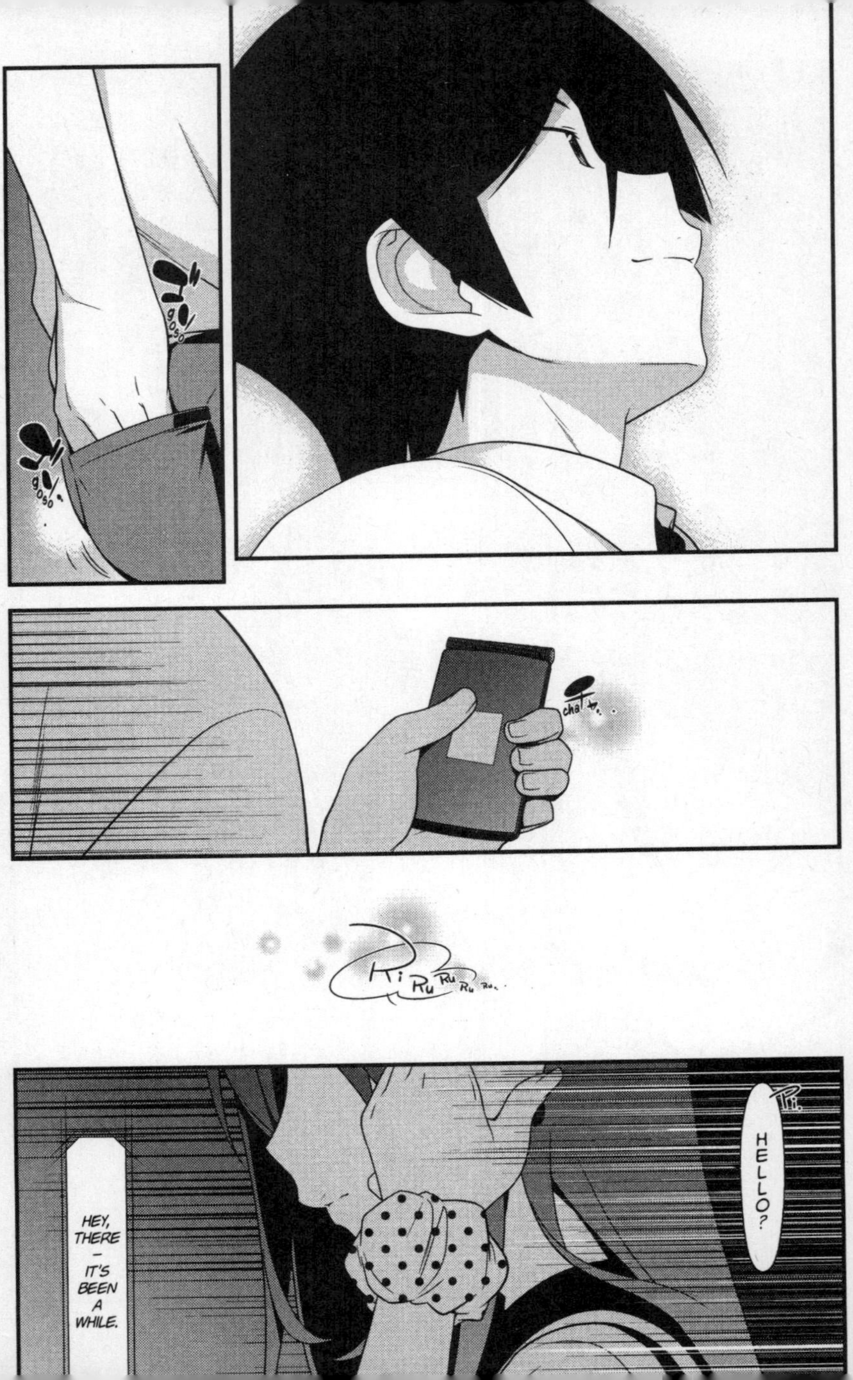
goso
goso
chat
RiRuRuRuRu
Pi.
HELLO?
HEY, THERE — IT'S BEEN A WHILE.

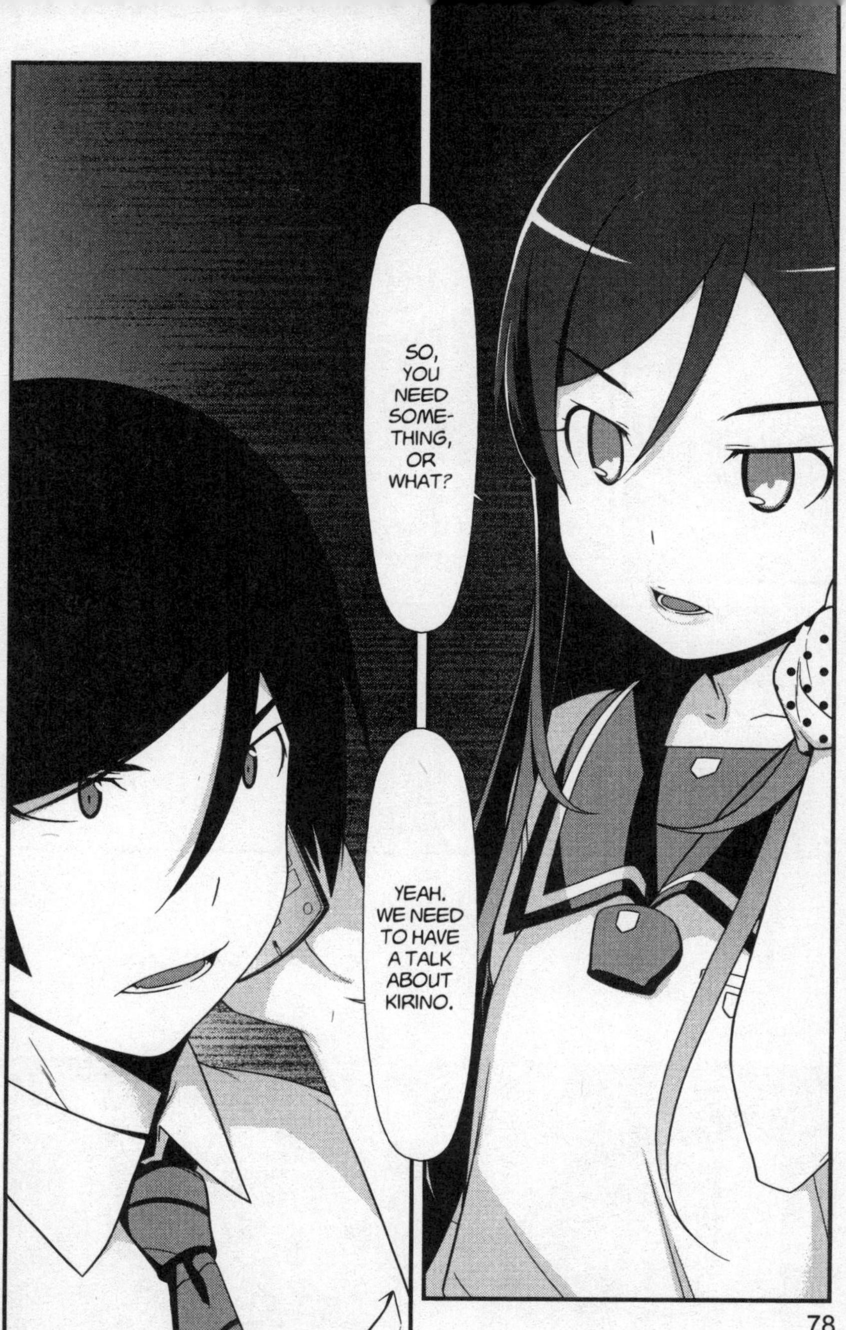
SO, YOU NEED SOMETHING, OR WHAT?
YEAH. WE NEED TO HAVE A TALK ABOUT KIRINO.

俺の妹が
こんなに
可愛いわけが
ない

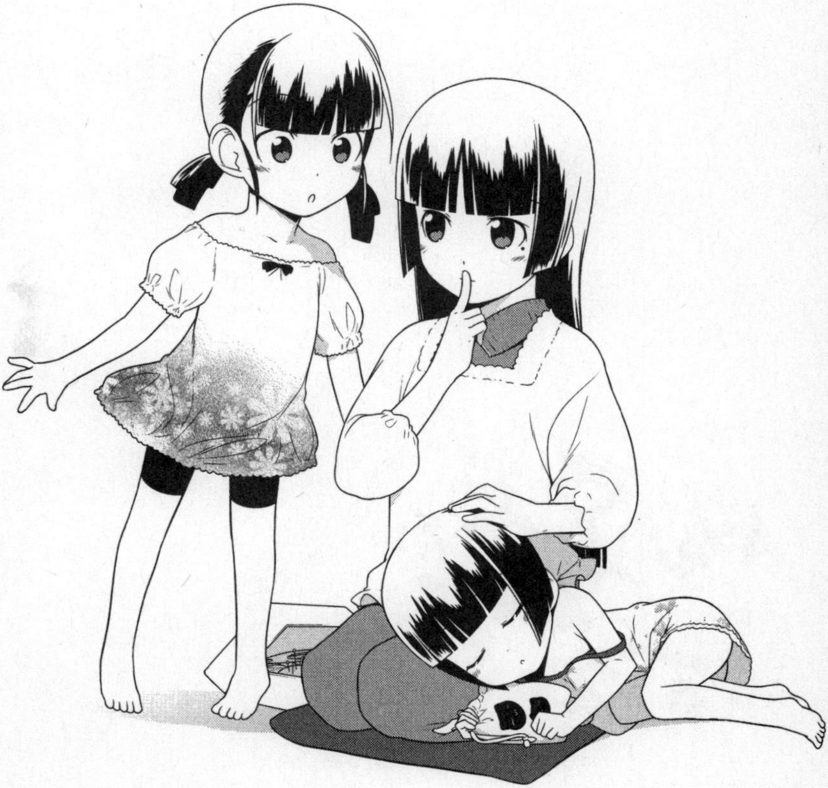

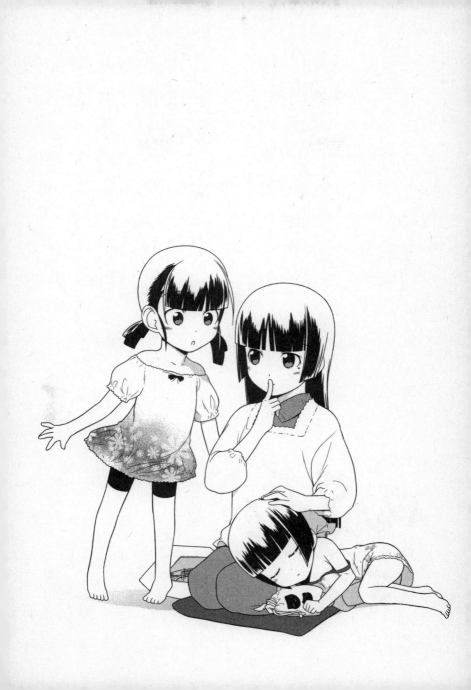

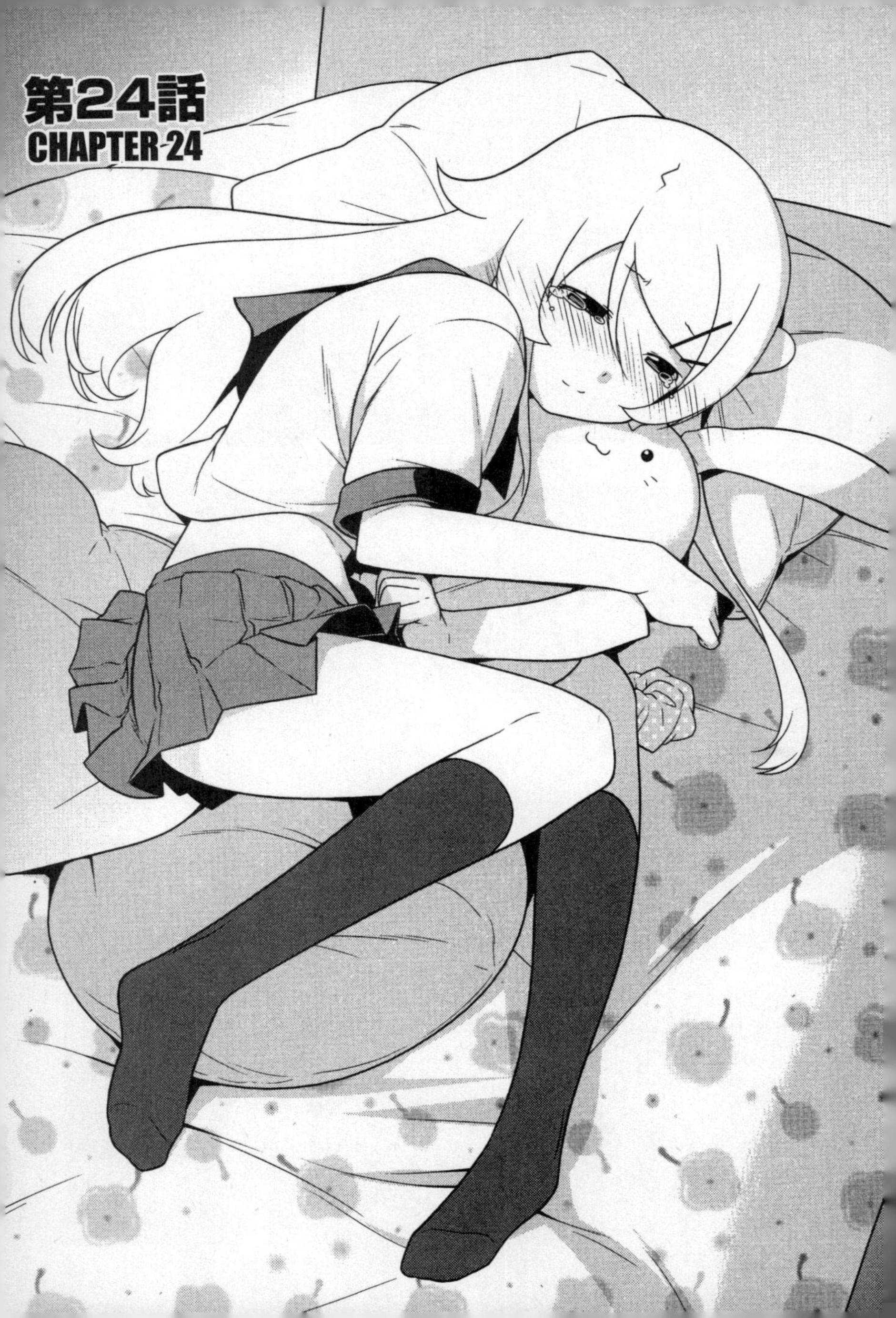
第24話
CHAPTER 24

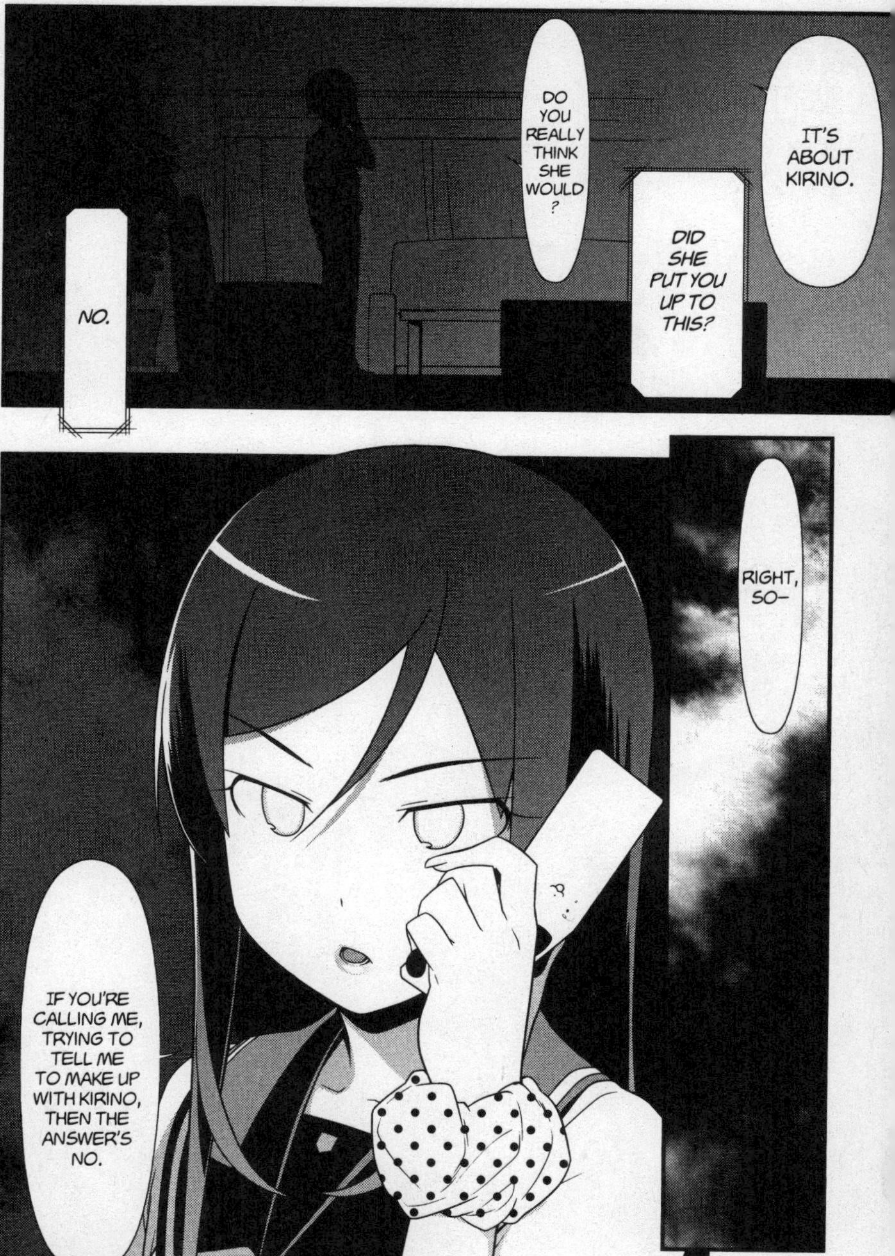
IT'S ABOUT KIRINO.
DID SHE PUT YOU UP TO THIS?
DO YOU REALLY THINK SHE WOULD?
NO.
RIGHT, SO–
IF YOU'RE CALLING ME, TRYING TO TELL ME TO MAKE UP WITH KIRINO, THEN THE ANSWER'S NO.

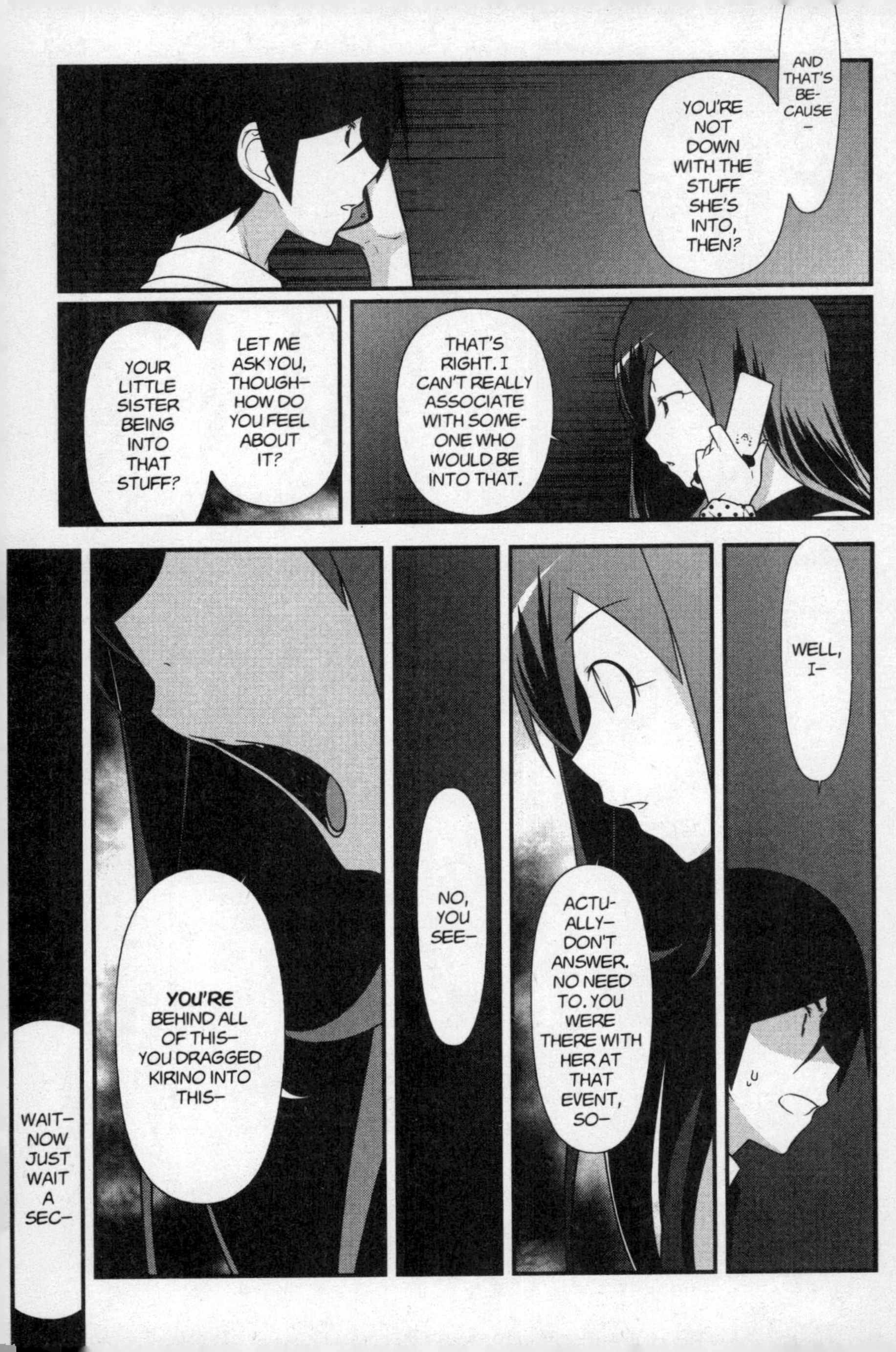
AND THAT'S BE-CAUSE—
YOU'RE NOT DOWN WITH THE STUFF SHE'S INTO, THEN?
THAT'S RIGHT. I CAN'T REALLY ASSOCIATE WITH SOME-ONE WHO WOULD BE INTO THAT.
LET ME ASK YOU, THOUGH—HOW DO YOU FEEL ABOUT IT?
YOUR LITTLE SISTER BEING INTO THAT STUFF?
WELL, I—
ACTU-ALLY—DON'T ANSWER. NO NEED TO. YOU WERE THERE WITH HER AT THAT EVENT, SO—
NO, YOU SEE—
YOU'RE BEHIND ALL OF THIS—YOU DRAGGED KIRINO INTO THIS—
WAIT—NOW JUST WAIT A SEC—

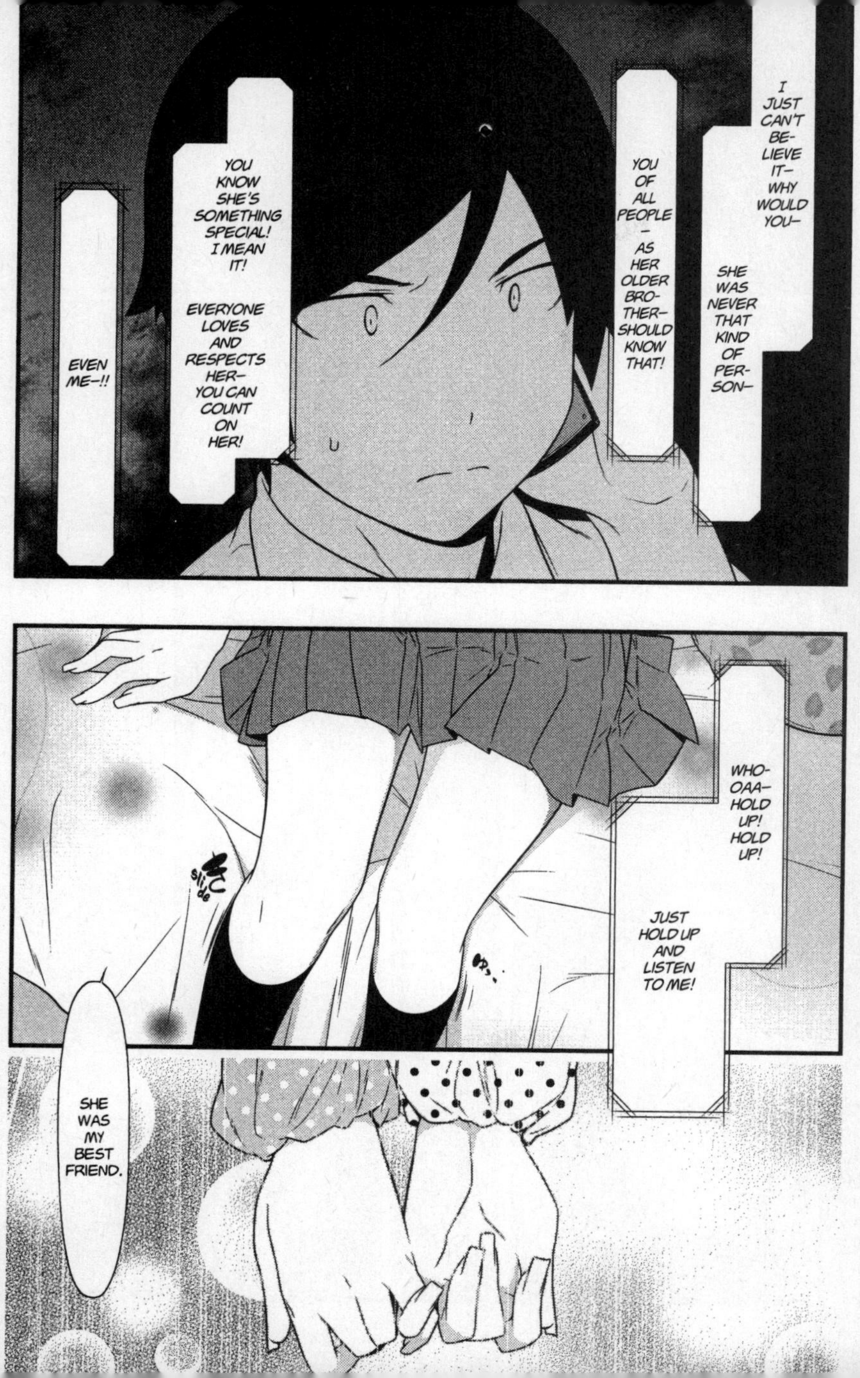
I JUST CAN'T BE-LIEVE IT—WHY WOULD YOU—
SHE WAS NEVER THAT KIND OF PER-SON—
YOU OF ALL PEOPLE—AS HER OLDER BRO-THER—SHOULD KNOW THAT!
YOU KNOW SHE'S SOMETHING SPECIAL! I MEAN IT!
EVERYONE LOVES AND RESPECTS HER—YOU CAN COUNT ON HER!
EVEN ME—!!
WHO-OAA—HOLD UP! HOLD UP!
JUST HOLD UP AND LISTEN TO ME!
slide
SHE WAS MY BEST FRIEND.

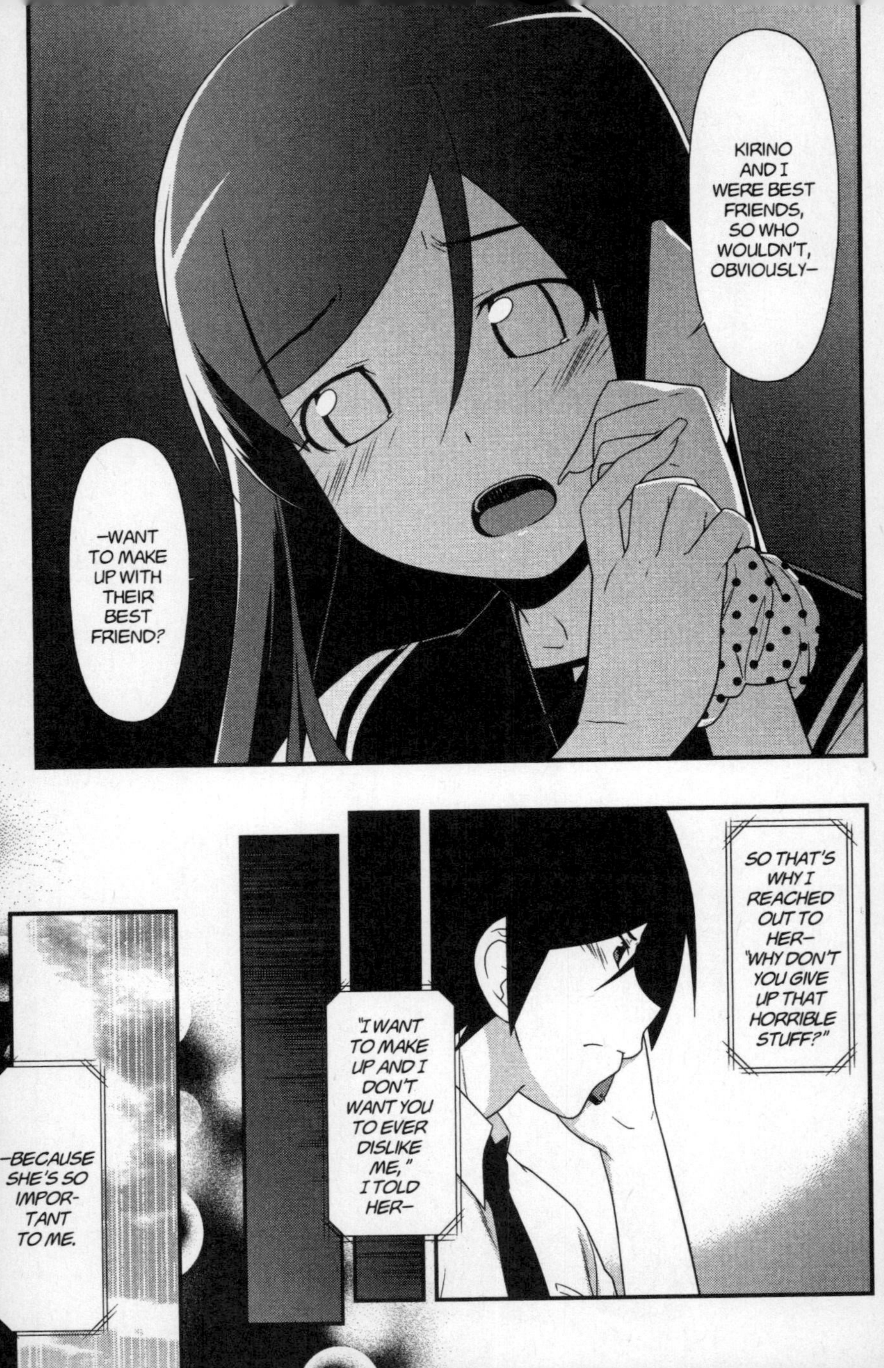
KIRINO AND I WERE BEST FRIENDS, SO WHO WOULDN'T, OBVIOUSLY—
—WANT TO MAKE UP WITH THEIR BEST FRIEND?
SO THAT'S WHY I REACHED OUT TO HER— "WHY DON'T YOU GIVE UP THAT HORRIBLE STUFF?"
"I WANT TO MAKE UP AND I DON'T WANT YOU TO EVER DISLIKE ME," I TOLD HER—
—BECAUSE SHE'S SO IMPOR-TANT TO ME.

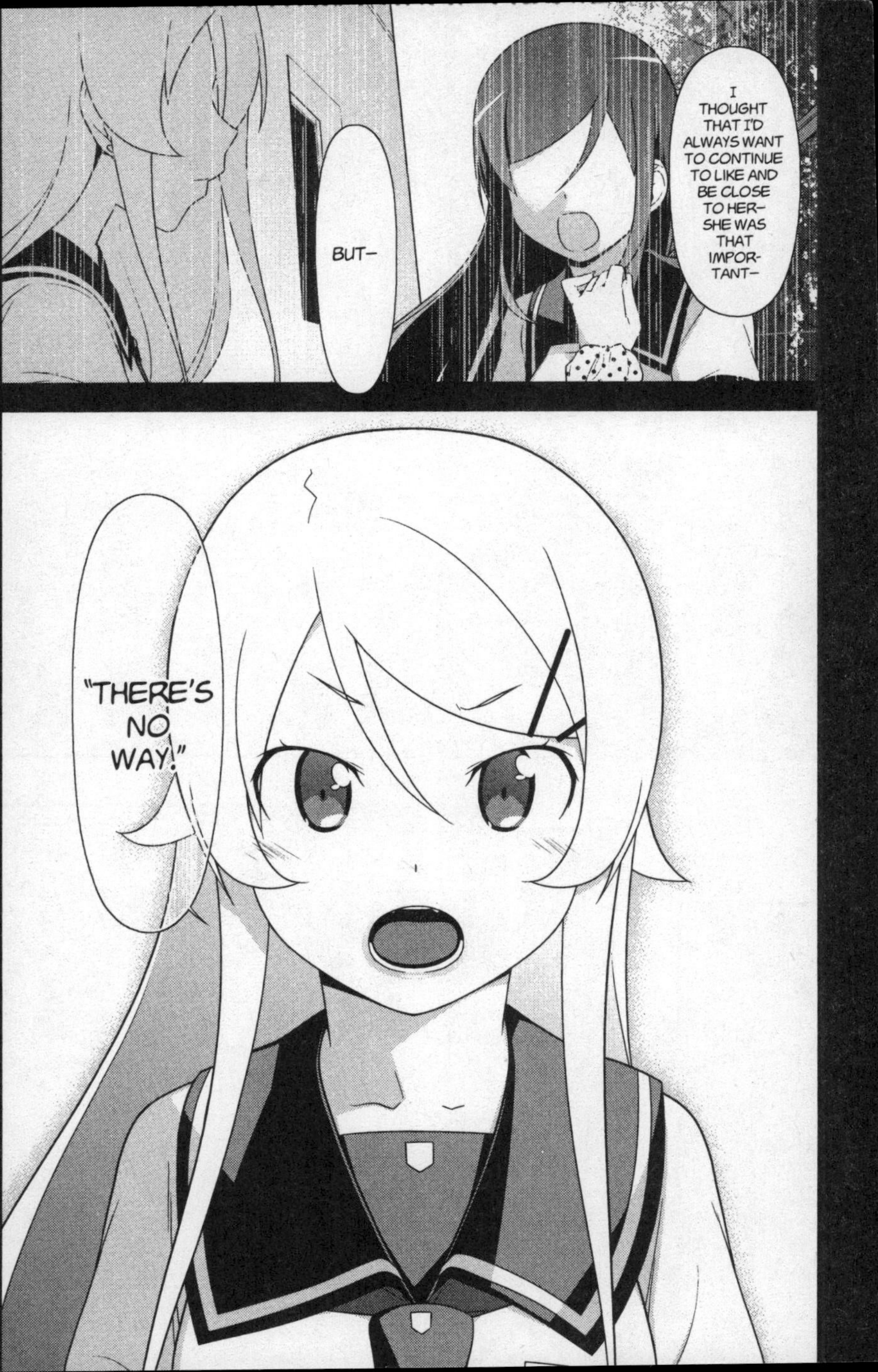
I THOUGHT THAT I'D ALWAYS WANT TO CONTINUE TO LIKE AND BE CLOSE TO HER- SHE WAS THAT IMPOR-TANT-
BUT-
"THERE'S NO WAY!"

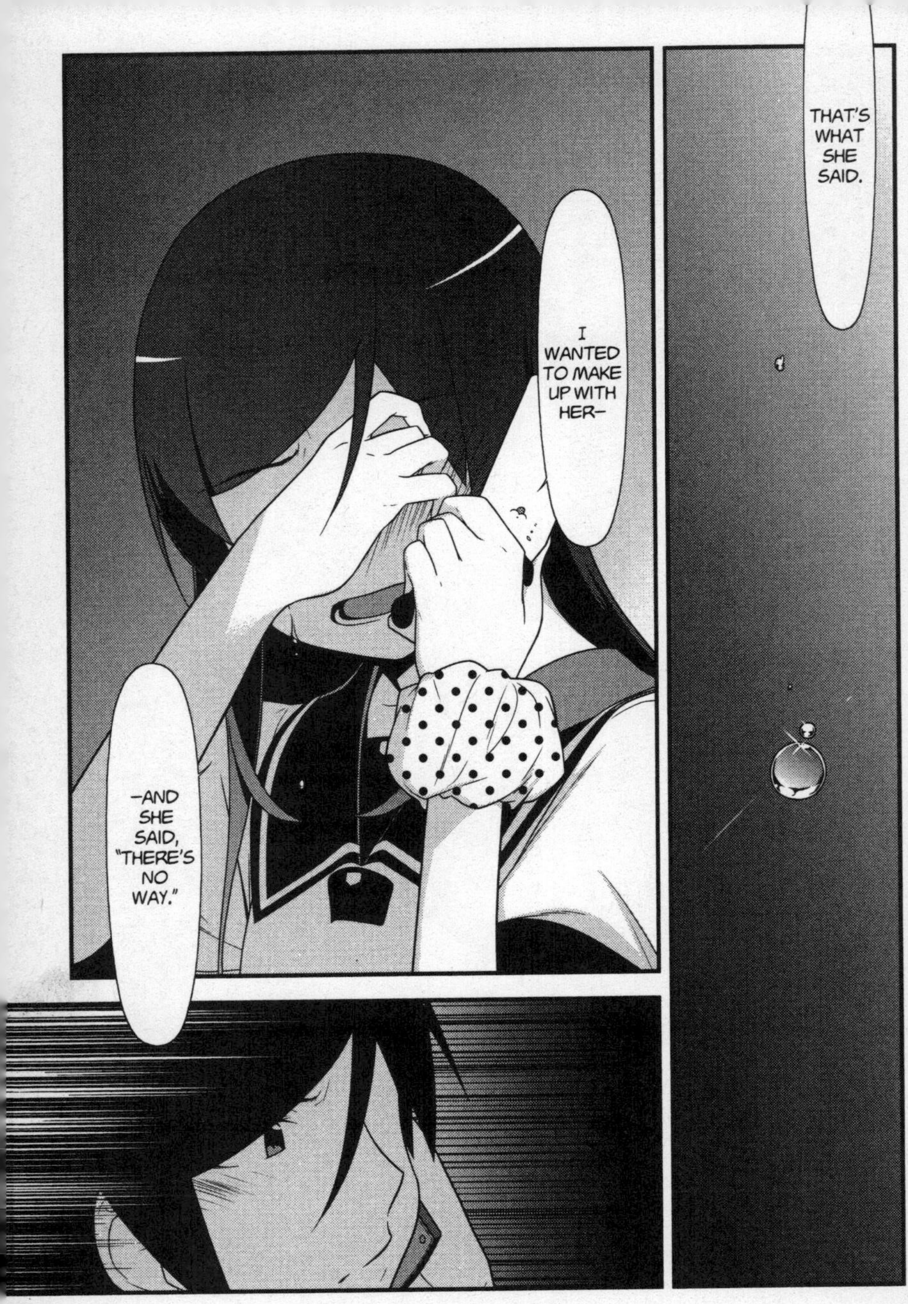
THAT'S WHAT SHE SAID.
I WANTED TO MAKE UP WITH HER–
–AND SHE SAID, "THERE'S NO WAY."

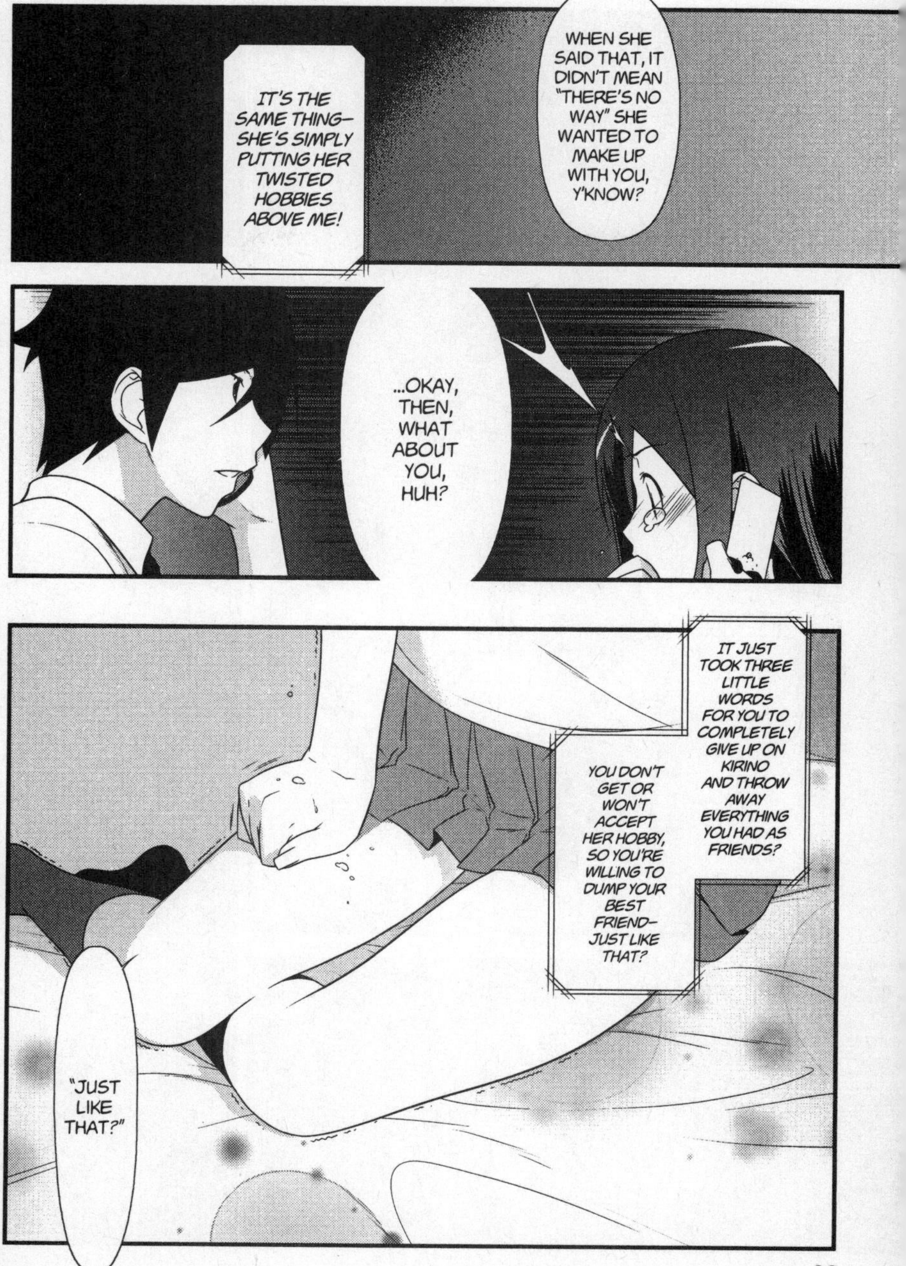
WHEN SHE SAID THAT, IT DIDN'T MEAN "THERE'S NO WAY" SHE WANTED TO MAKE UP WITH YOU, Y'KNOW?
IT'S THE SAME THING– SHE'S SIMPLY PUTTING HER TWISTED HOBBIES ABOVE ME!
...OKAY, THEN, WHAT ABOUT YOU, HUH?
IT JUST TOOK THREE LITTLE WORDS FOR YOU TO COMPLETELY GIVE UP ON KIRINO AND THROW AWAY EVERYTHING YOU HAD AS FRIENDS?
YOU DON'T GET OR WON'T ACCEPT HER HOBBY, SO YOU'RE WILLING TO DUMP YOUR BEST FRIEND– JUST LIKE THAT?
"JUST LIKE THAT?"

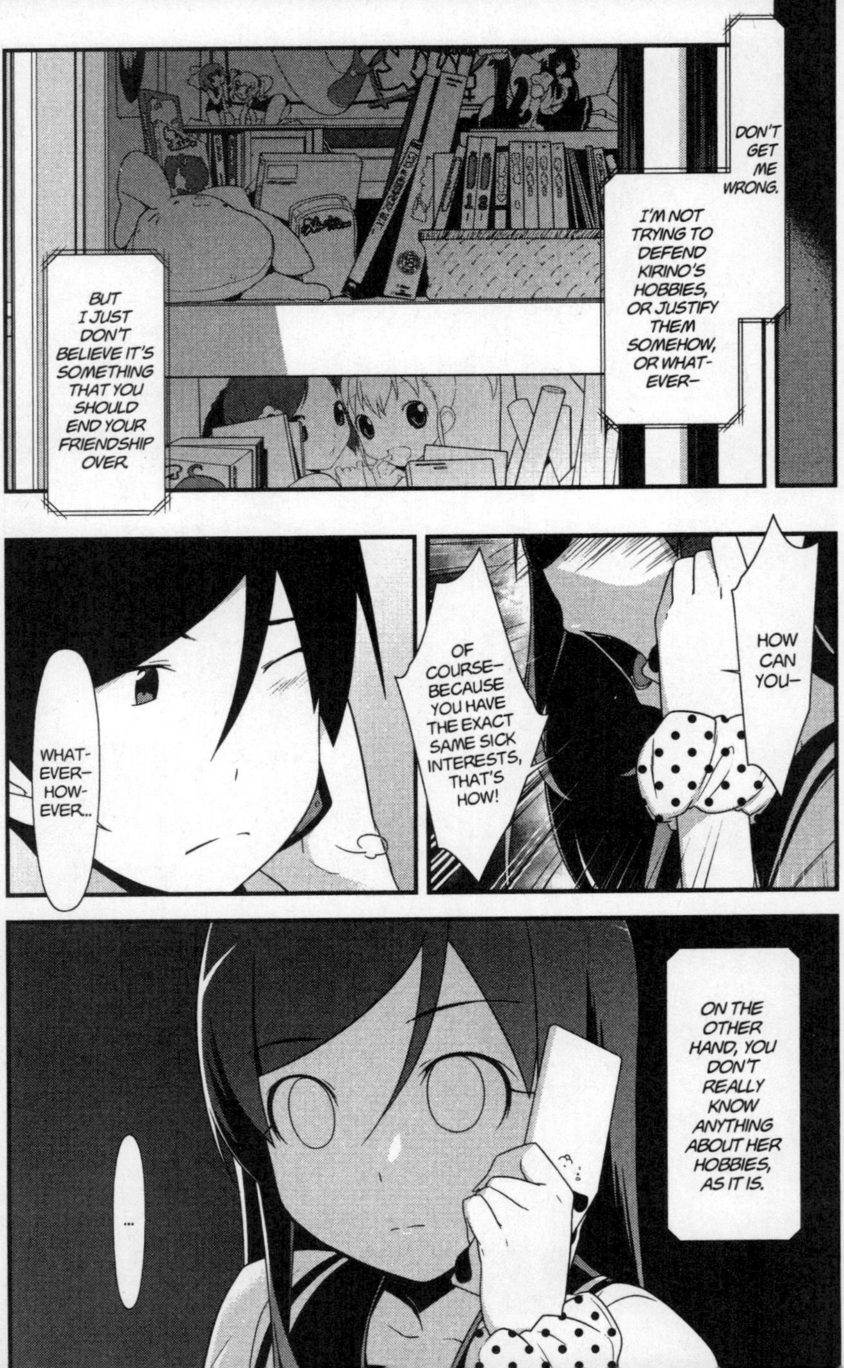
DON'T GET ME WRONG.
I'M NOT TRYING TO DEFEND KIRINO'S HOBBIES, OR JUSTIFY THEM SOMEHOW, OR WHAT-EVER—
BUT I JUST DON'T BELIEVE IT'S SOMETHING THAT YOU SHOULD END YOUR FRIENDSHIP OVER.
HOW CAN YOU—
OF COURSE—BECAUSE YOU HAVE THE EXACT SAME SICK INTERESTS, THAT'S HOW!
WHAT-EVER—HOW-EVER...
ON THE OTHER HAND, YOU DON'T REALLY KNOW ANYTHING ABOUT HER HOBBIES, AS IT IS.
...

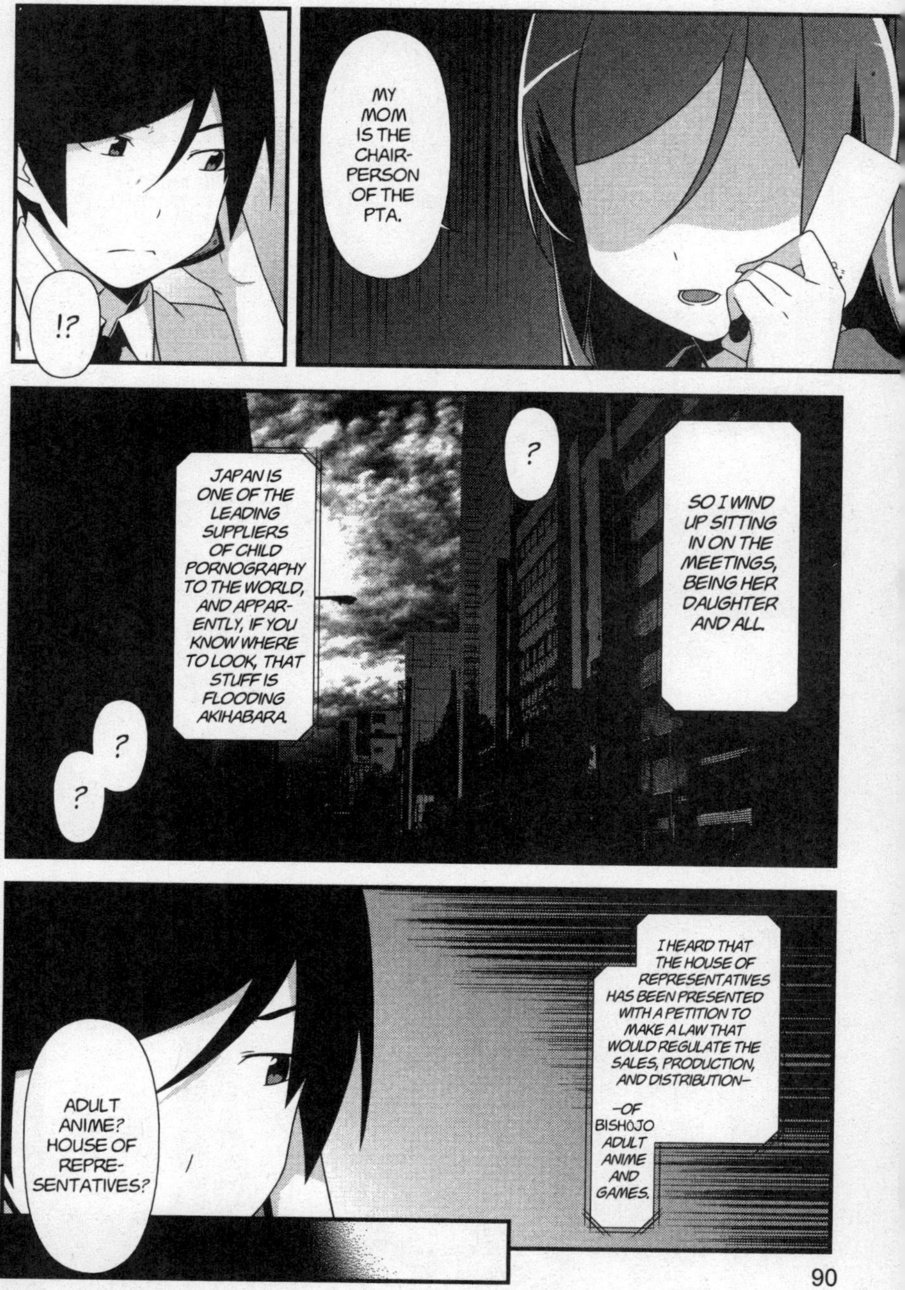
MY MOM IS THE CHAIR-PERSON OF THE PTA.
!?
SO I WIND UP SITTING IN ON THE MEETINGS, BEING HER DAUGHTER AND ALL.
?
JAPAN IS ONE OF THE LEADING SUPPLIERS OF CHILD PORNOGRAPHY TO THE WORLD, AND APPAR-ENTLY, IF YOU KNOW WHERE TO LOOK, THAT STUFF IS FLOODING AKIHABARA.
?
?
I HEARD THAT THE HOUSE OF REPRESENTATIVES HAS BEEN PRESENTED WITH A PETITION TO MAKE A LAW THAT WOULD REGULATE THE SALES, PRODUCTION, AND DISTRIBUTION–
–OF BISHŌJO ADULT ANIME AND GAMES.
ADULT ANIME? HOUSE OF REPRE-SENTATIVES?

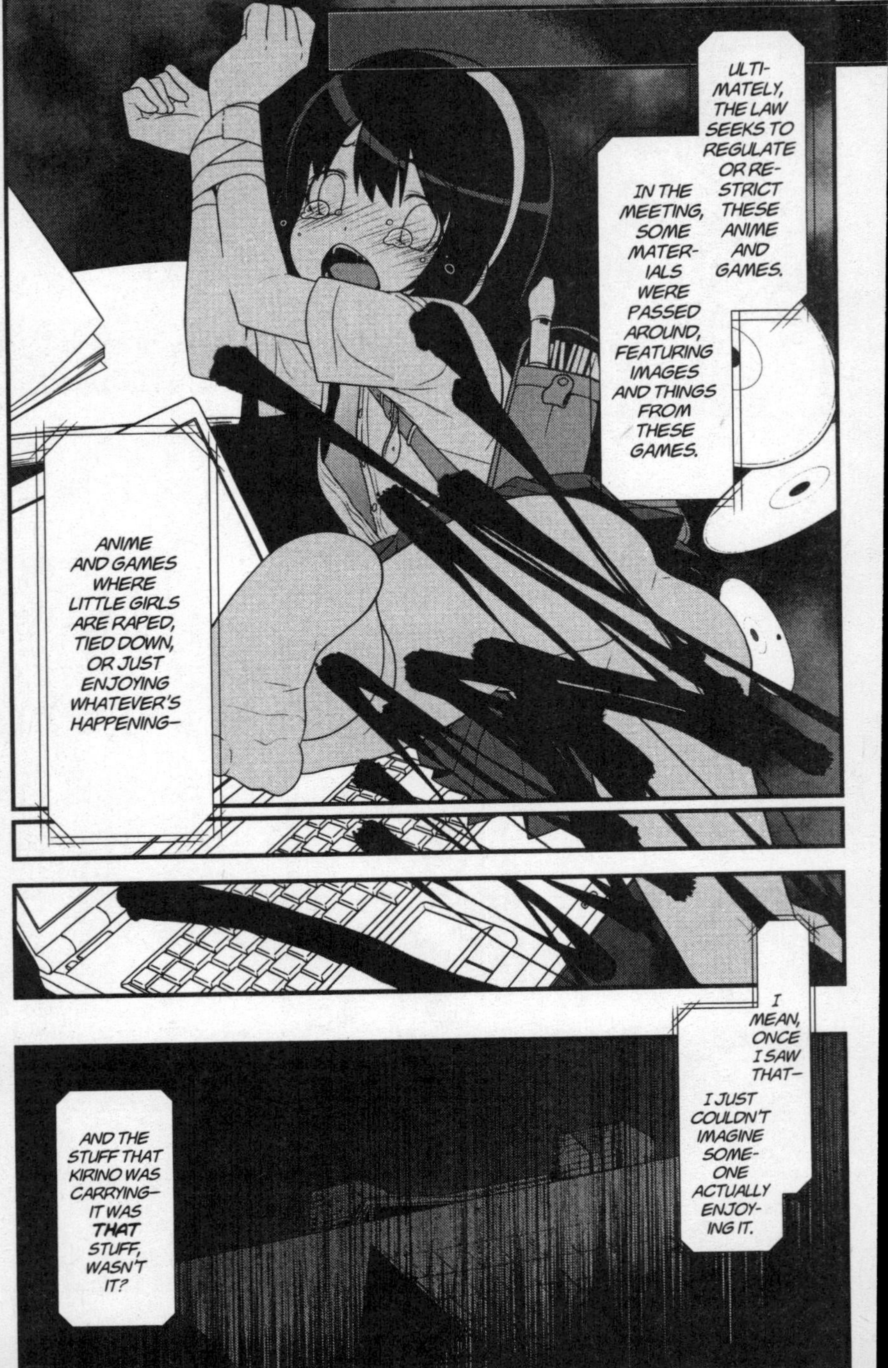
ULTI-MATELY, THE LAW SEEKS TO REGULATE OR RE-STRICT THESE ANIME AND GAMES.
IN THE MEETING, SOME MATER-IALS WERE PASSED AROUND, FEATURING IMAGES AND THINGS FROM THESE GAMES.
ANIME AND GAMES WHERE LITTLE GIRLS ARE RAPED, TIED DOWN, OR JUST ENJOYING WHATEVER'S HAPPENING—
I MEAN, ONCE I SAW THAT—
I JUST COULDN'T IMAGINE SOME-ONE ACTUALLY ENJOY-ING IT.
AND THE STUFF THAT KIRINO WAS CARRYING— IT WAS **THAT** STUFF, WASN'T IT?

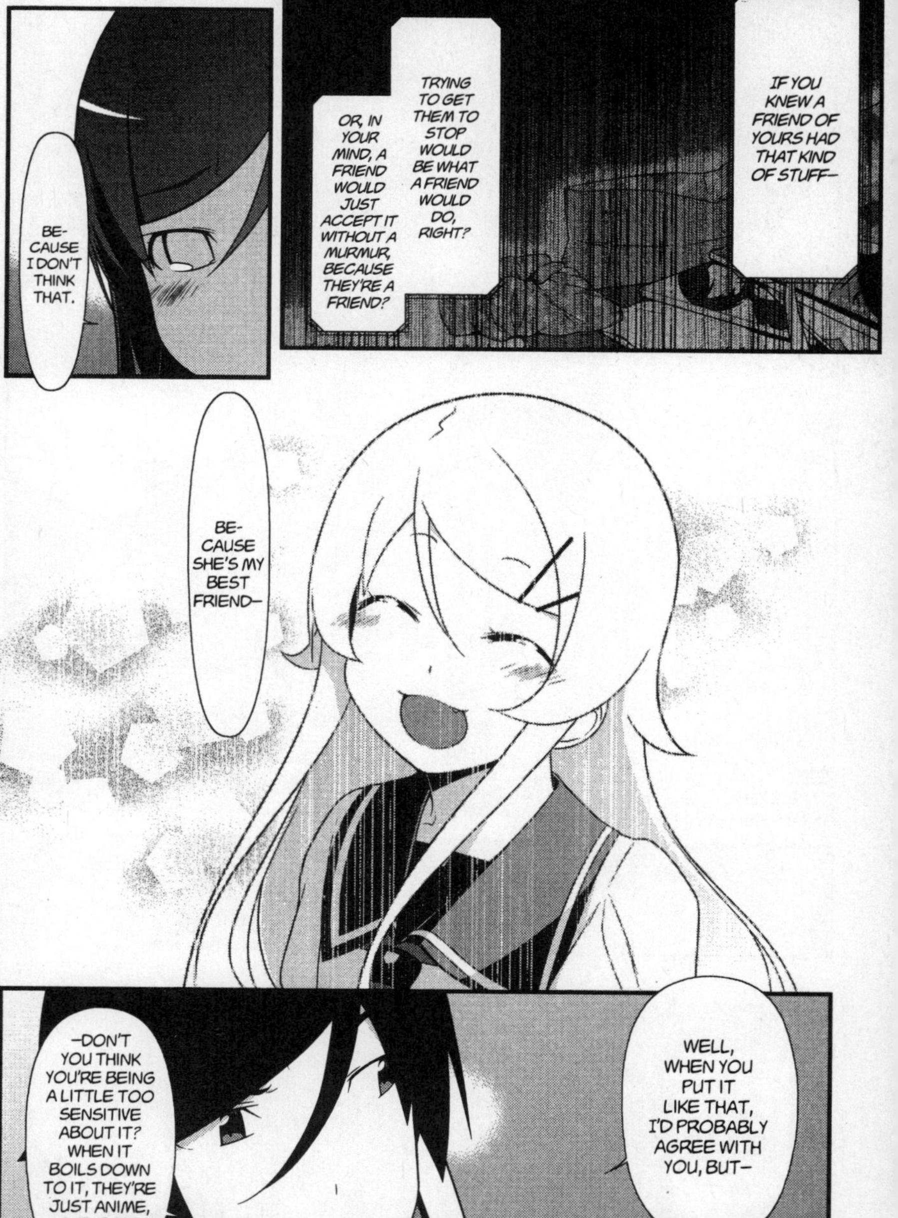
IF YOU KNEW A FRIEND OF YOURS HAD THAT KIND OF STUFF—
TRYING TO GET THEM TO STOP WOULD BE WHAT A FRIEND WOULD DO, RIGHT?
OR, IN YOUR MIND, A FRIEND WOULD JUST ACCEPT IT WITHOUT A MURMUR, BECAUSE THEY'RE A FRIEND?
BE-CAUSE I DON'T THINK THAT.
BE-CAUSE SHE'S MY BEST FRIEND—
WELL, WHEN YOU PUT IT LIKE THAT, I'D PROBABLY AGREE WITH YOU, BUT—
—DON'T YOU THINK YOU'RE BEING A LITTLE TOO SENSITIVE ABOUT IT? WHEN IT BOILS DOWN TO IT, THEY'RE JUST ANIME, AND JUST GAMES.

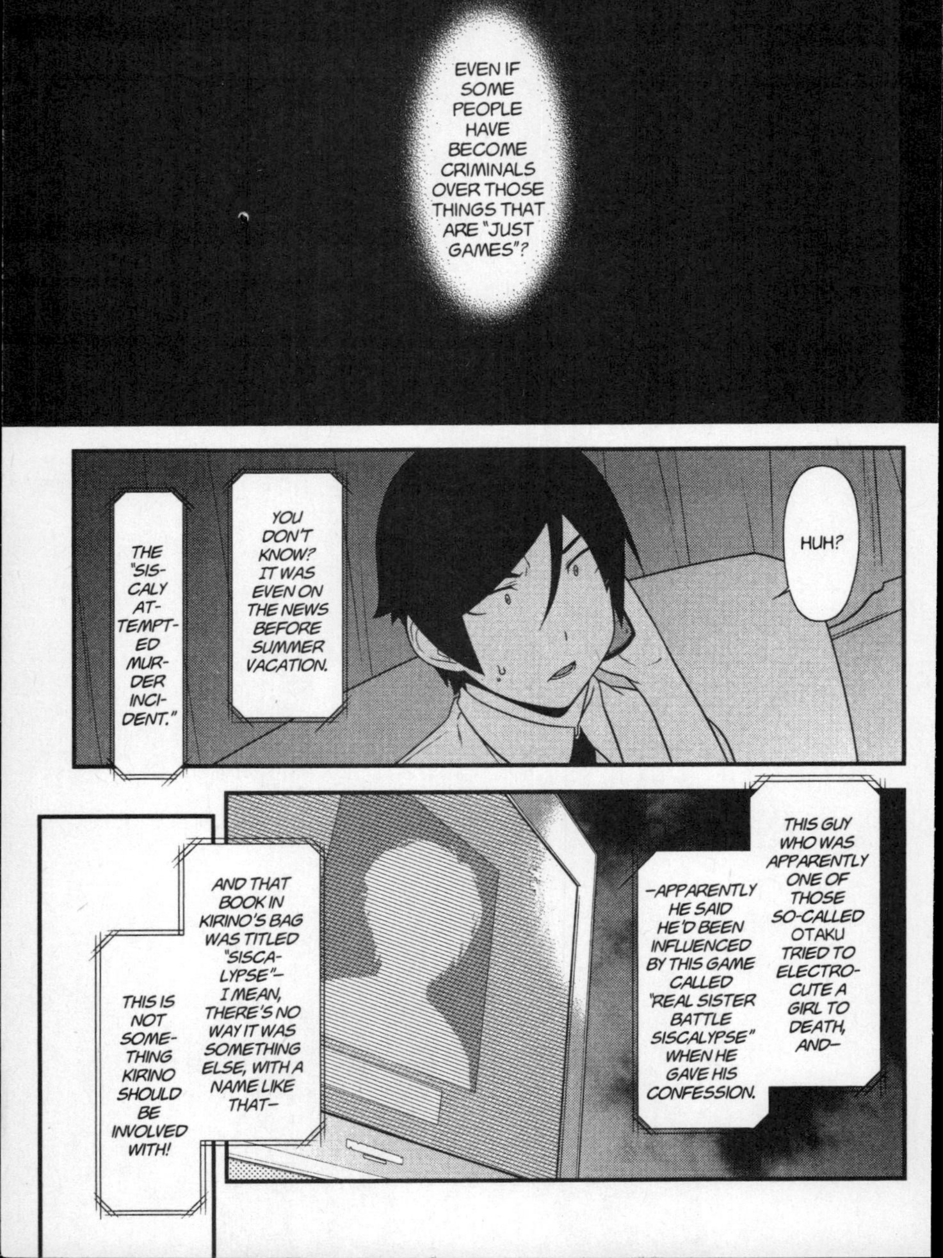
EVEN IF SOME PEOPLE HAVE BECOME CRIMINALS OVER THOSE THINGS THAT ARE "JUST GAMES"?
HUH?
YOU DON'T KNOW? IT WAS EVEN ON THE NEWS BEFORE SUMMER VACATION.
THE "SIS-CALY AT-TEMPT-ED MUR-DER INCI-DENT."
THIS GUY WHO WAS APPARENTLY ONE OF THOSE SO-CALLED OTAKU TRIED TO ELECTRO-CUTE A GIRL TO DEATH, AND—
—APPARENTLY HE SAID HE'D BEEN INFLUENCED BY THIS GAME CALLED "REAL SISTER BATTLE SISCALYPSE" WHEN HE GAVE HIS CONFESSION.
AND THAT BOOK IN KIRINO'S BAG WAS TITLED "SISCA-LYPSE"— I MEAN, THERE'S NO WAY IT WAS SOMETHING ELSE, WITH A NAME LIKE THAT—
THIS IS NOT SOME-THING KIRINO SHOULD BE INVOLVED WITH!

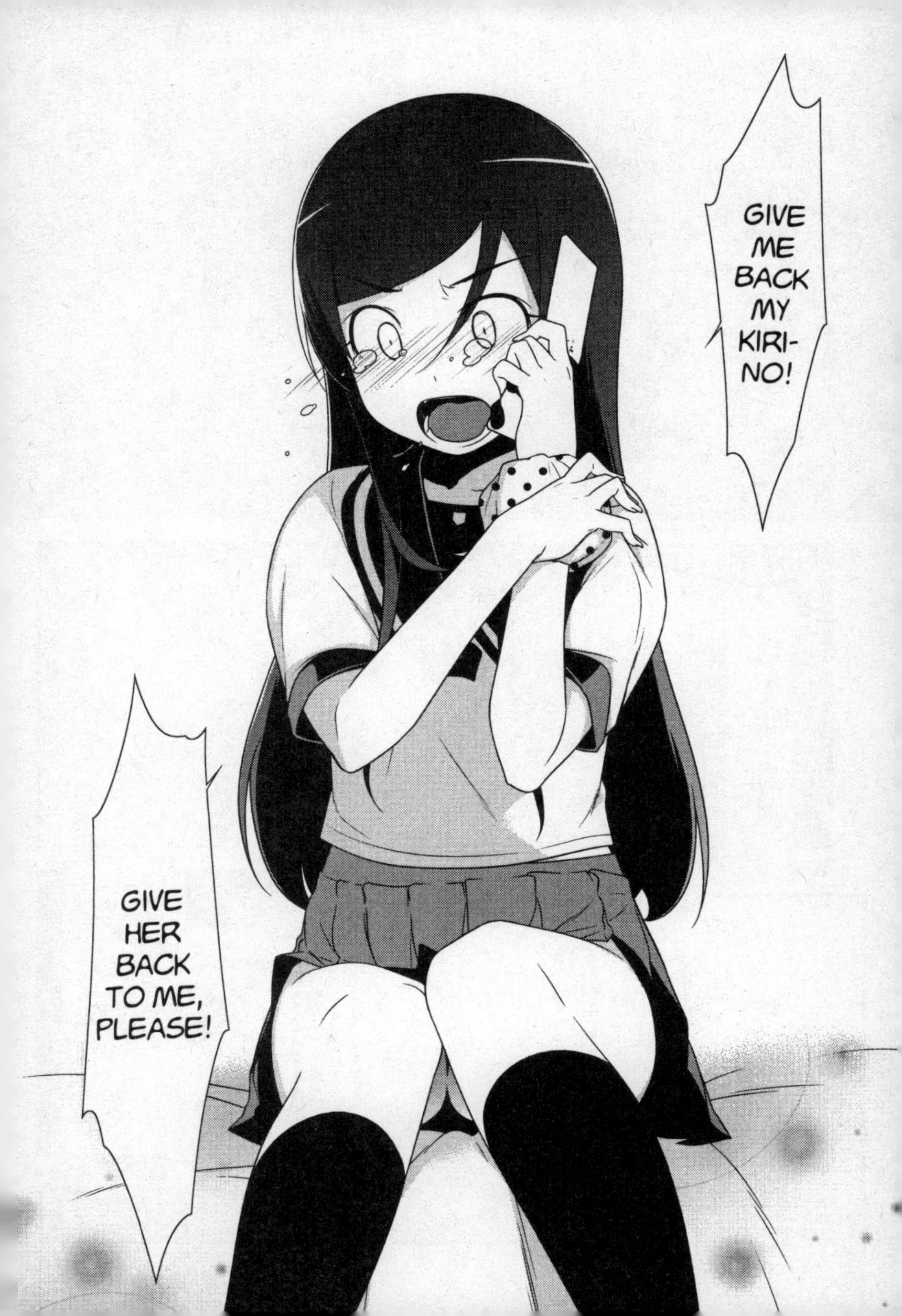
GIVE ME BACK MY KIRI-NO!
GIVE HER BACK TO ME, PLEASE!

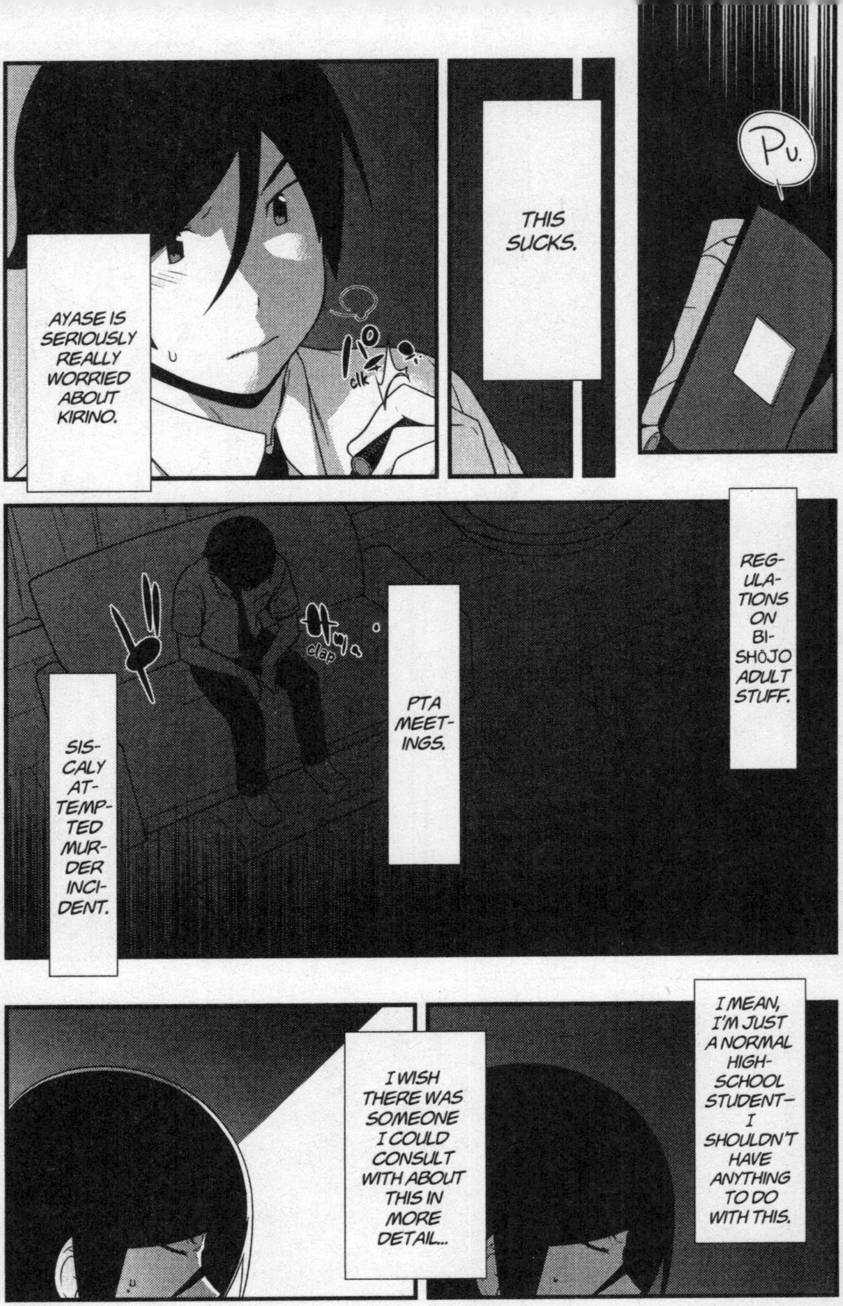
Pu.
THIS SUCKS.
AYASE IS SERIOUSLY REALLY WORRIED ABOUT KIRINO.
clk
REGULATIONS ON BISHŌJO ADULT STUFF.
PTA MEETINGS.
clap
SISCALY ATTEMPTED MURDER INCIDENT.
I MEAN, I'M JUST A NORMAL HIGH-SCHOOL STUDENT— I SHOULDN'T HAVE ANYTHING TO DO WITH THIS.
I WISH THERE WAS SOMEONE I COULD CONSULT WITH ABOUT THIS IN MORE DETAIL...

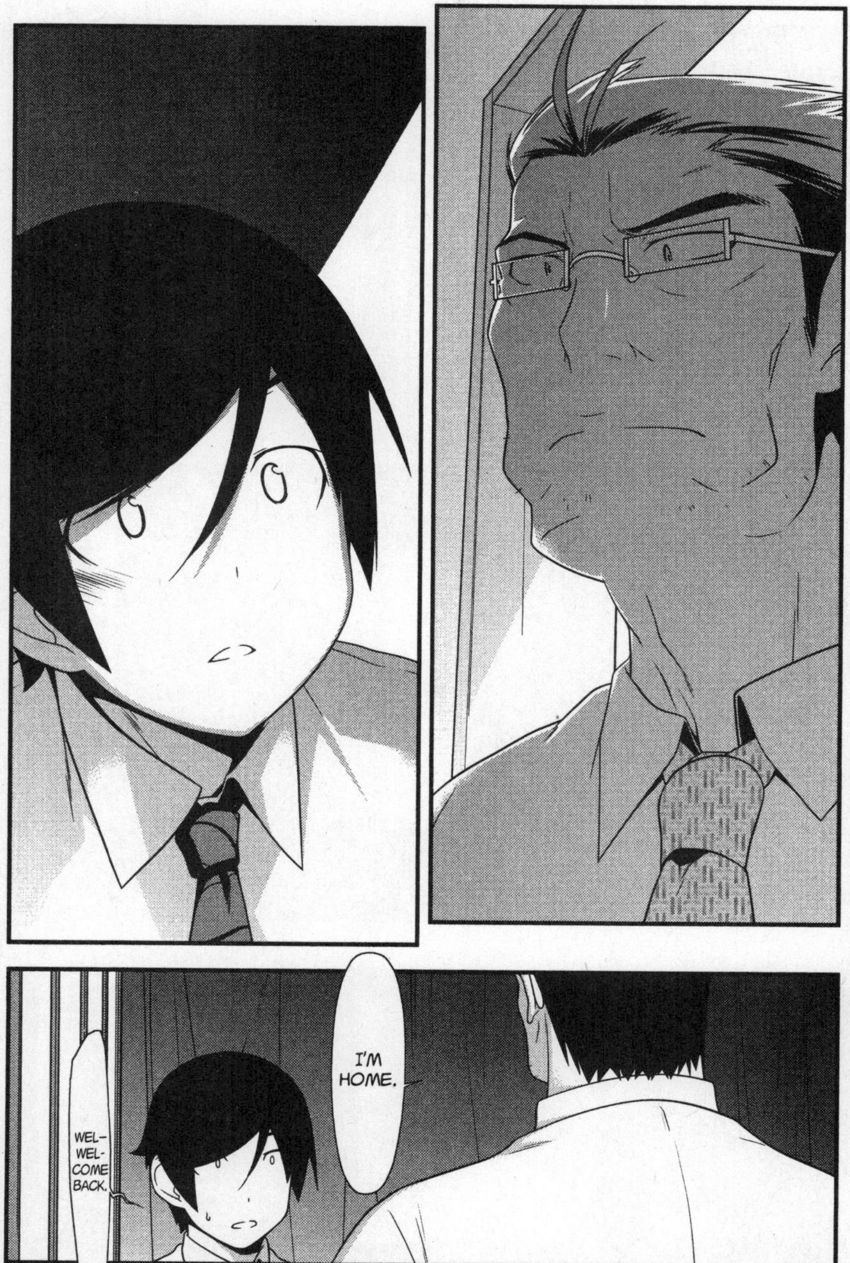
I'M HOME.
WEL- WEL-COME BACK.

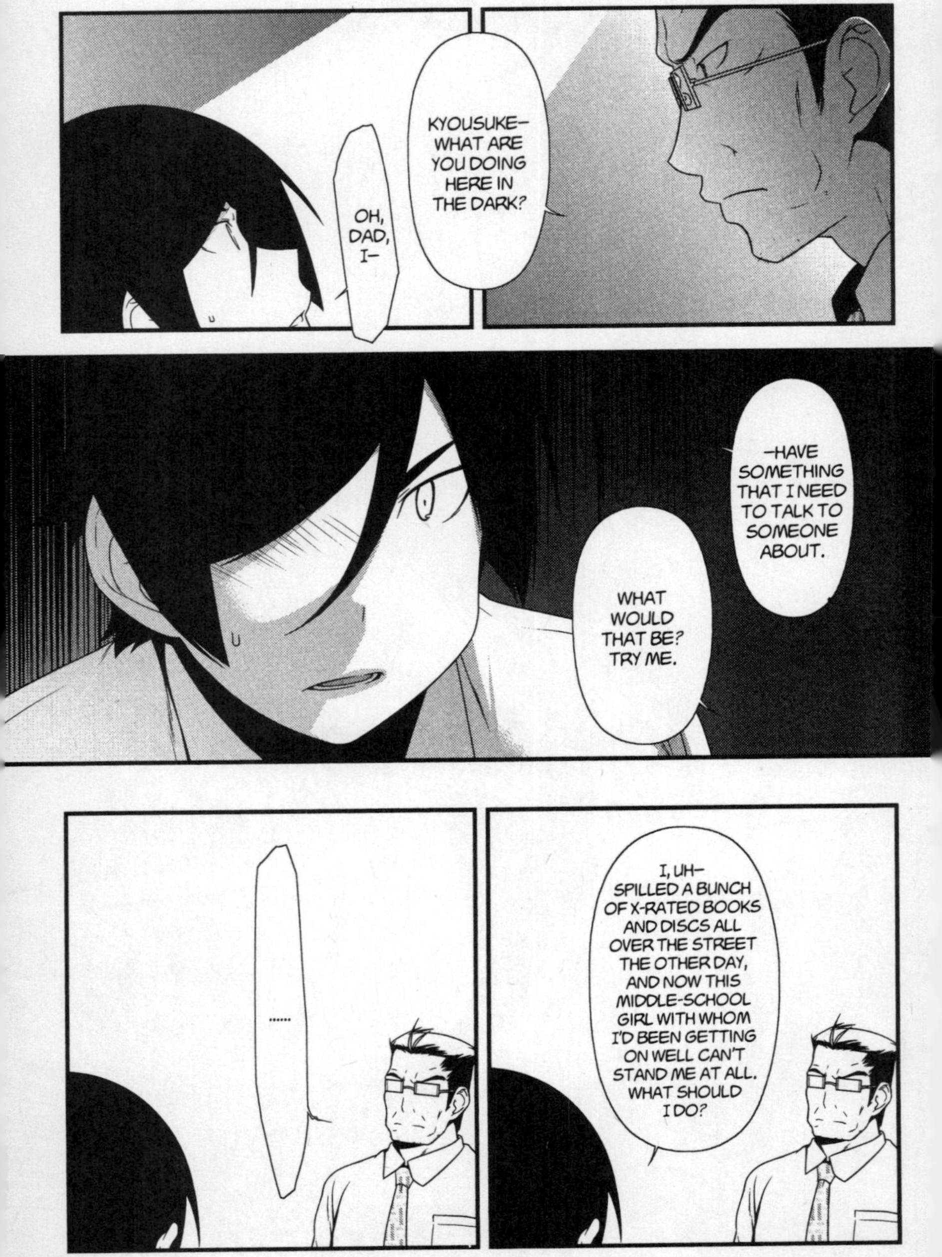
KYOUSUKE— WHAT ARE YOU DOING HERE IN THE DARK?
OH, DAD, I—
—HAVE SOMETHING THAT I NEED TO TALK TO SOMEONE ABOUT.
WHAT WOULD THAT BE? TRY ME.
I, UH— SPILLED A BUNCH OF X-RATED BOOKS AND DISCS ALL OVER THE STREET THE OTHER DAY, AND NOW THIS MIDDLE-SCHOOL GIRL WITH WHOM I'D BEEN GETTING ON WELL CAN'T STAND ME AT ALL. WHAT SHOULD I DO?
......

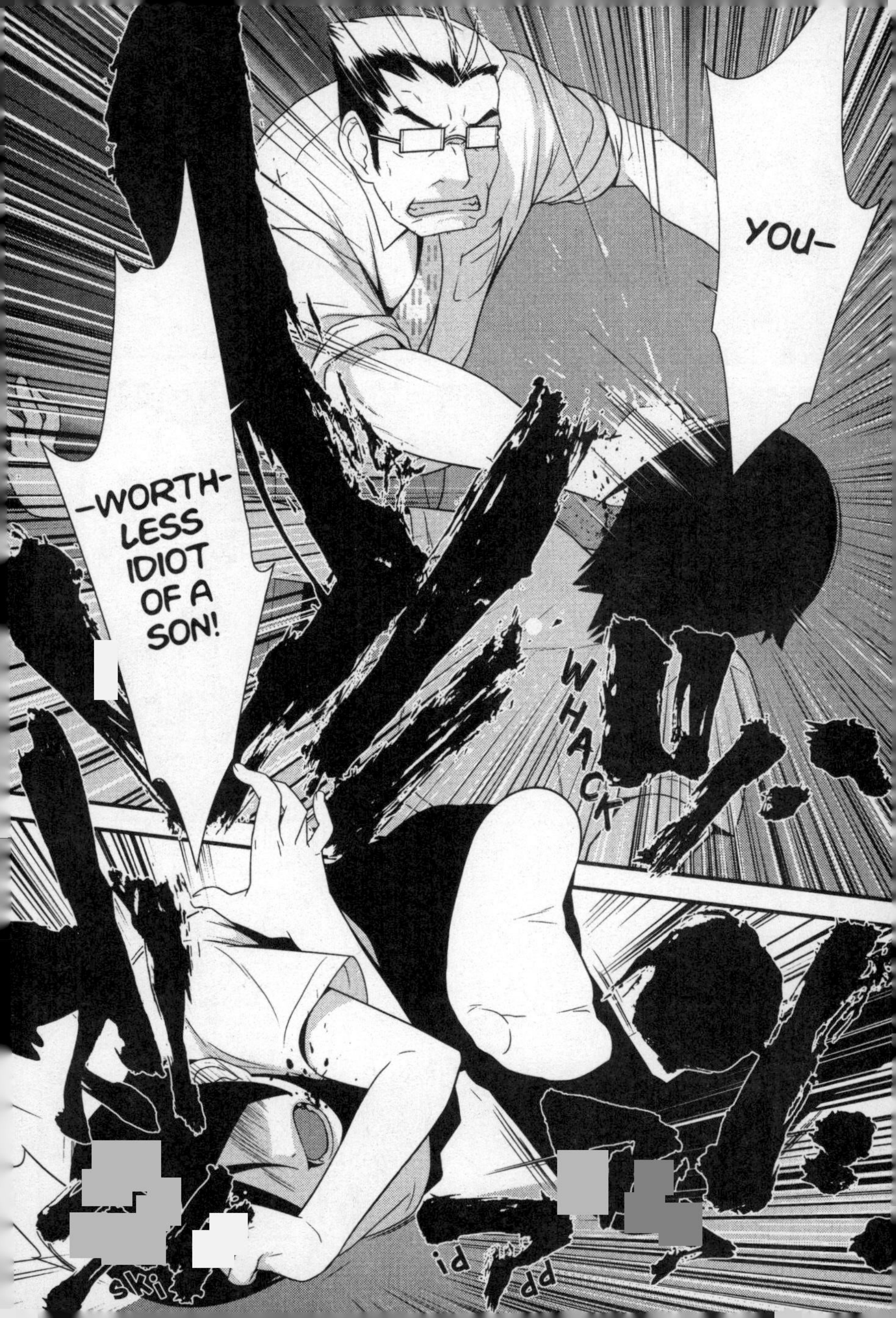
YOU-
-WORTH-LESS IDIOT OF A SON!
WHACK
ski

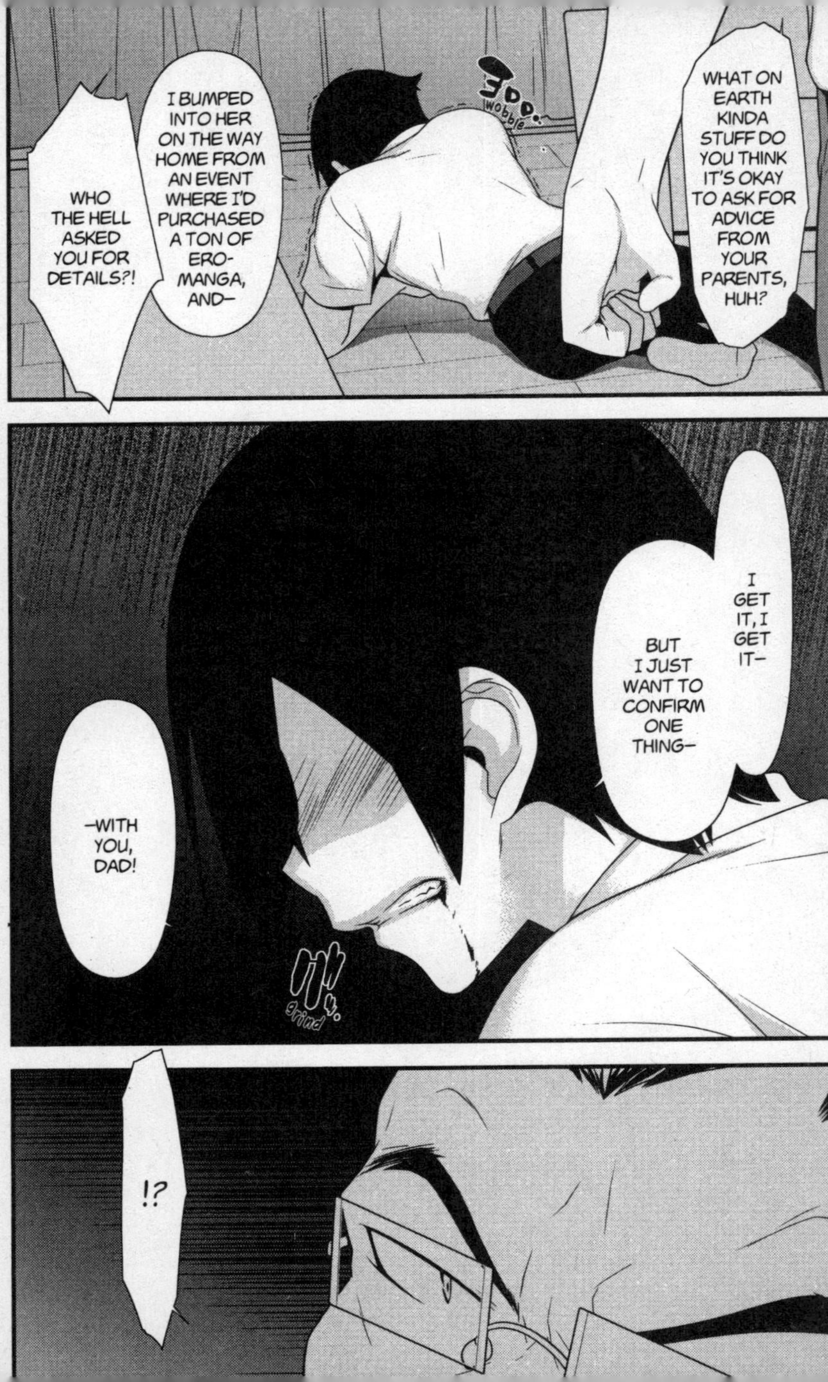
WHAT ON EARTH KINDA STUFF DO YOU THINK IT'S OKAY TO ASK FOR ADVICE FROM YOUR PARENTS, HUH?
wobble
I BUMPED INTO HER ON THE WAY HOME FROM AN EVENT WHERE I'D PURCHASED A TON OF ERO-MANGA, AND—
WHO THE HELL ASKED YOU FOR DETAILS?!
I GET IT, I GET IT—
BUT I JUST WANT TO CONFIRM ONE THING—
—WITH YOU, DAD!
grind
!?

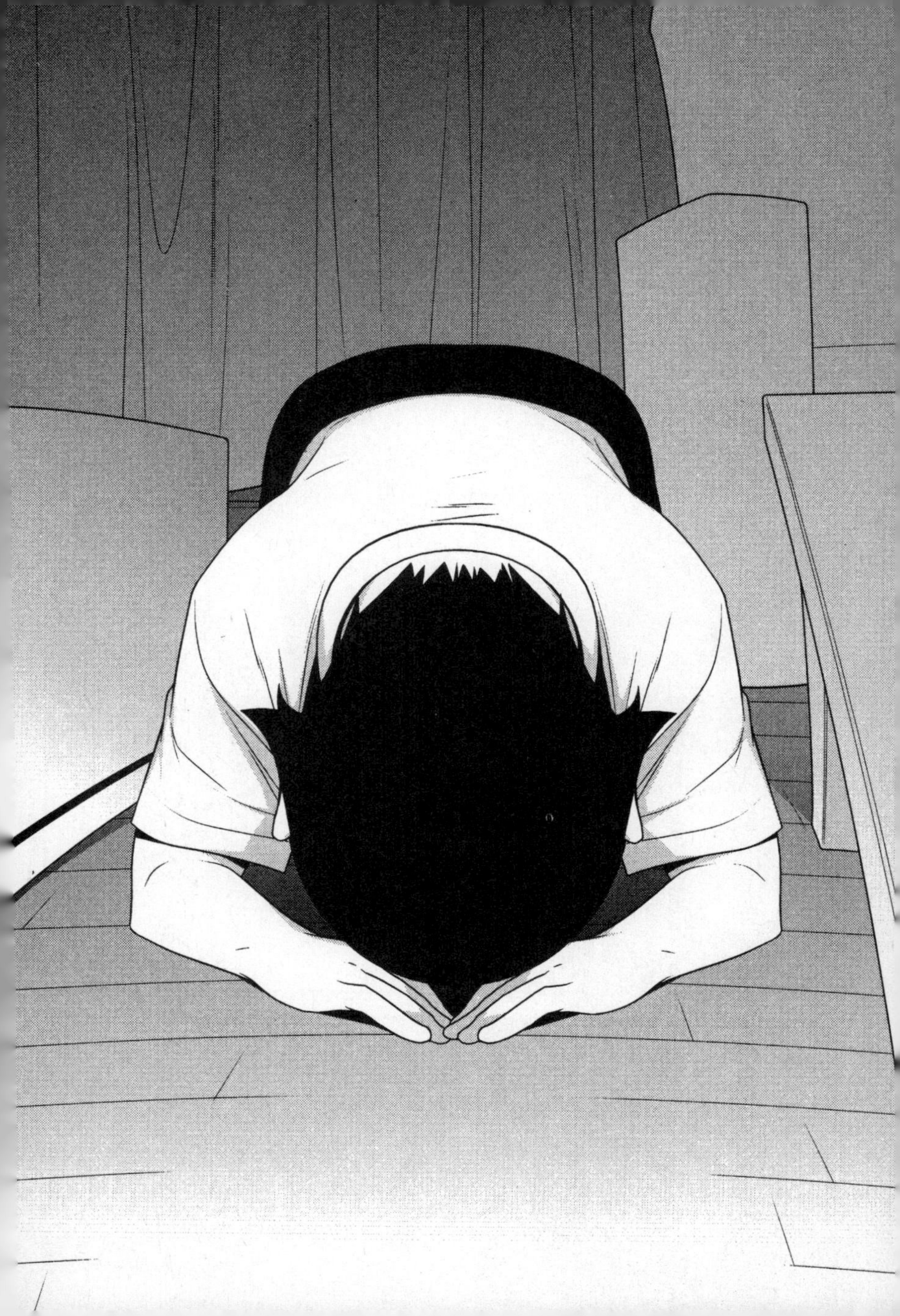

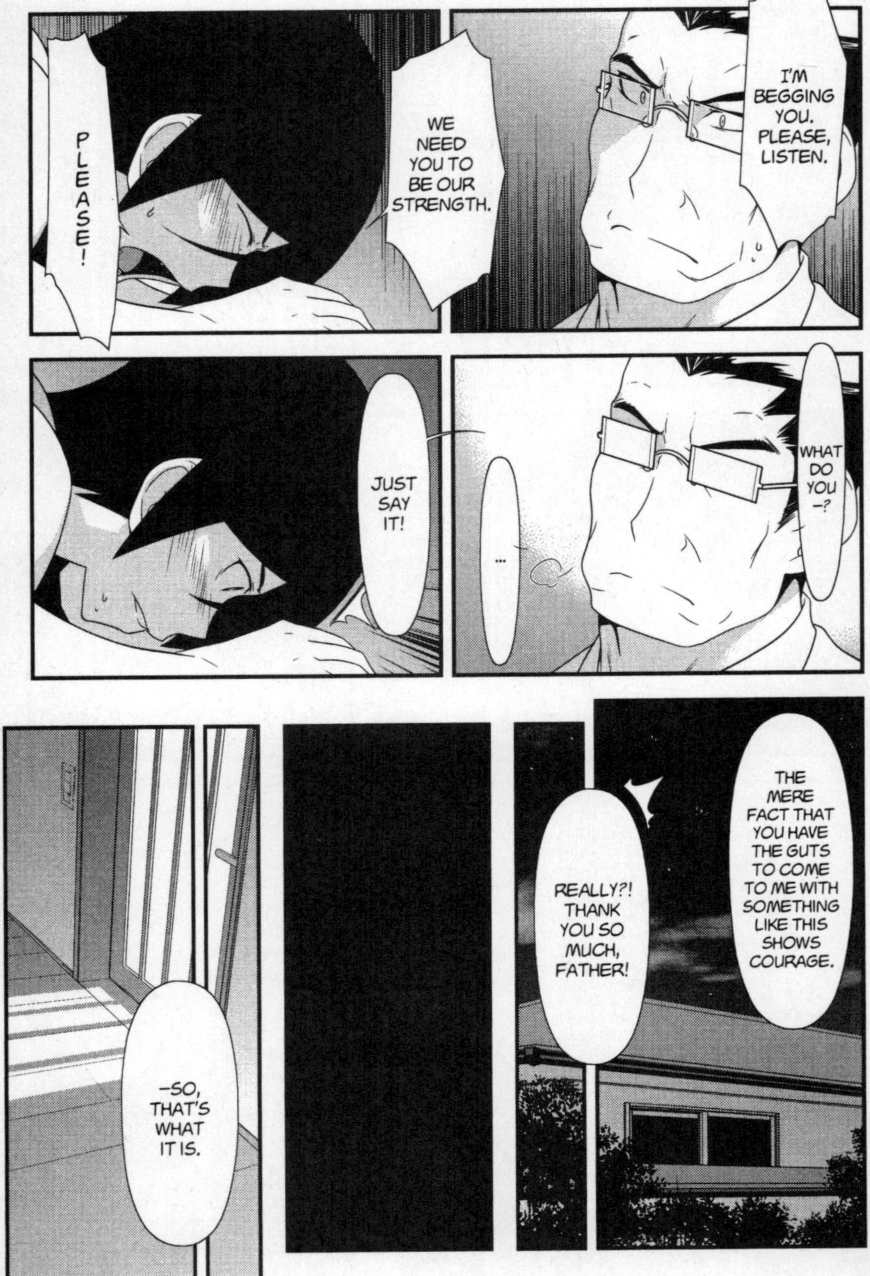
I'M BEGGING YOU. PLEASE, LISTEN.
WE NEED YOU TO BE OUR STRENGTH.
PLEASE!
WHAT DO YOU–?
...
JUST SAY IT!
THE MERE FACT THAT YOU HAVE THE GUTS TO COME TO ME WITH SOMETHING LIKE THIS SHOWS COURAGE.
REALLY?! THANK YOU SO MUCH, FATHER!
–SO, THAT'S WHAT IT IS.

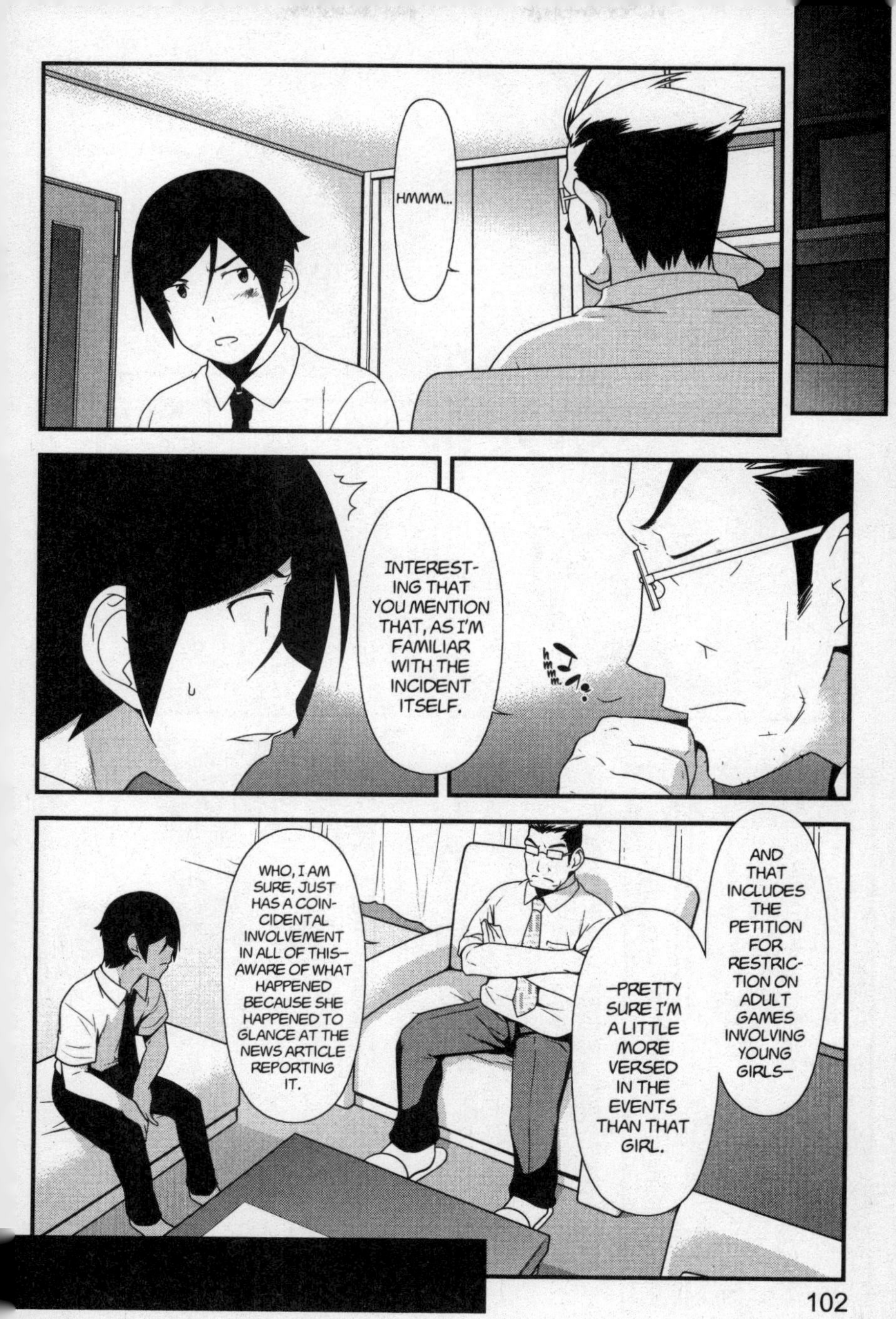
HMMM...
INTERESTING THAT YOU MENTION THAT, AS I'M FAMILIAR WITH THE INCIDENT ITSELF.
hmmm.
AND THAT INCLUDES THE PETITION FOR RESTRICTION ON ADULT GAMES INVOLVING YOUNG GIRLS—
—PRETTY SURE I'M A LITTLE MORE VERSED IN THE EVENTS THAN THAT GIRL.
WHO, I AM SURE, JUST HAS A COINCIDENTAL INVOLVEMENT IN ALL OF THIS—AWARE OF WHAT HAPPENED BECAUSE SHE HAPPENED TO GLANCE AT THE NEWS ARTICLE REPORTING IT.

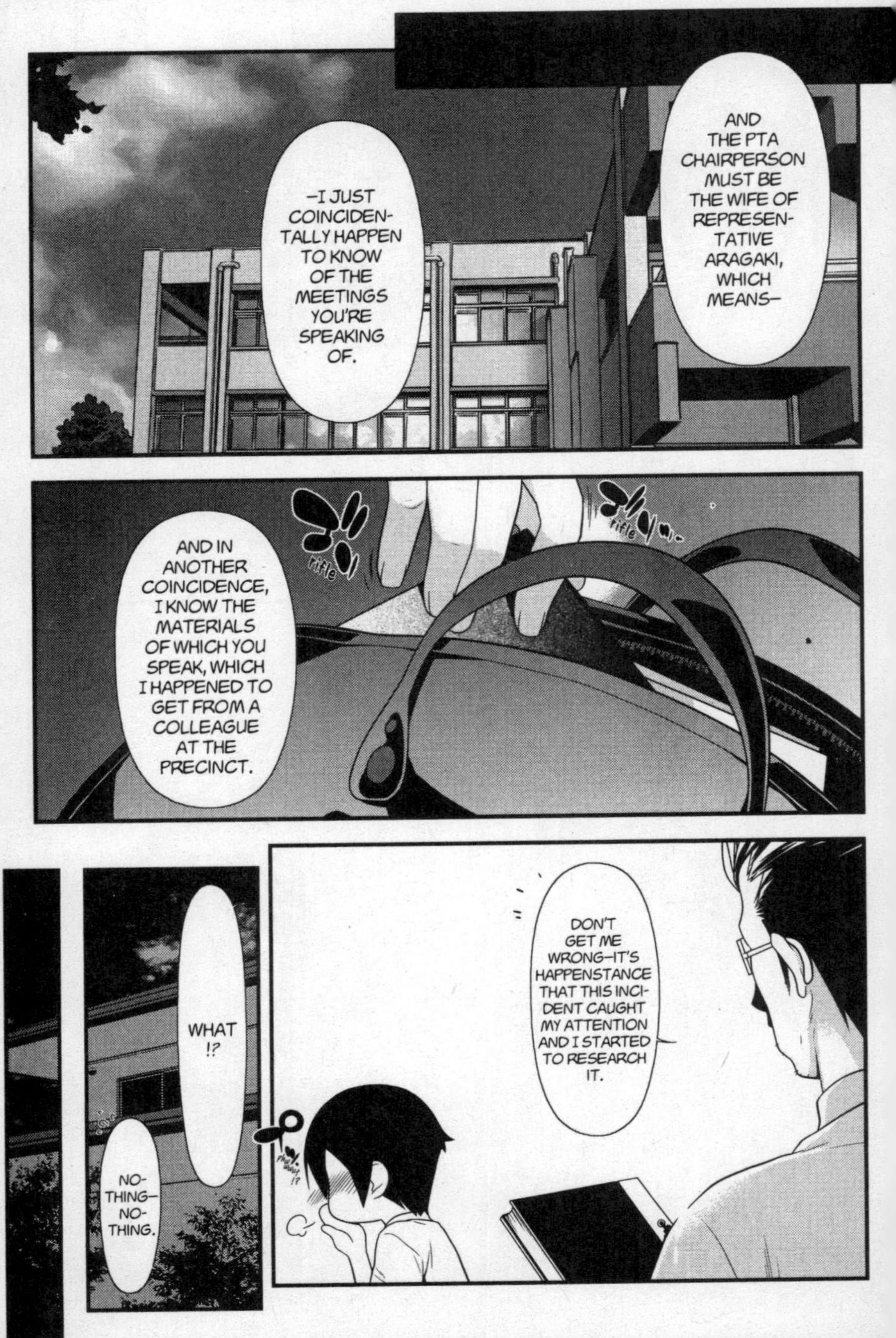
AND THE PTA CHAIRPERSON MUST BE THE WIFE OF REPRESEN-TATIVE ARAGAKI, WHICH MEANS—
—I JUST COINCIDEN-TALLY HAPPEN TO KNOW OF THE MEETINGS YOU'RE SPEAKING OF.
rifle
rifle
AND IN ANOTHER COINCIDENCE, I KNOW THE MATERIALS OF WHICH YOU SPEAK, WHICH I HAPPENED TO GET FROM A COLLEAGUE AT THE PRECINCT.
DON'T GET ME WRONG—IT'S HAPPENSTANCE THAT THIS INCI-DENT CAUGHT MY ATTENTION AND I STARTED TO RESEARCH IT.
WHAT !?
NO-THING— NO-THING.

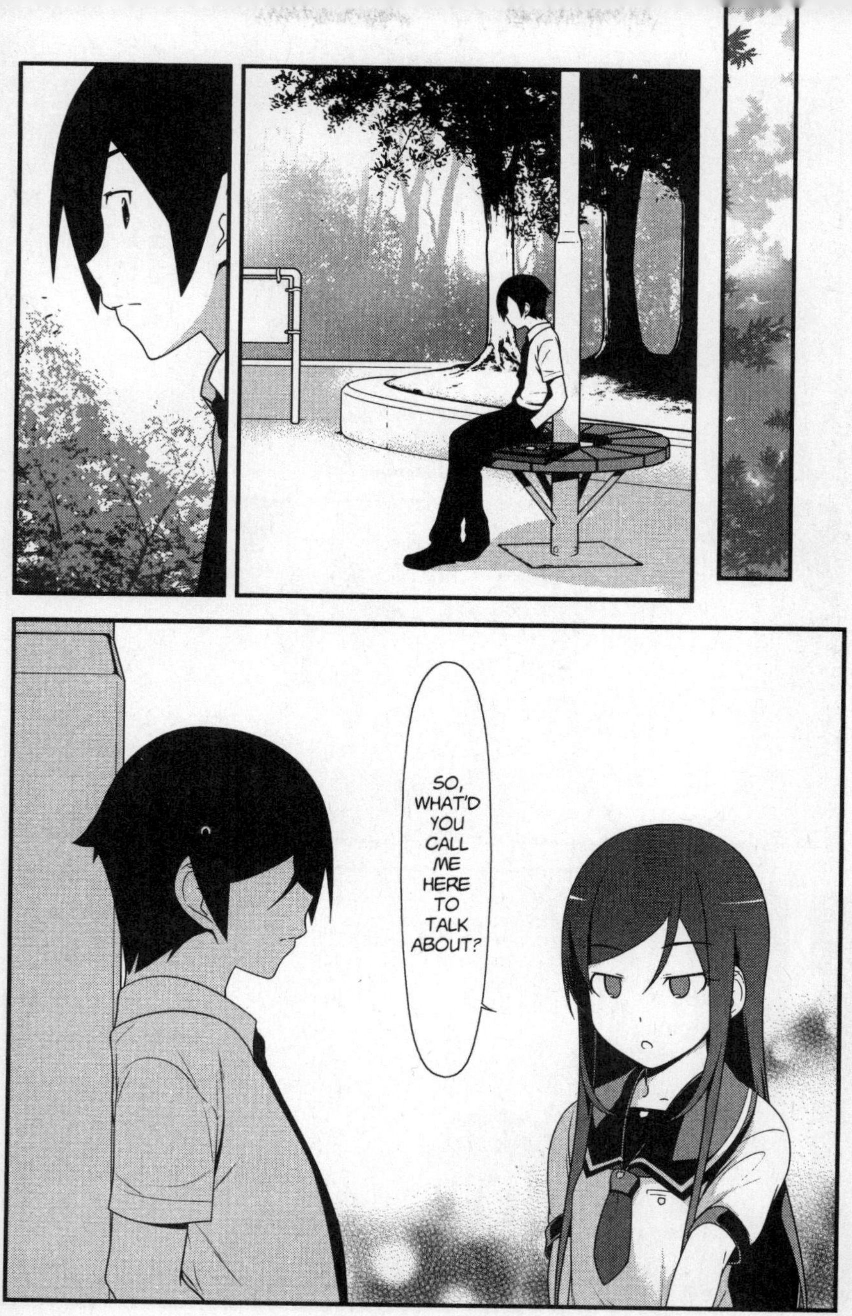
SO, WHAT'D YOU CALL ME HERE TO TALK ABOUT?

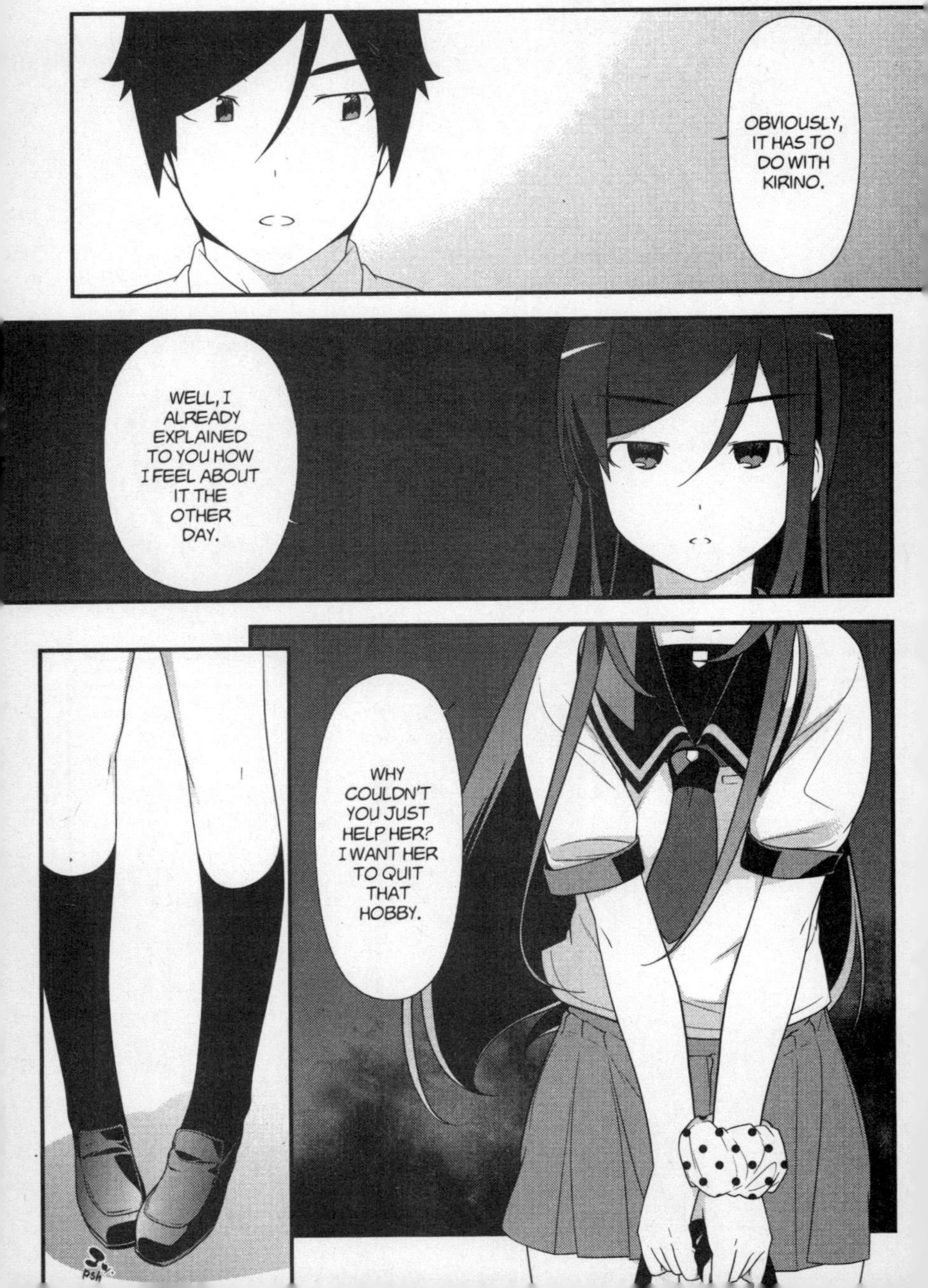
OBVIOUSLY, IT HAS TO DO WITH KIRINO.
WELL, I ALREADY EXPLAINED TO YOU HOW I FEEL ABOUT IT THE OTHER DAY.
WHY COULDN'T YOU JUST HELP HER? I WANT HER TO QUIT THAT HOBBY.
psh

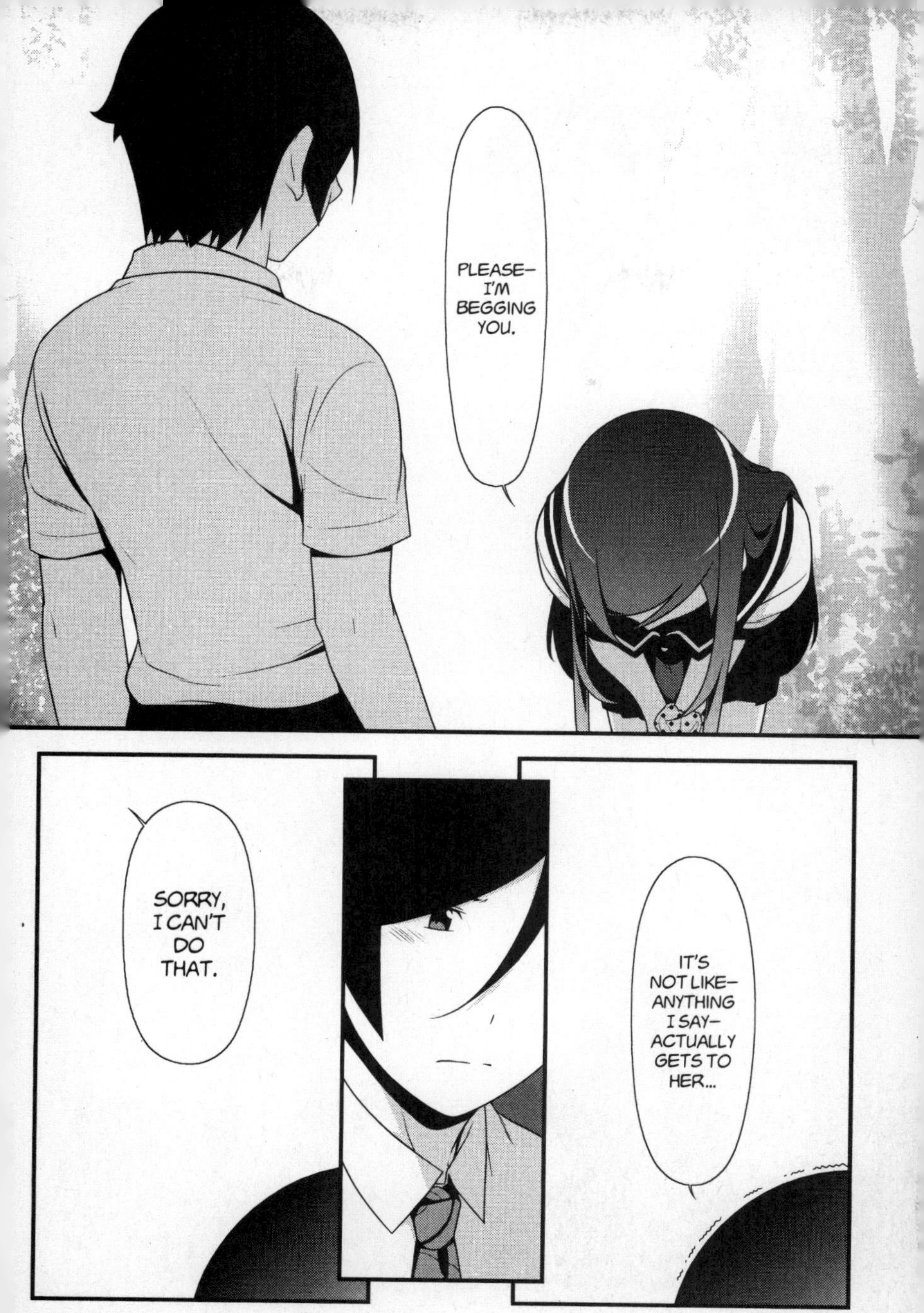
PLEASE— I'M BEGGING YOU.
IT'S NOT LIKE— ANYTHING I SAY— ACTUALLY GETS TO HER...
SORRY, I CAN'T DO THAT.

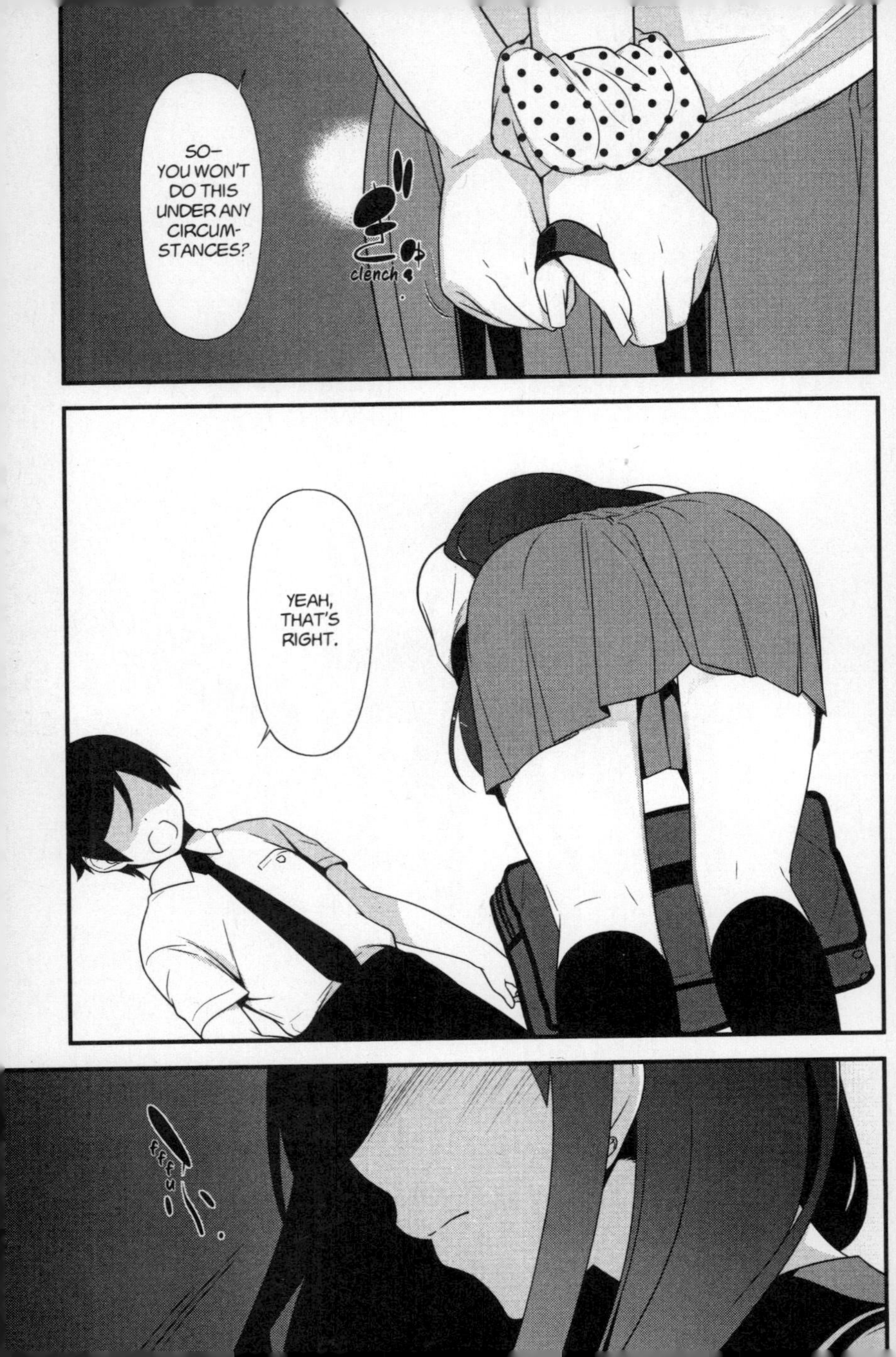
SO— YOU WON'T DO THIS UNDER ANY CIRCUM- STANCES?
clench
YEAH, THAT'S RIGHT.
fffu

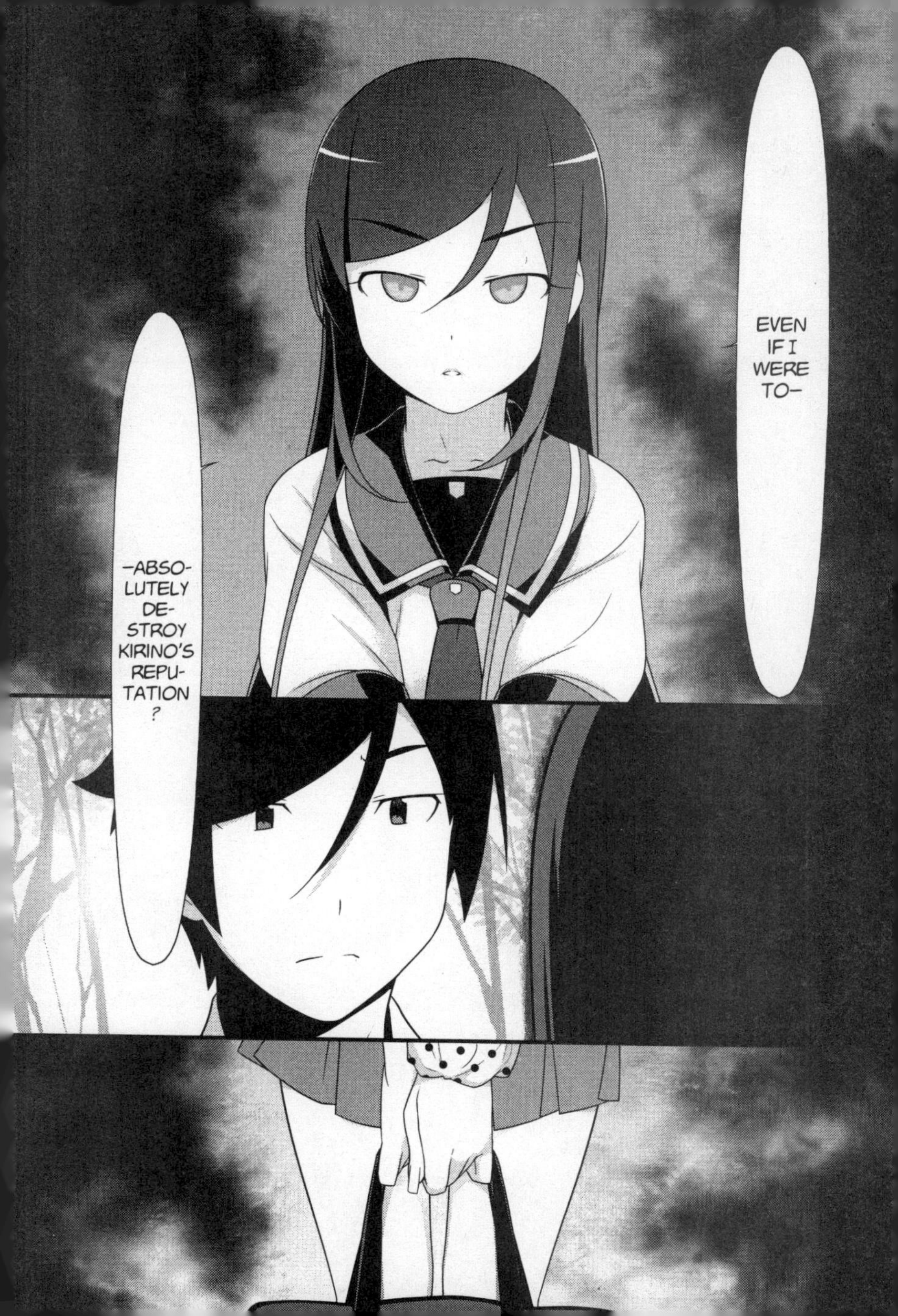
EVEN IF I WERE TO—
—ABSOLUTELY DE-STROY KIRINO'S REPU-TATION?

俺の妹が
こんなに
可愛いわけが、
ない

CHAPTER 25
第25話

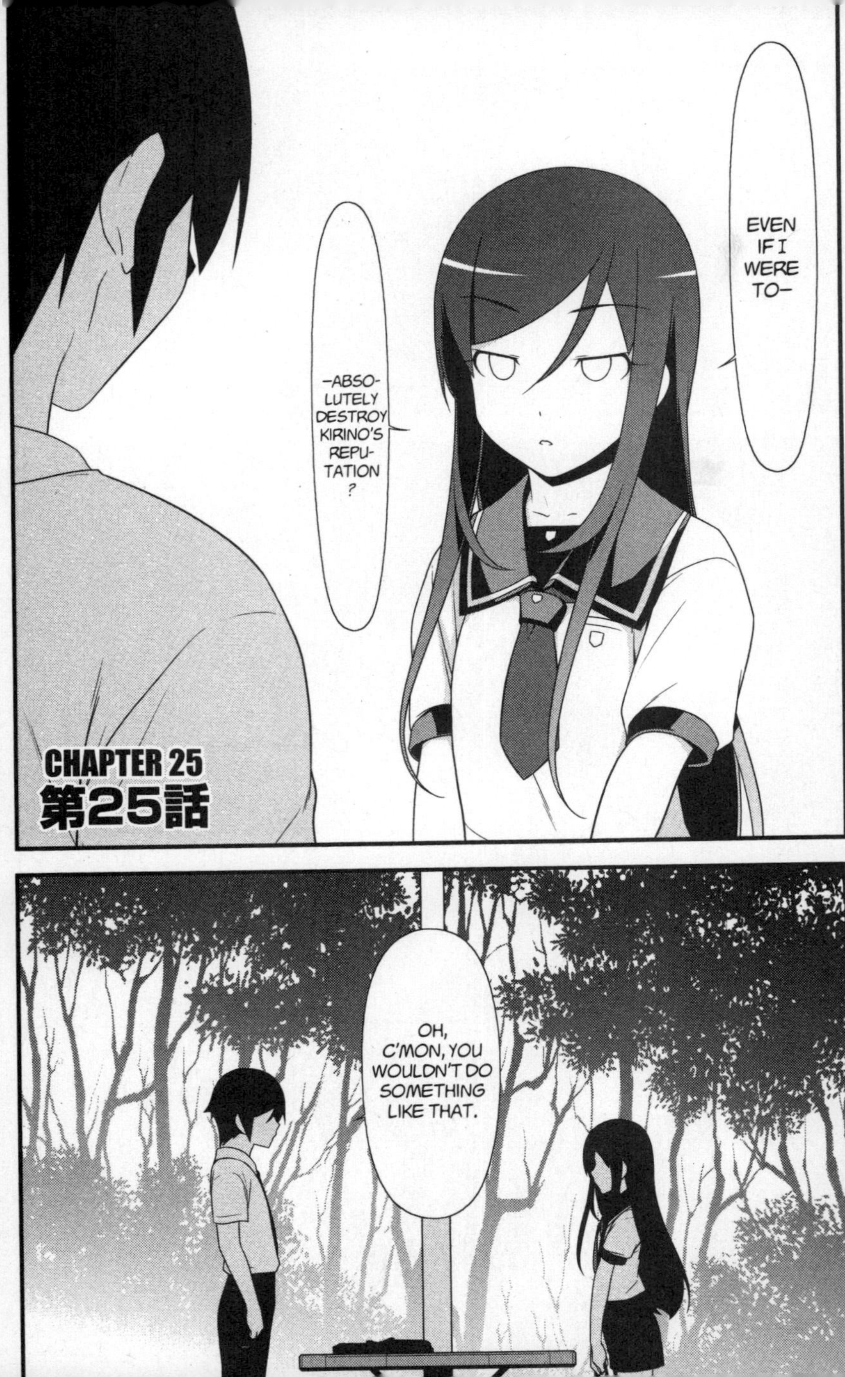

EVEN IF I WERE TO—
—ABSOLUTELY DESTROY KIRINO'S REPUTATION?
OH, C'MON, YOU WOULDN'T DO SOMETHING LIKE THAT.

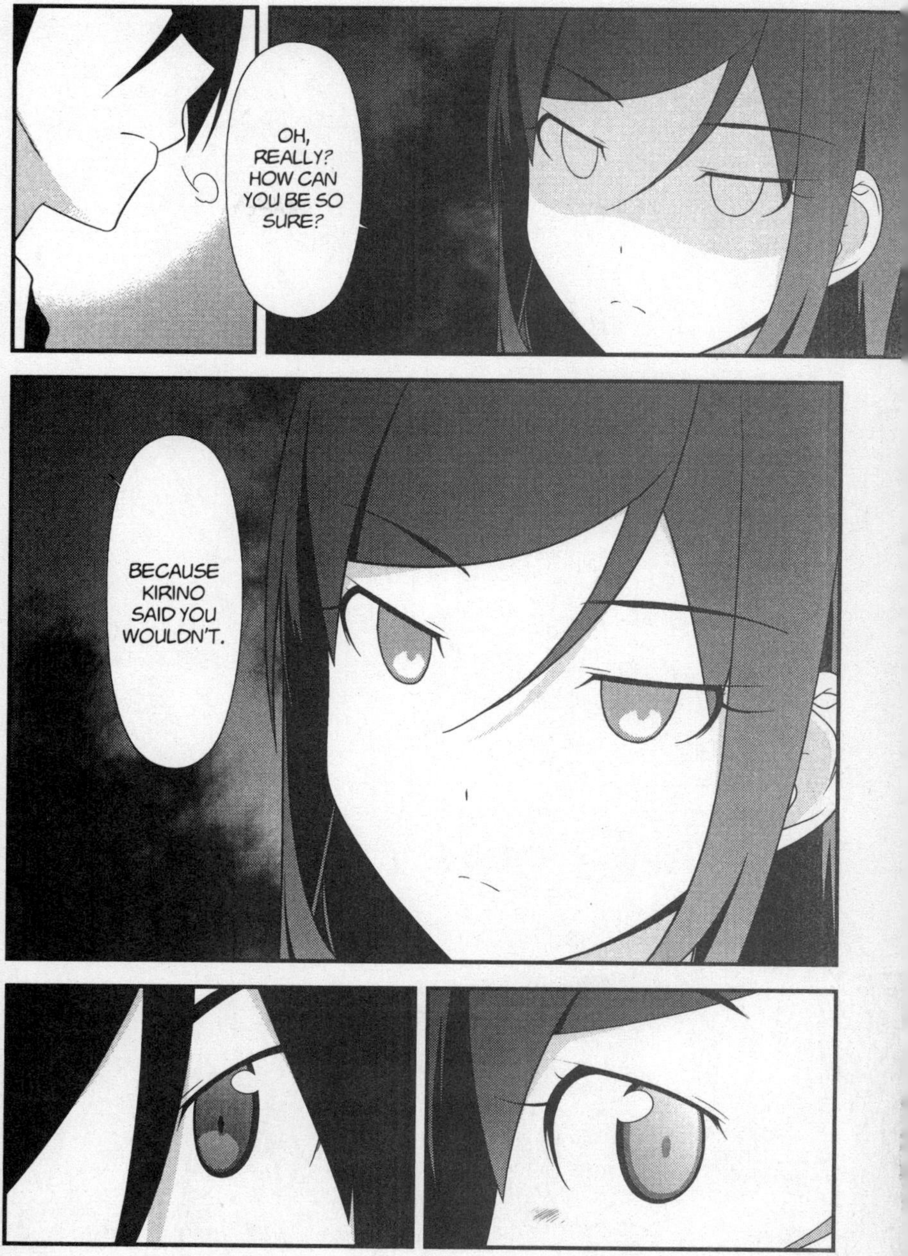
OH, REALLY? HOW CAN YOU BE SO SURE?
BECAUSE KIRINO SAID YOU WOULDN'T.

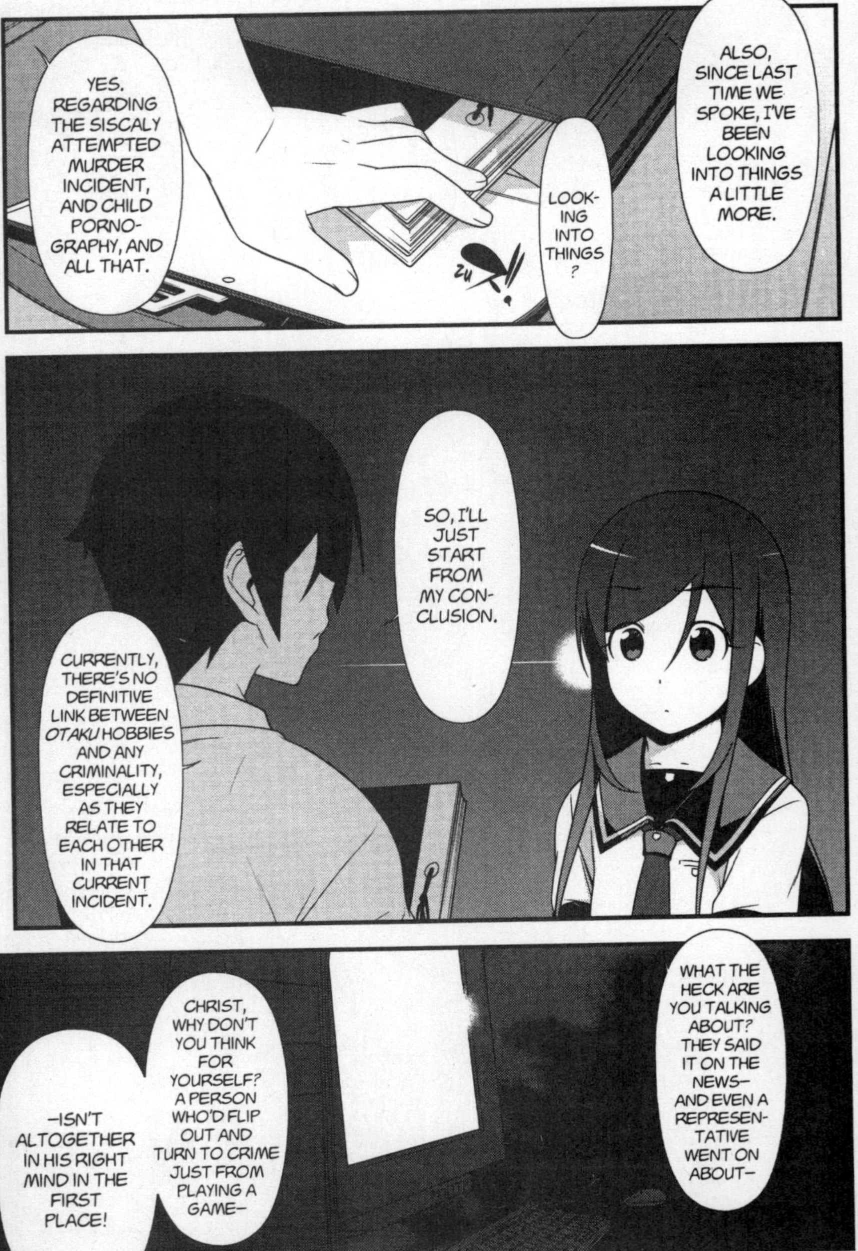
ALSO, SINCE LAST TIME WE SPOKE, I'VE BEEN LOOKING INTO THINGS A LITTLE MORE.
LOOKING INTO THINGS?
ZU
YES. REGARDING THE SISCALY ATTEMPTED MURDER INCIDENT, AND CHILD PORNOGRAPHY, AND ALL THAT.
SO, I'LL JUST START FROM MY CONCLUSION.
CURRENTLY, THERE'S NO DEFINITIVE LINK BETWEEN *OTAKU* HOBBIES AND ANY CRIMINALITY, ESPECIALLY AS THEY RELATE TO EACH OTHER IN THAT CURRENT INCIDENT.
WHAT THE HECK ARE YOU TALKING ABOUT? THEY SAID IT ON THE NEWS— AND EVEN A REPRESENTATIVE WENT ON ABOUT—
CHRIST, WHY DON'T YOU THINK FOR YOURSELF? A PERSON WHO'D FLIP OUT AND TURN TO CRIME JUST FROM PLAYING A GAME—
—ISN'T ALTOGETHER IN HIS RIGHT MIND IN THE FIRST PLACE!

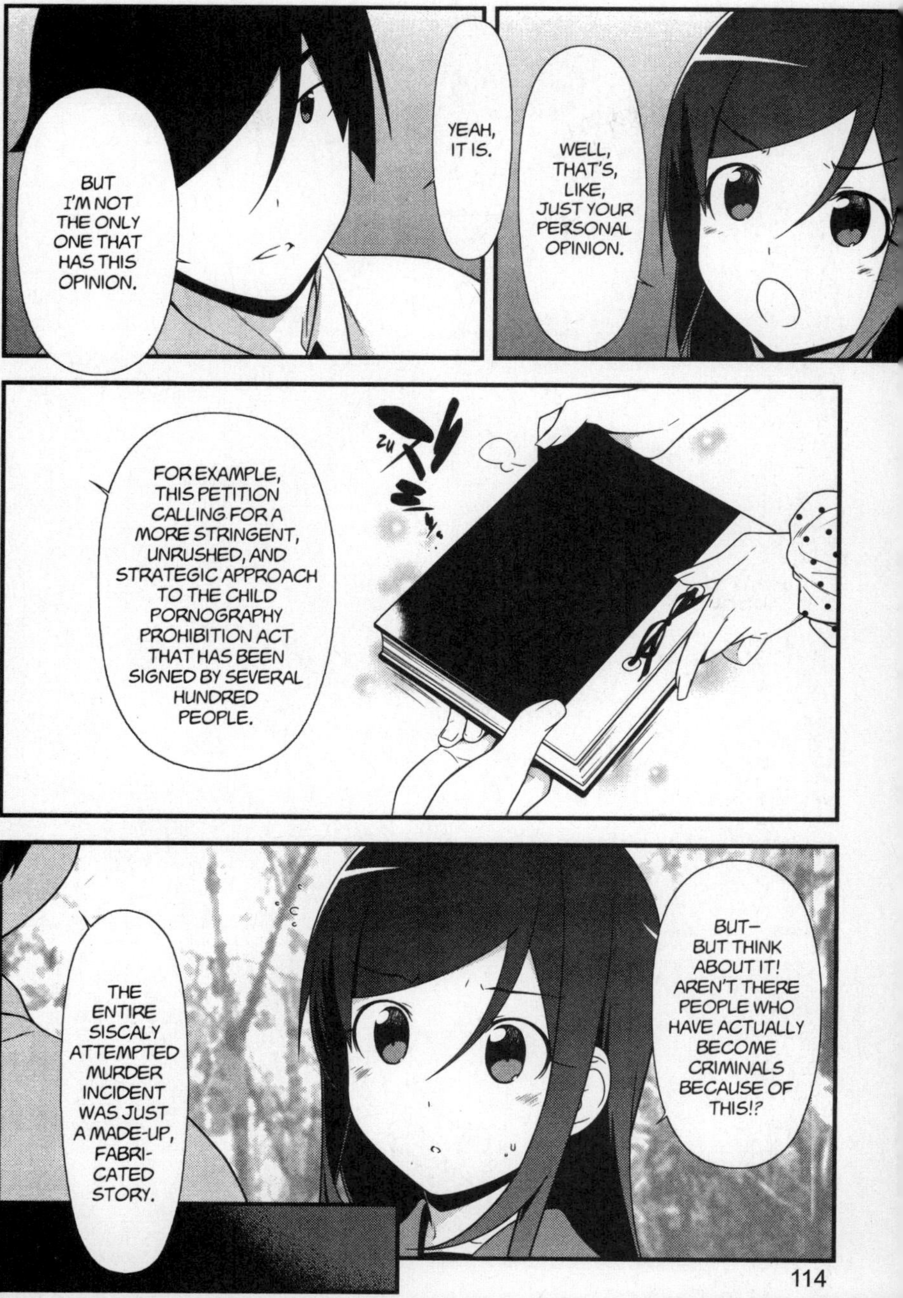
WELL, THAT'S, LIKE, JUST YOUR PERSONAL OPINION.
YEAH, IT IS.
BUT I'M NOT THE ONLY ONE THAT HAS THIS OPINION.
ZU
FOR EXAMPLE, THIS PETITION CALLING FOR A MORE STRINGENT, UNRUSHED, AND STRATEGIC APPROACH TO THE CHILD PORNOGRAPHY PROHIBITION ACT THAT HAS BEEN SIGNED BY SEVERAL HUNDRED PEOPLE.
BUT— BUT THINK ABOUT IT! AREN'T THERE PEOPLE WHO HAVE ACTUALLY BECOME CRIMINALS BECAUSE OF THIS!?
THE ENTIRE SISCALY ATTEMPTED MURDER INCIDENT WAS JUST A MADE-UP, FABRICATED STORY.

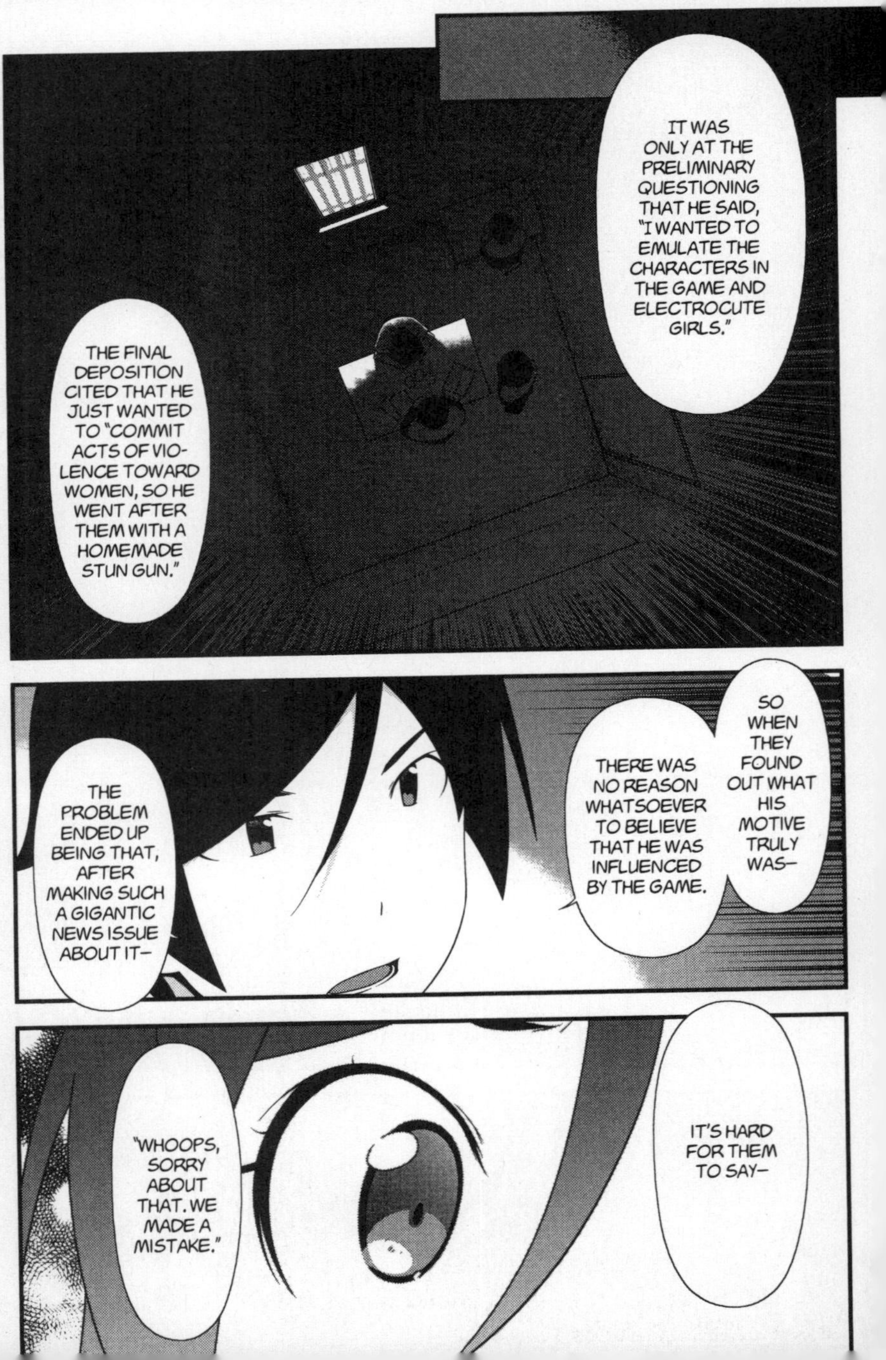
IT WAS ONLY AT THE PRELIMINARY QUESTIONING THAT HE SAID, "I WANTED TO EMULATE THE CHARACTERS IN THE GAME AND ELECTROCUTE GIRLS."
THE FINAL DEPOSITION CITED THAT HE JUST WANTED TO "COMMIT ACTS OF VIOLENCE TOWARD WOMEN, SO HE WENT AFTER THEM WITH A HOMEMADE STUN GUN."
SO WHEN THEY FOUND OUT WHAT HIS MOTIVE TRULY WAS—
THERE WAS NO REASON WHATSOEVER TO BELIEVE THAT HE WAS INFLUENCED BY THE GAME.
THE PROBLEM ENDED UP BEING THAT, AFTER MAKING SUCH A GIGANTIC NEWS ISSUE ABOUT IT—
IT'S HARD FOR THEM TO SAY—
"WHOOPS, SORRY ABOUT THAT. WE MADE A MISTAKE."

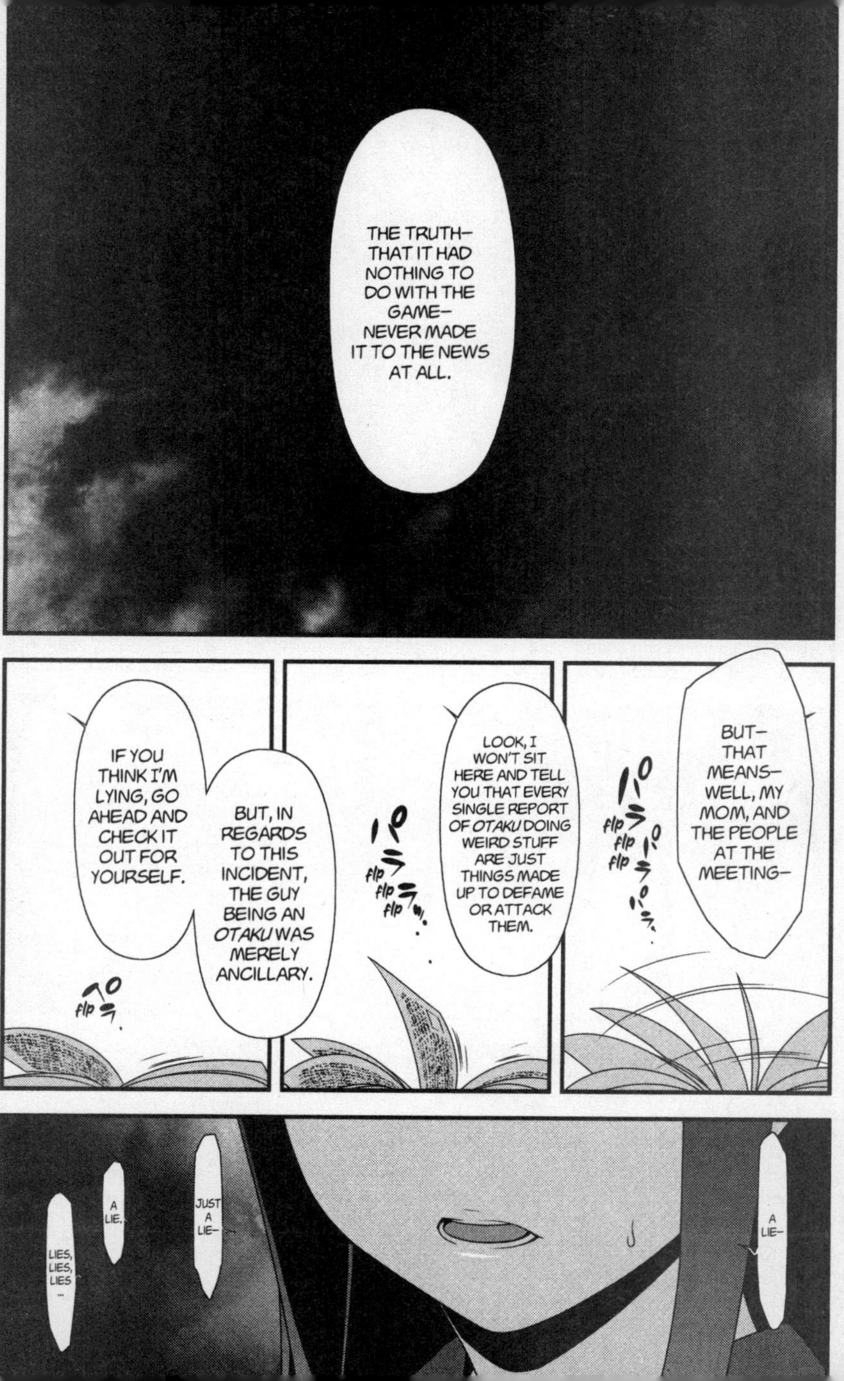
THE TRUTH— THAT IT HAD NOTHING TO DO WITH THE GAME— NEVER MADE IT TO THE NEWS AT ALL.
BUT— THAT MEANS— WELL, MY MOM, AND THE PEOPLE AT THE MEETING—
flp flp flp
LOOK, I WON'T SIT HERE AND TELL YOU THAT EVERY SINGLE REPORT OF *OTAKU* DOING WEIRD STUFF ARE JUST THINGS MADE UP TO DEFAME OR ATTACK THEM.
flp flp flp
BUT, IN REGARDS TO THIS INCIDENT, THE GUY BEING AN *OTAKU* WAS MERELY ANCILLARY.
IF YOU THINK I'M LYING, GO AHEAD AND CHECK IT OUT FOR YOURSELF.
flp
A LIE—
JUST A LIE—
A LIE.
LIES, LIES, LIES ...

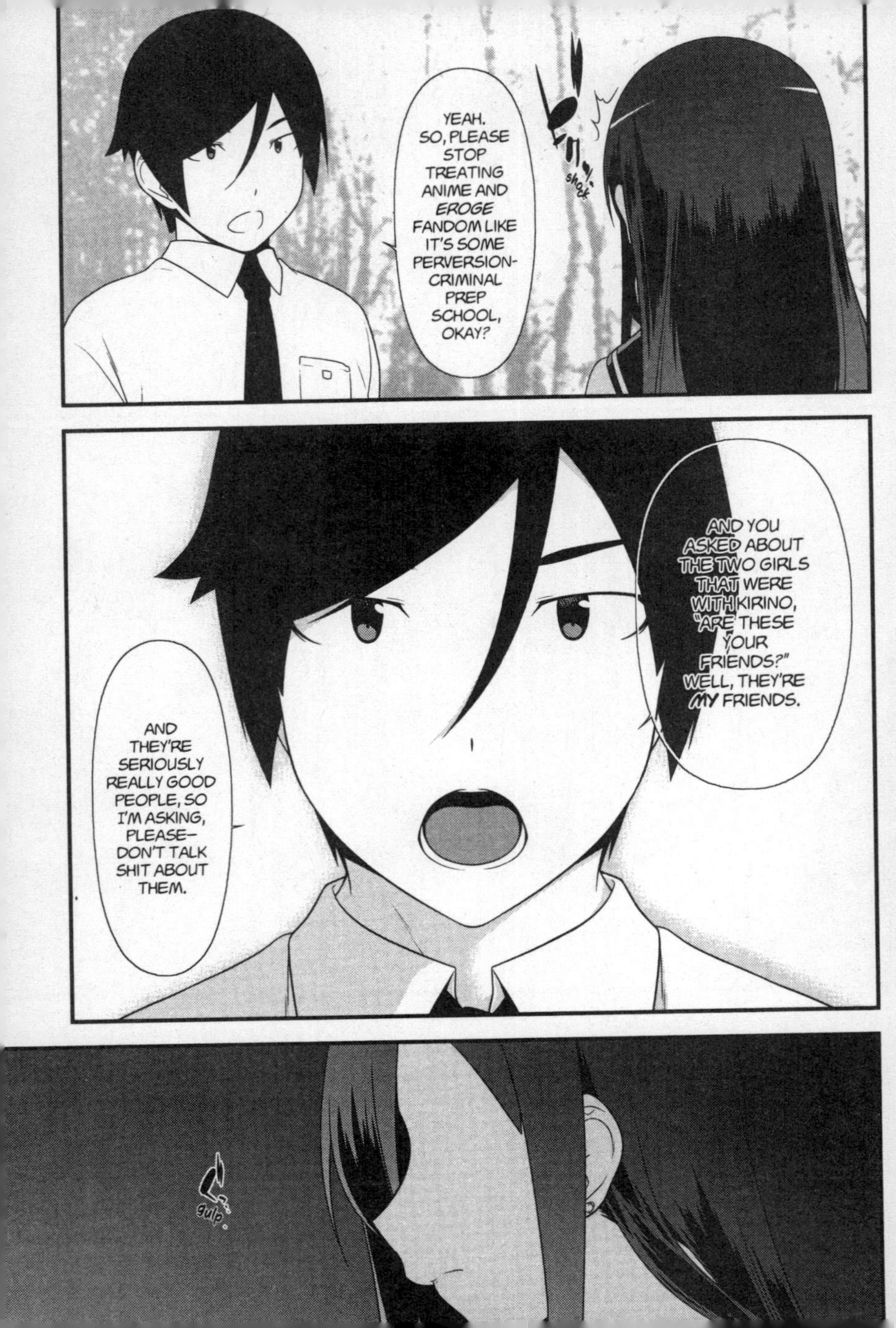
shock
YEAH. SO, PLEASE STOP TREATING ANIME AND *EROGE* FANDOM LIKE IT'S SOME PERVERSION-CRIMINAL PREP SCHOOL, OKAY?
AND YOU ASKED ABOUT THE TWO GIRLS THAT WERE WITH KIRINO, "ARE THESE YOUR FRIENDS?" WELL, THEY'RE *MY* FRIENDS.
AND THEY'RE SERIOUSLY REALLY GOOD PEOPLE, SO I'M ASKING, PLEASE— DON'T TALK SHIT ABOUT THEM.
gulp

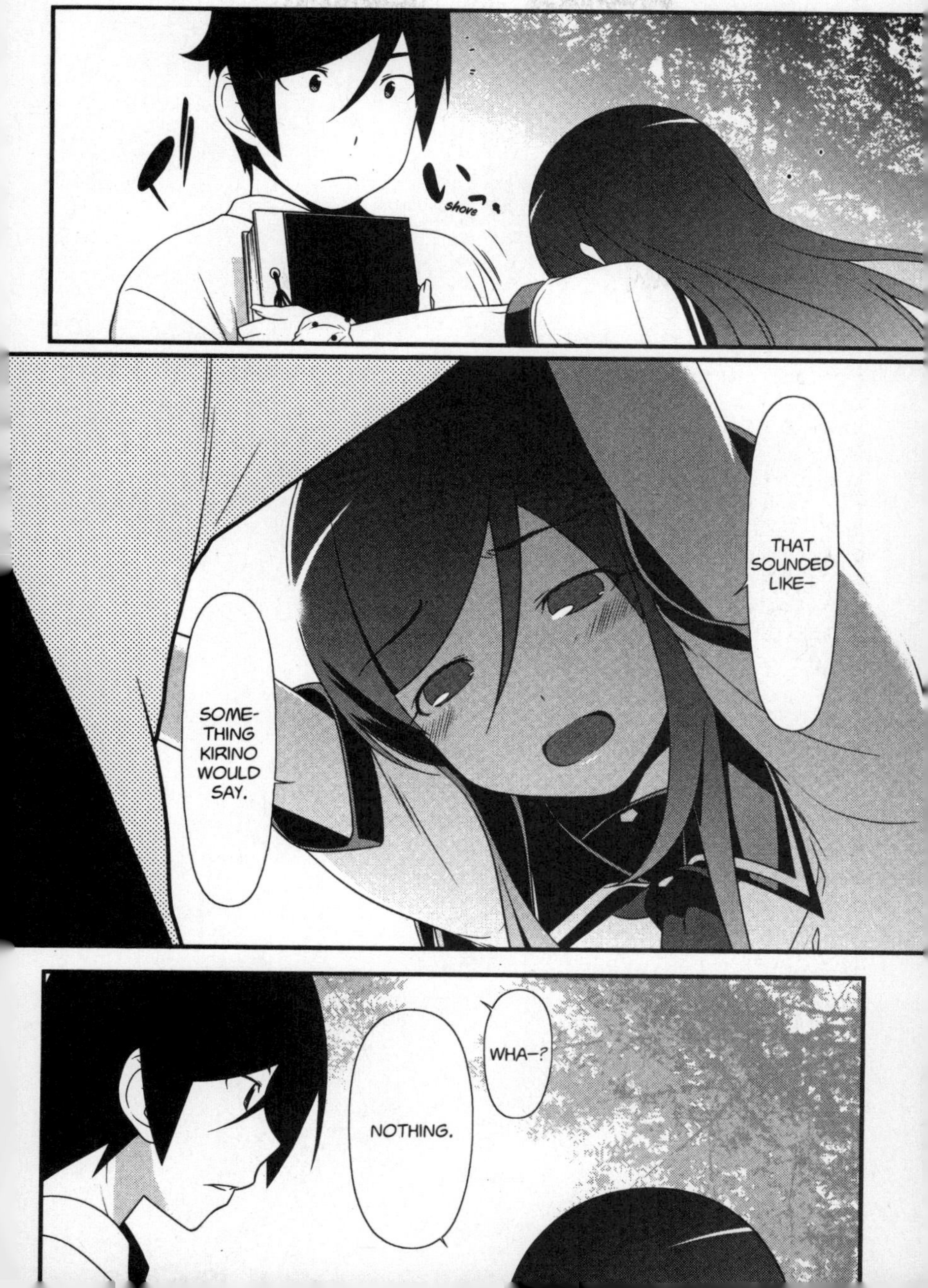
shove
THAT SOUNDED LIKE-
SOME-THING KIRINO WOULD SAY.
WHA-?
NOTHING.

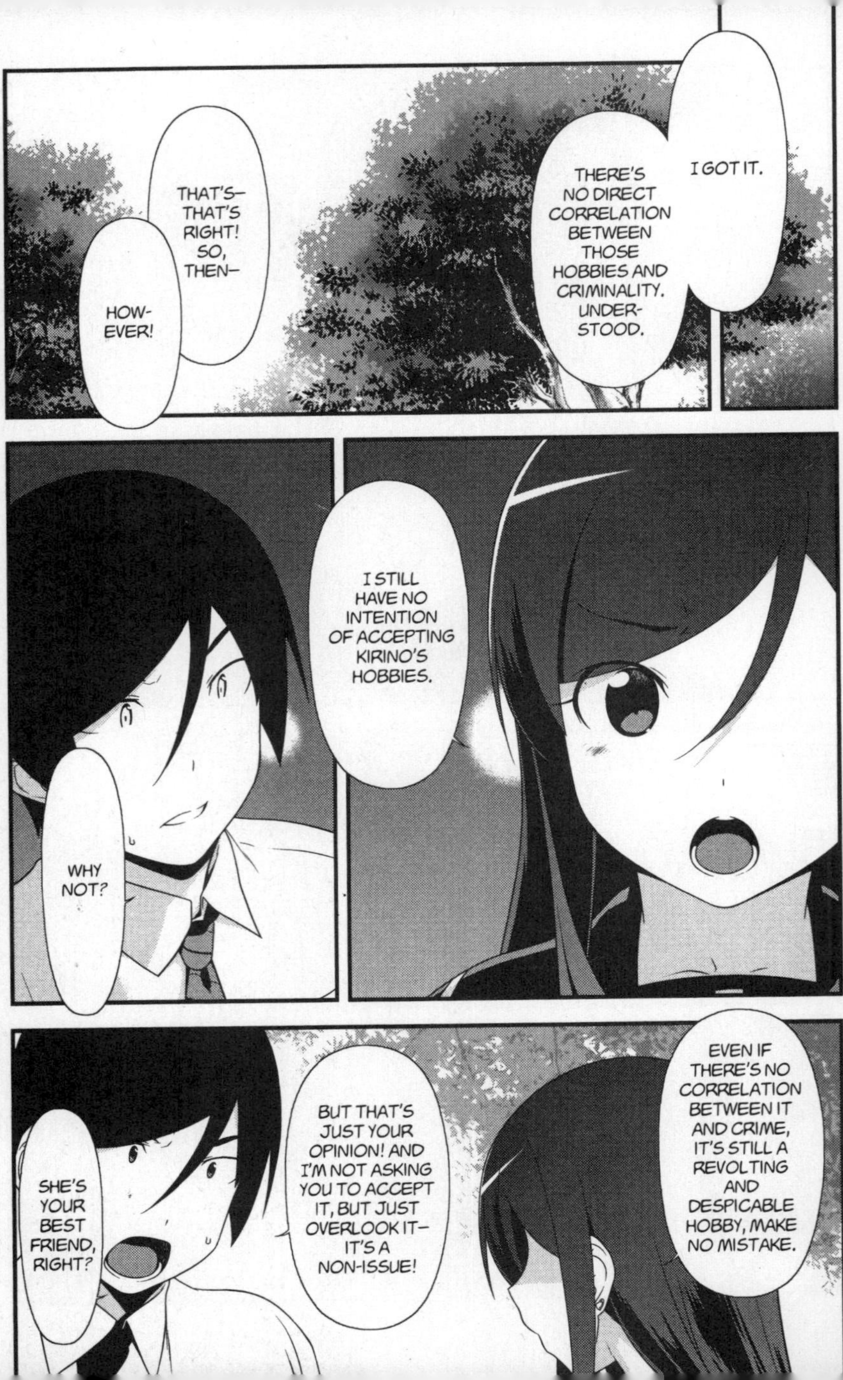
I GOT IT.
THERE'S NO DIRECT CORRELATION BETWEEN THOSE HOBBIES AND CRIMINALITY. UNDER-STOOD.
THAT'S— THAT'S RIGHT! SO, THEN–
HOW-EVER!
I STILL HAVE NO INTENTION OF ACCEPTING KIRINO'S HOBBIES.
WHY NOT?
EVEN IF THERE'S NO CORRELATION BETWEEN IT AND CRIME, IT'S STILL A REVOLTING AND DESPICABLE HOBBY, MAKE NO MISTAKE.
BUT THAT'S JUST YOUR OPINION! AND I'M NOT ASKING YOU TO ACCEPT IT, BUT JUST OVERLOOK IT— IT'S A NON-ISSUE!
SHE'S YOUR BEST FRIEND, RIGHT?

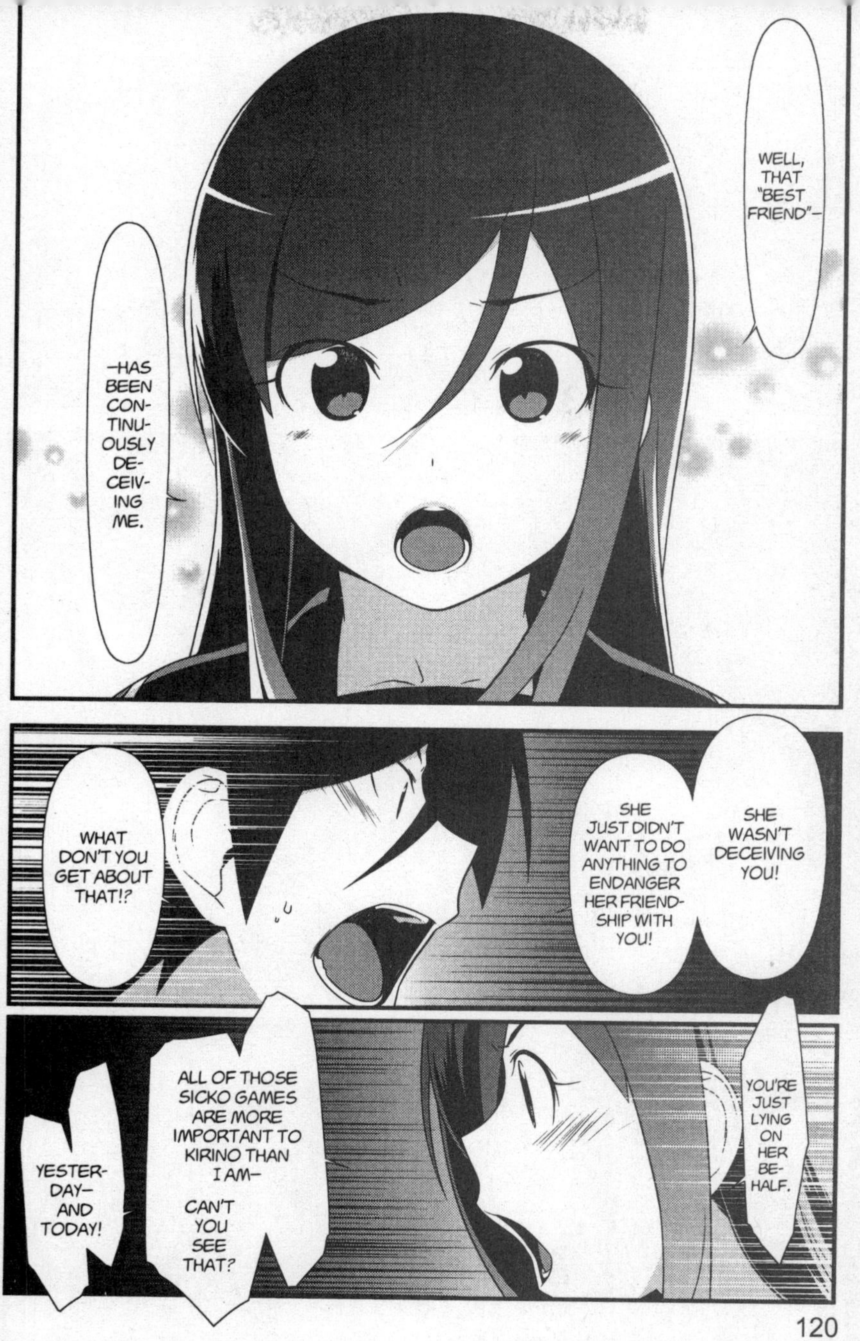
WELL, THAT "BEST FRIEND"—
—HAS BEEN CONTINUOUSLY DECEIVING ME.
SHE WASN'T DECEIVING YOU!
SHE JUST DIDN'T WANT TO DO ANYTHING TO ENDANGER HER FRIENDSHIP WITH YOU!
WHAT DON'T YOU GET ABOUT THAT!?
YOU'RE JUST LYING ON HER BEHALF.
ALL OF THOSE SICKO GAMES ARE MORE IMPORTANT TO KIRINO THAN I AM—
CAN'T YOU SEE THAT?
YESTERDAY— AND TODAY!

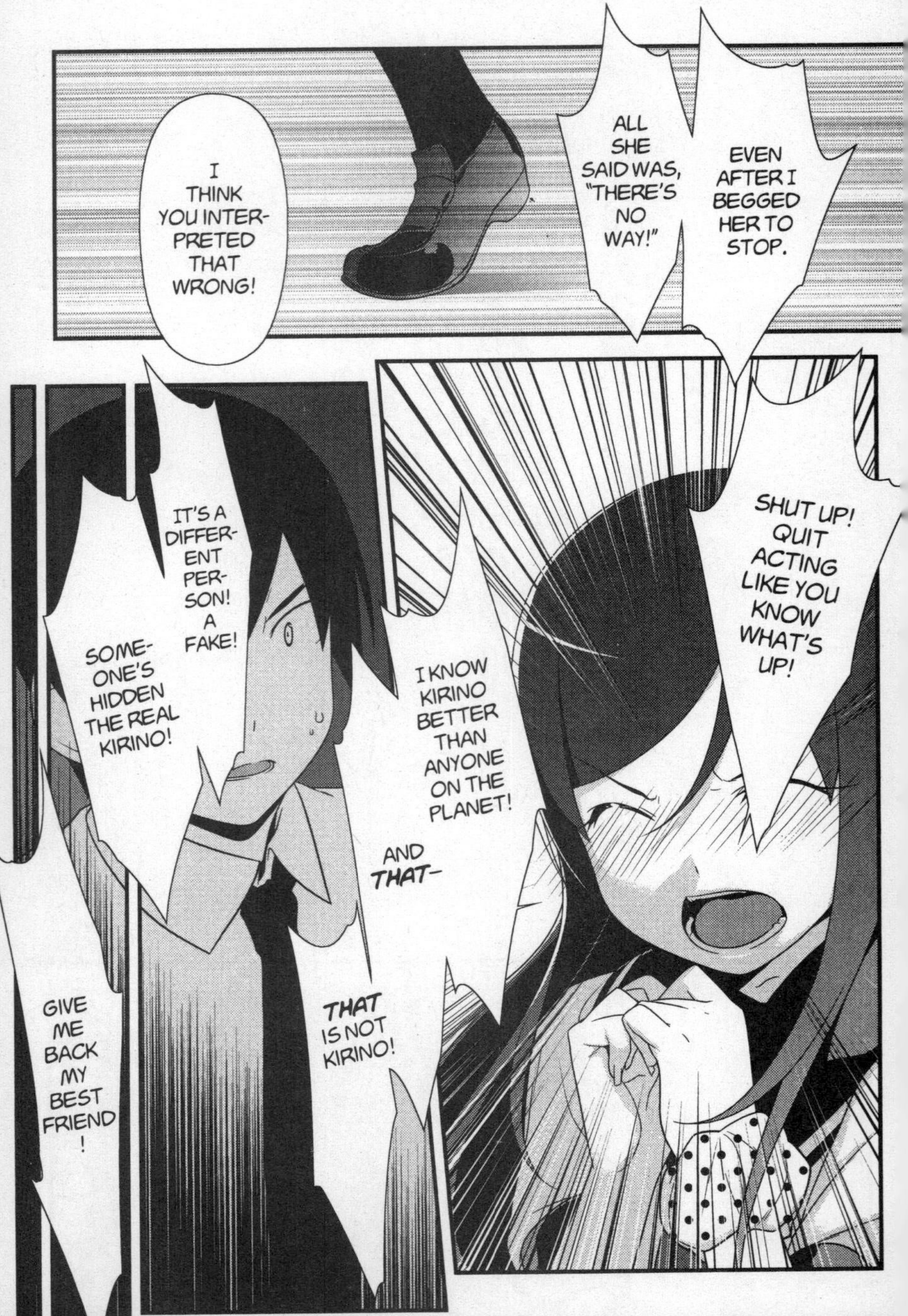
EVEN AFTER I BEGGED HER TO STOP.
ALL SHE SAID WAS, "THERE'S NO WAY!"
I THINK YOU INTERPRETED THAT WRONG!
SHUT UP! QUIT ACTING LIKE YOU KNOW WHAT'S UP!
I KNOW KIRINO BETTER THAN ANYONE ON THE PLANET!
AND *THAT*-
THAT IS NOT KIRINO!
IT'S A DIFFERENT PERSON! A FAKE!
SOMEONE'S HIDDEN THE REAL KIRINO!
GIVE ME BACK MY BEST FRIEND!

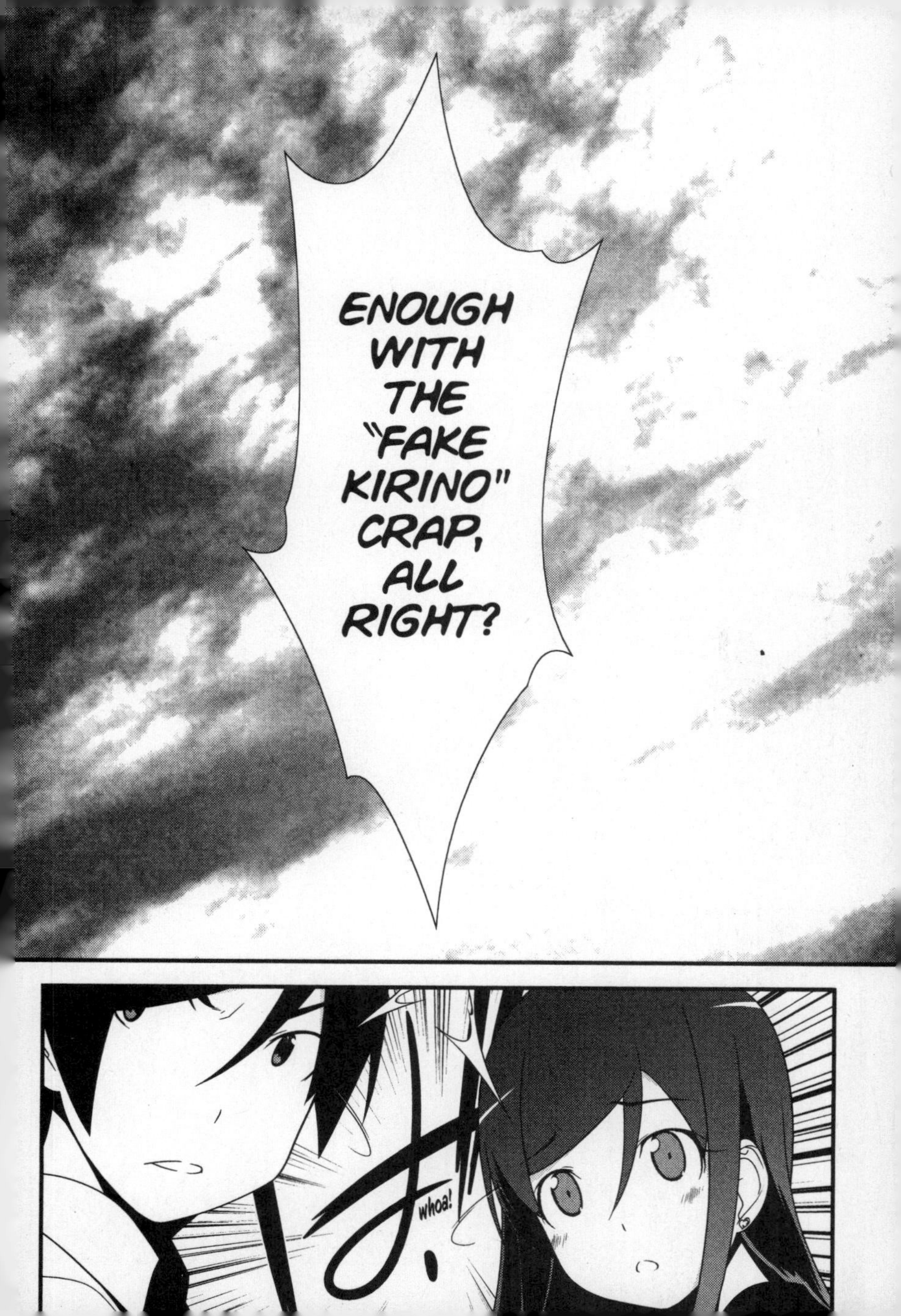
ENOUGH WITH THE "FAKE KIRINO" CRAP, ALL RIGHT?
whoa!

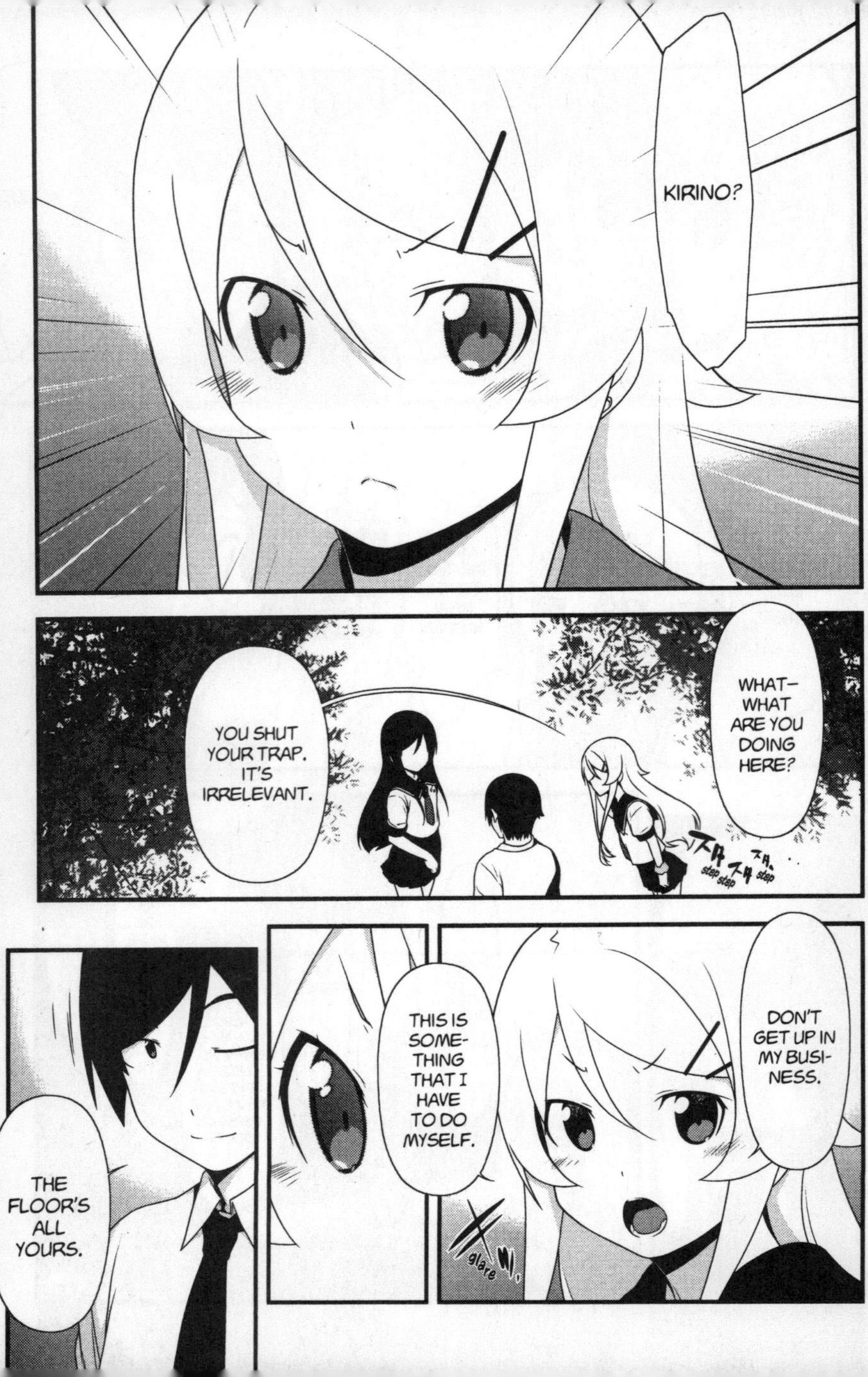
KIRINO?
WHAT— WHAT ARE YOU DOING HERE?
step step step
YOU SHUT YOUR TRAP. IT'S IRRELEVANT.
DON'T GET UP IN MY BUSI- NESS.
THIS IS SOME- THING THAT I HAVE TO DO MYSELF.
glare
THE FLOOR'S ALL YOURS.

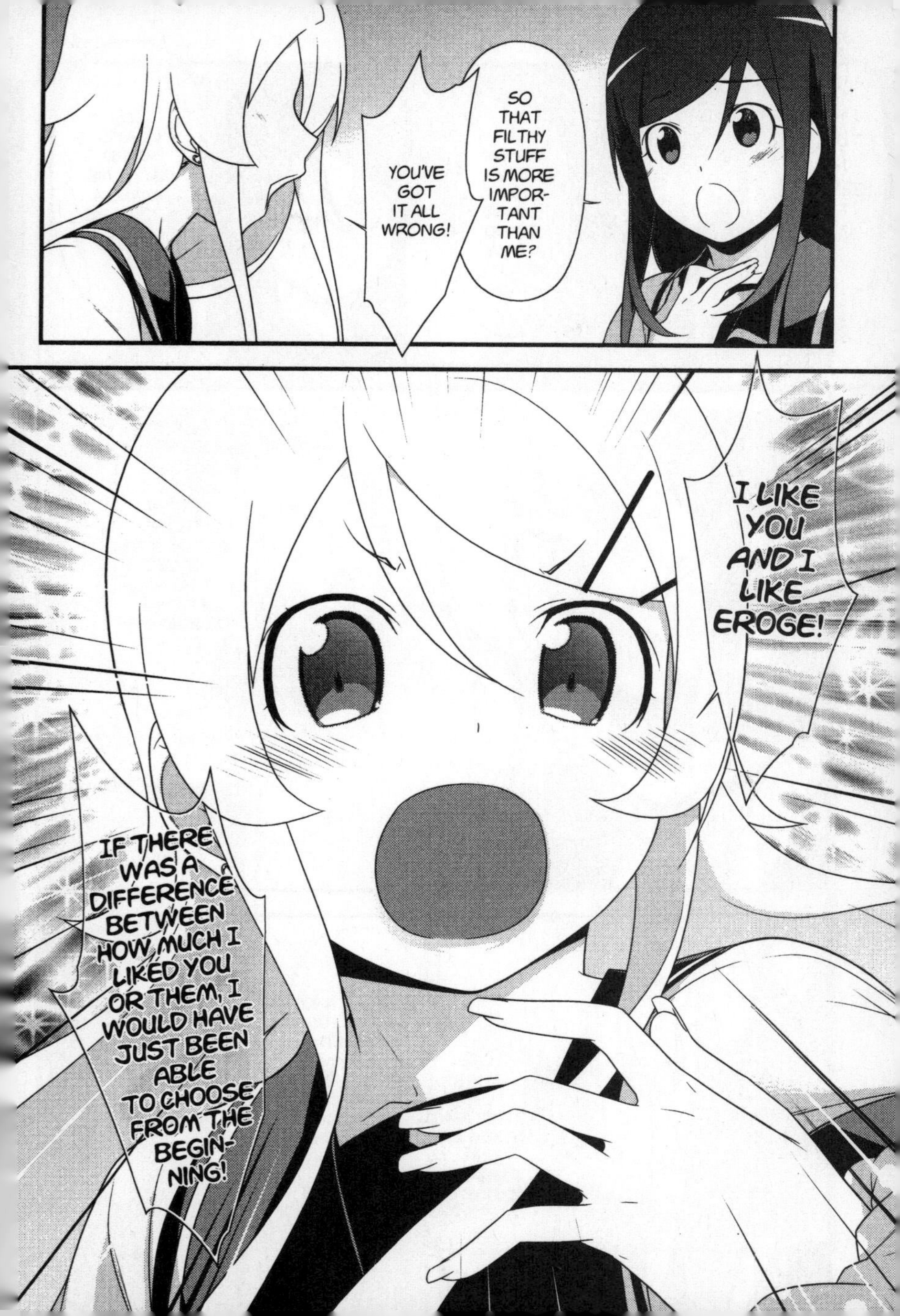
SO THAT FILTHY STUFF IS MORE IMPOR-TANT THAN ME?
YOU'VE GOT IT ALL WRONG!
I LIKE YOU AND I LIKE EROGE!
IF THERE WAS A DIFFERENCE BETWEEN HOW MUCH I LIKED YOU OR THEM, I WOULD HAVE JUST BEEN ABLE TO CHOOSE FROM THE BEGIN-NING!

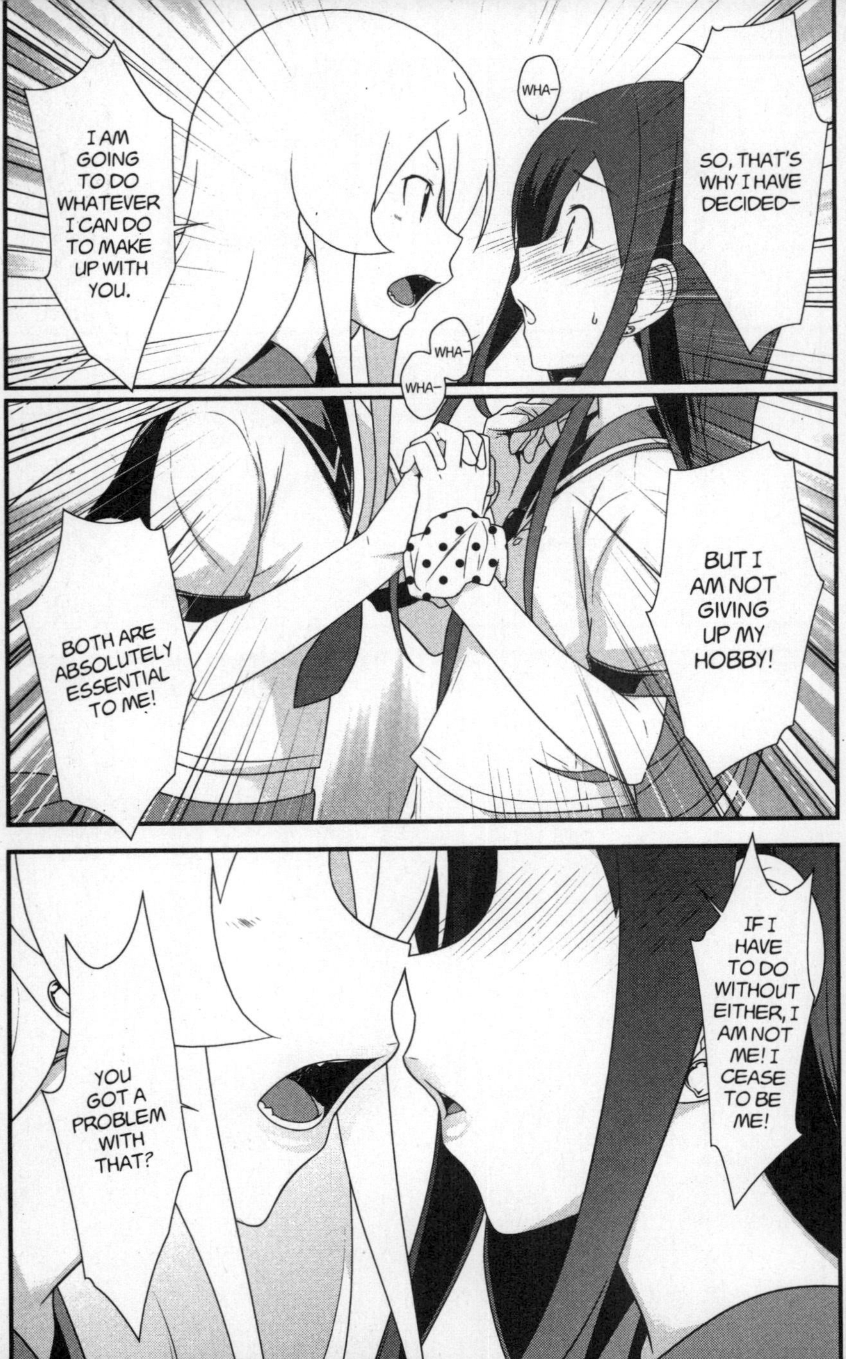
SO, THAT'S WHY I HAVE DECIDED–
WHA–
I AM GOING TO DO WHATEVER I CAN DO TO MAKE UP WITH YOU.
WHA–
WHA–
BUT I AM NOT GIVING UP MY HOBBY!
BOTH ARE ABSOLUTELY ESSENTIAL TO ME!
IF I HAVE TO DO WITHOUT EITHER, I AM NOT ME! I CEASE TO BE ME!
YOU GOT A PROBLEM WITH THAT?

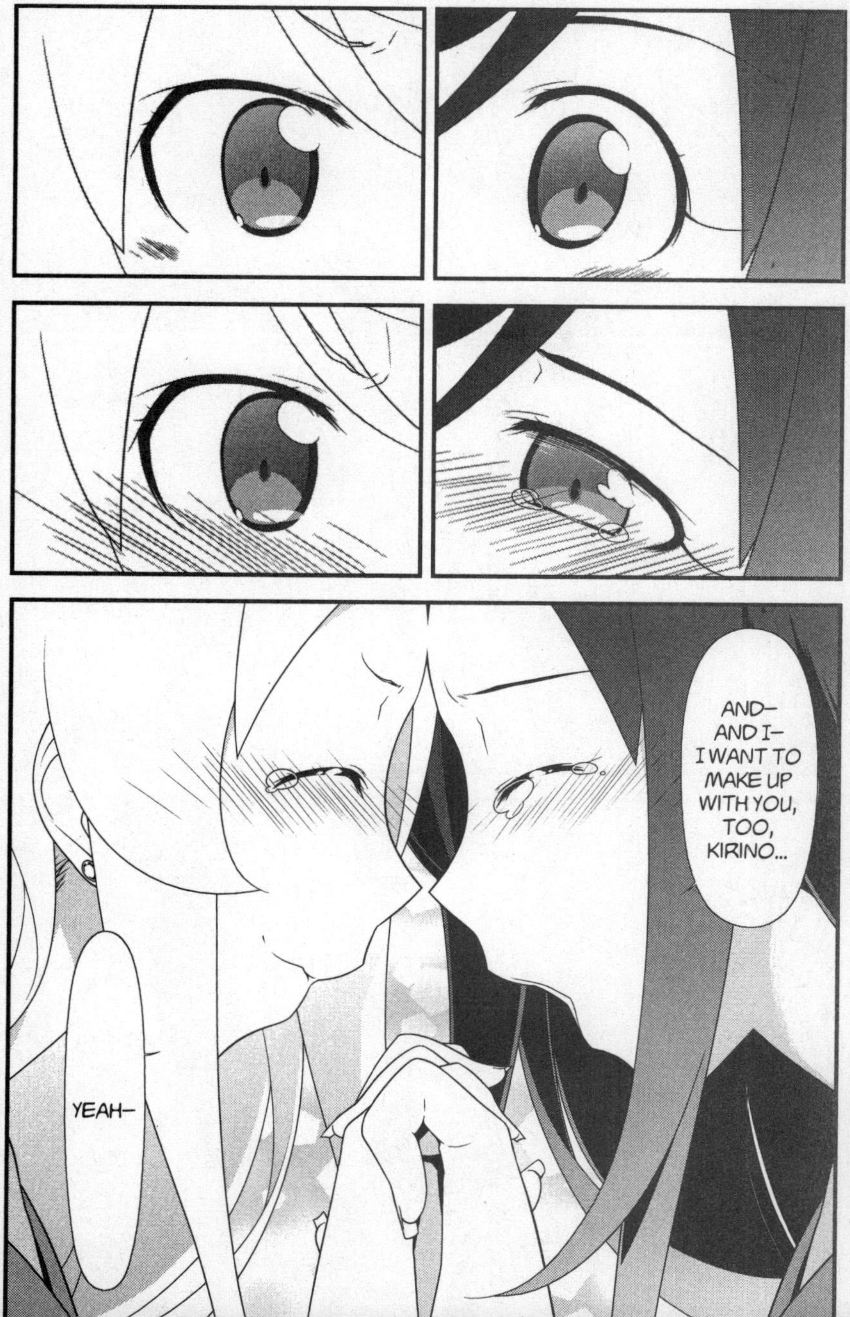
AND— AND I— I WANT TO MAKE UP WITH YOU, TOO, KIRINO...
YEAH—

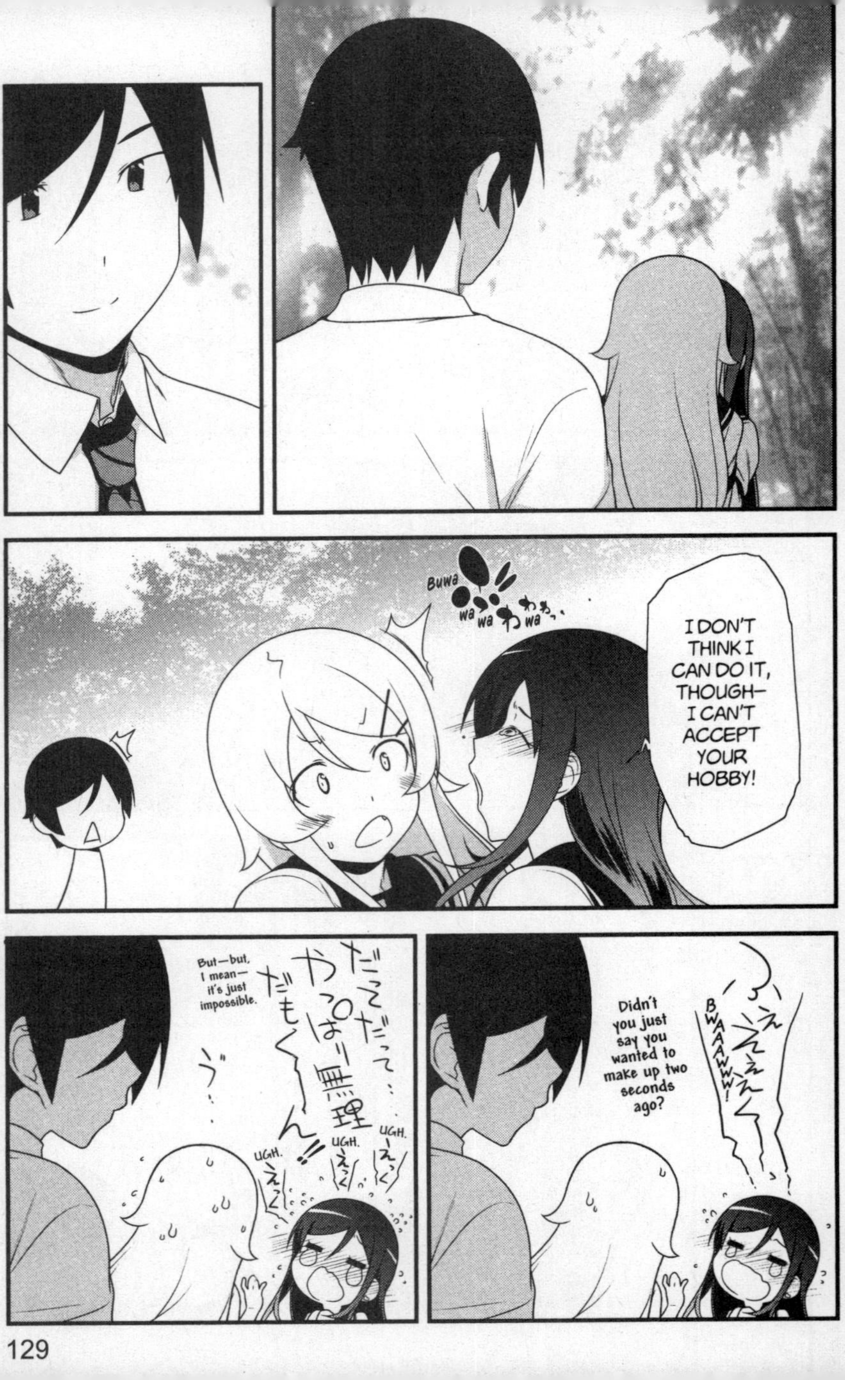
Buwa wa wa wa
I DON'T THINK I CAN DO IT, THOUGH— I CAN'T ACCEPT YOUR HOBBY!
Didn't you just say you wanted to make up two seconds ago?
BWAAAAWW!
But—but, I mean— it's just impossible.
UGH.
UGH.
UGH.

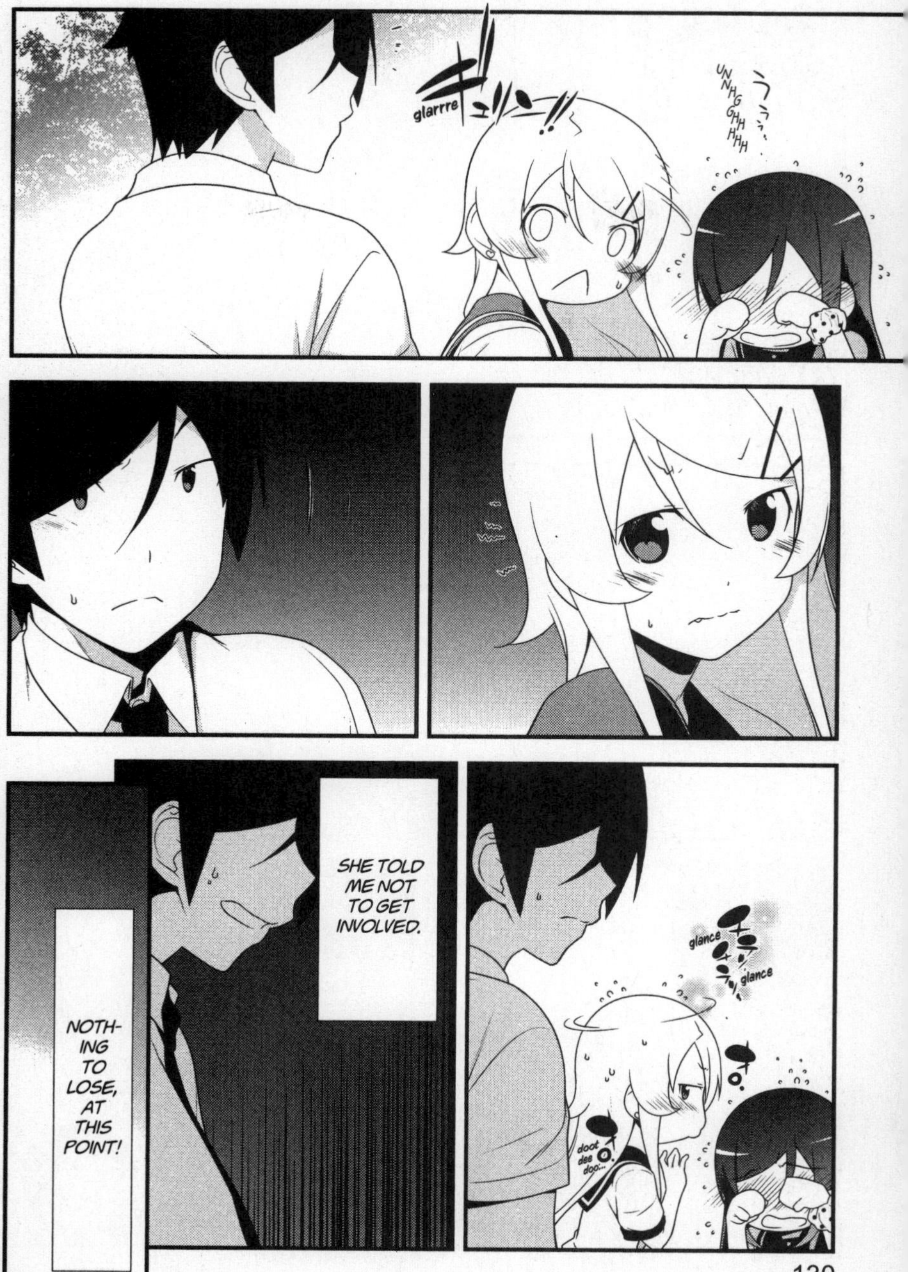
glarrre
UNNHGGHHHHH
glance
glance
doot dee doo...
SHE TOLD ME NOT TO GET INVOLVED.
NOTHING TO LOSE, AT THIS POINT!

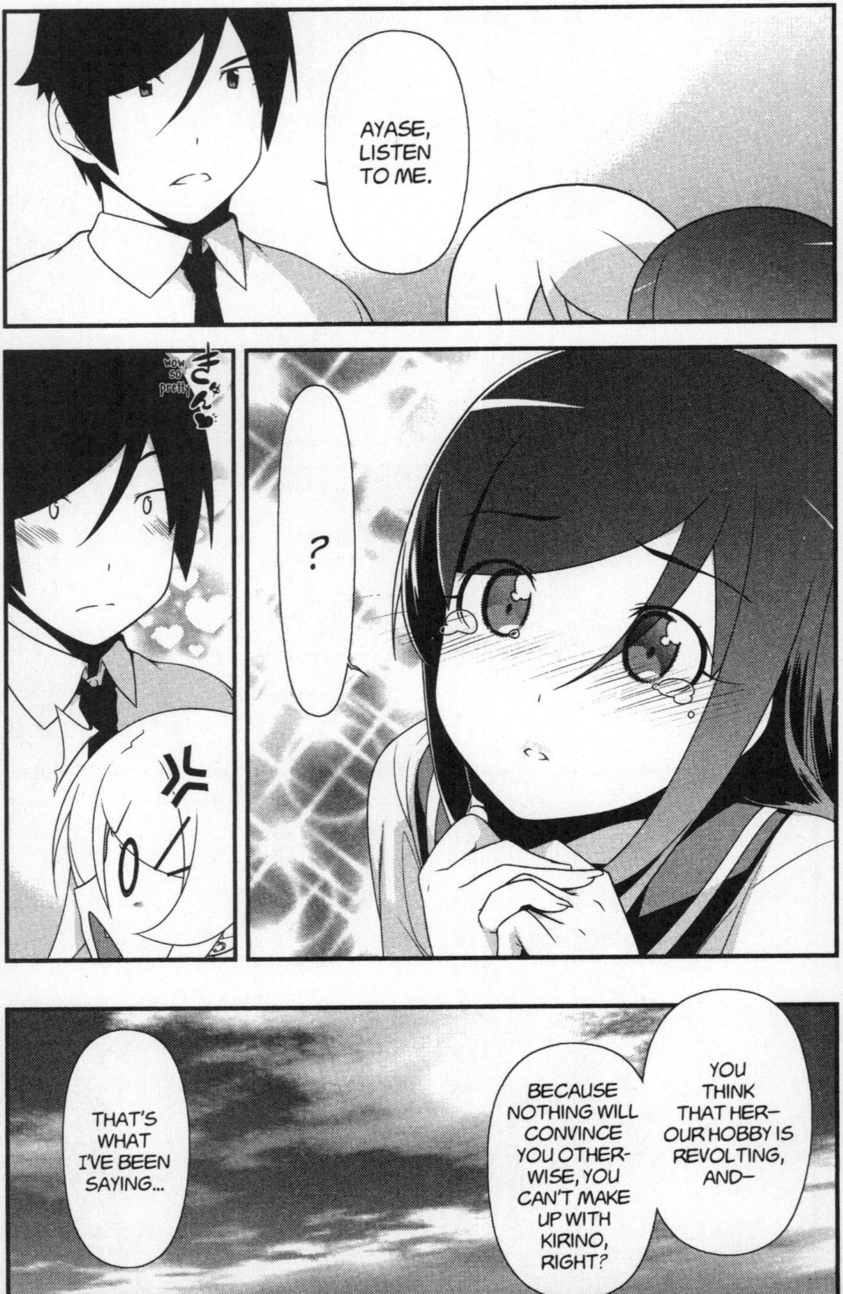
AYASE, LISTEN TO ME.
?
きゅん
wow, so pretty
YOU THINK THAT HER— OUR HOBBY IS REVOLTING, AND—
BECAUSE NOTHING WILL CONVINCE YOU OTHER-WISE, YOU CAN'T MAKE UP WITH KIRINO, RIGHT?
THAT'S WHAT I'VE BEEN SAYING...

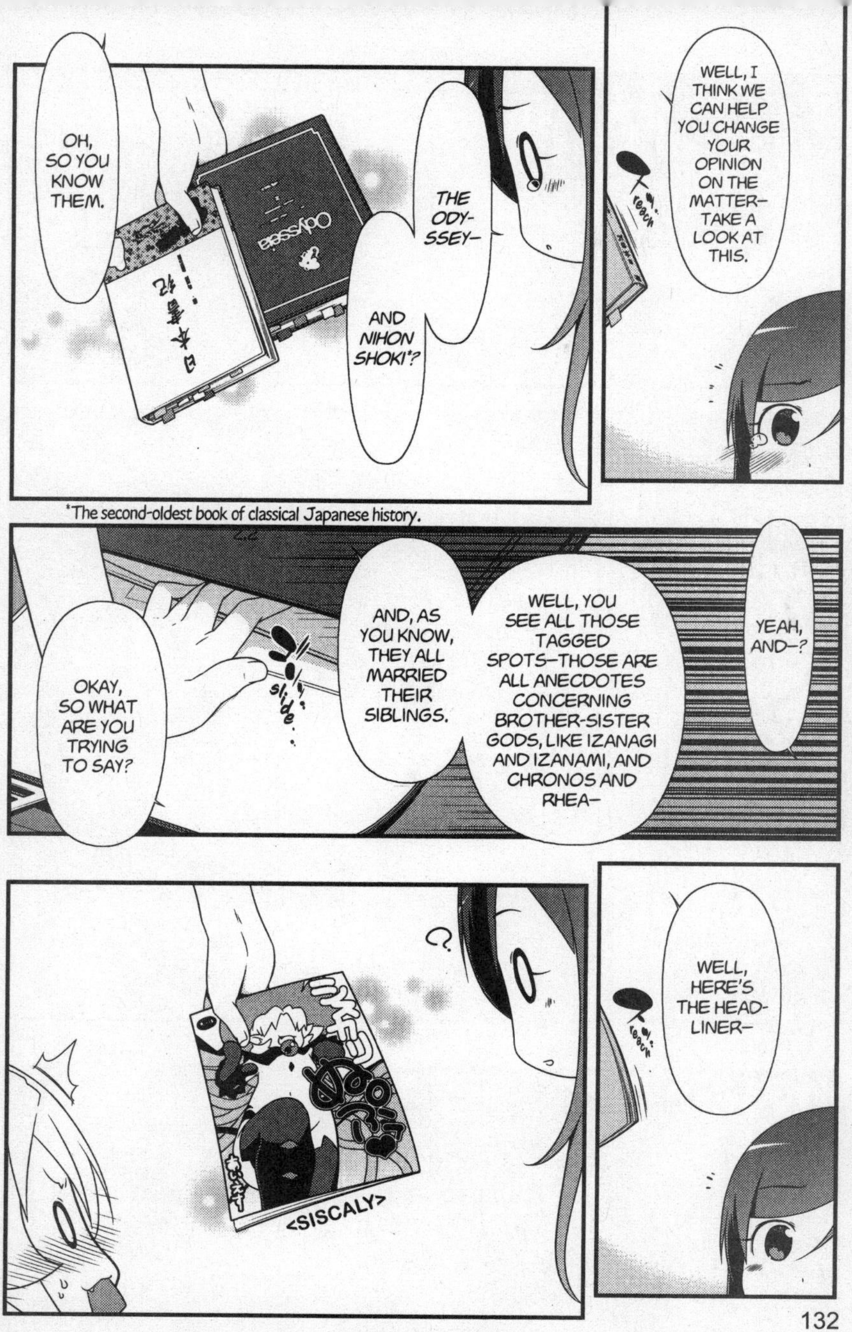
WELL, I THINK WE CAN HELP YOU CHANGE YOUR OPINION ON THE MATTER—TAKE A LOOK AT THIS.
reach
THE ODY-SSEY—
AND NIHON SHOKI*?
OH, SO YOU KNOW THEM.
YEAH, AND—?
WELL, YOU SEE ALL THOSE TAGGED SPOTS—THOSE ARE ALL ANECDOTES CONCERNING BROTHER-SISTER GODS, LIKE IZANAGI AND IZANAMI, AND CHRONOS AND RHEA—
AND, AS YOU KNOW, THEY ALL MARRIED THEIR SIBLINGS.
slide
OKAY, SO WHAT ARE YOU TRYING TO SAY?
WELL, HERE'S THE HEAD-LINER—
reach
<SISCALY>

*The second-oldest book of classical Japanese history.

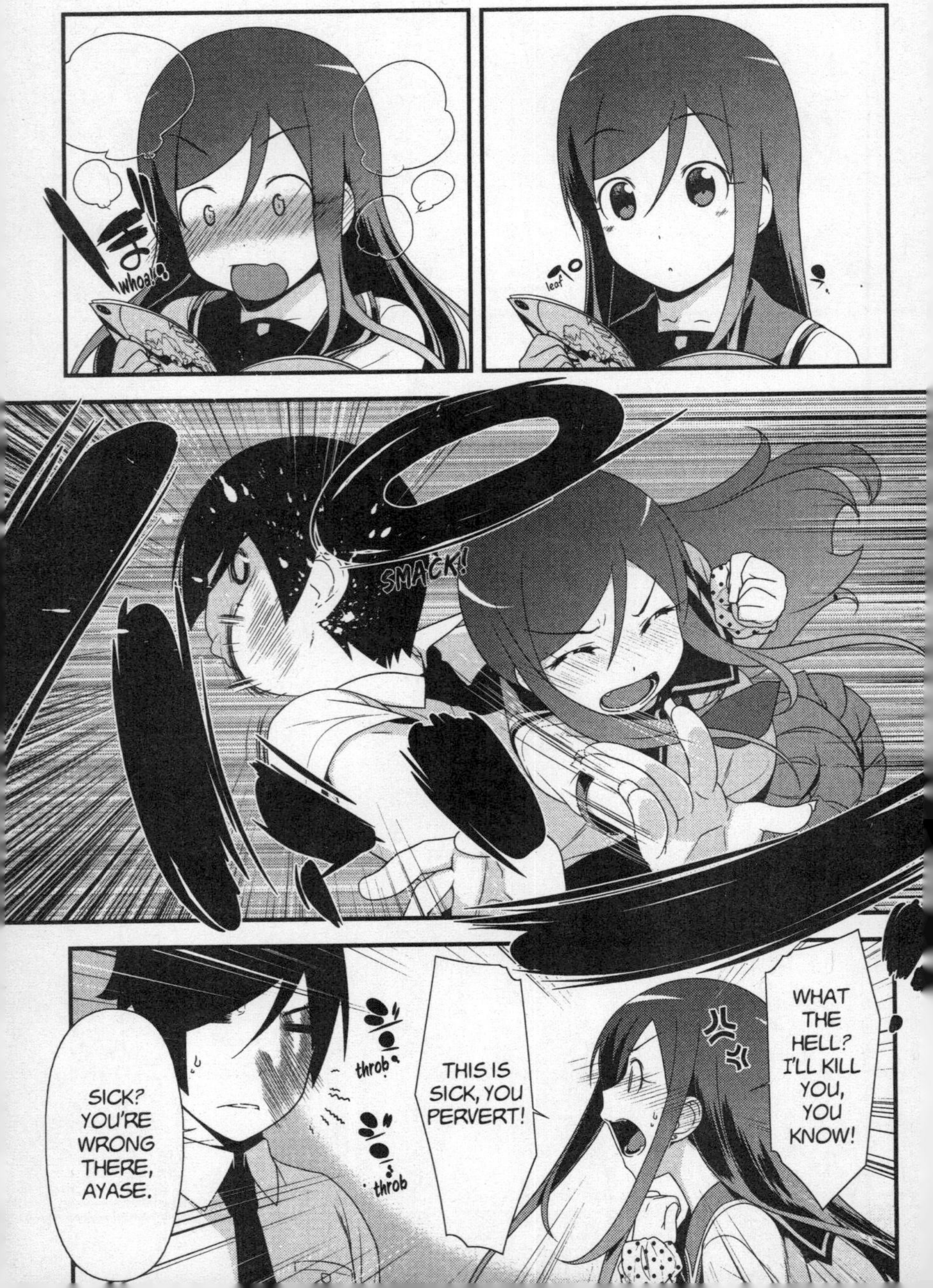
leaf
whoa!?
SMACK!
WHAT THE HELL? I'LL KILL YOU, YOU KNOW!
THIS IS SICK, YOU PERVERT!
throb
throb
SICK? YOU'RE WRONG THERE, AYASE.

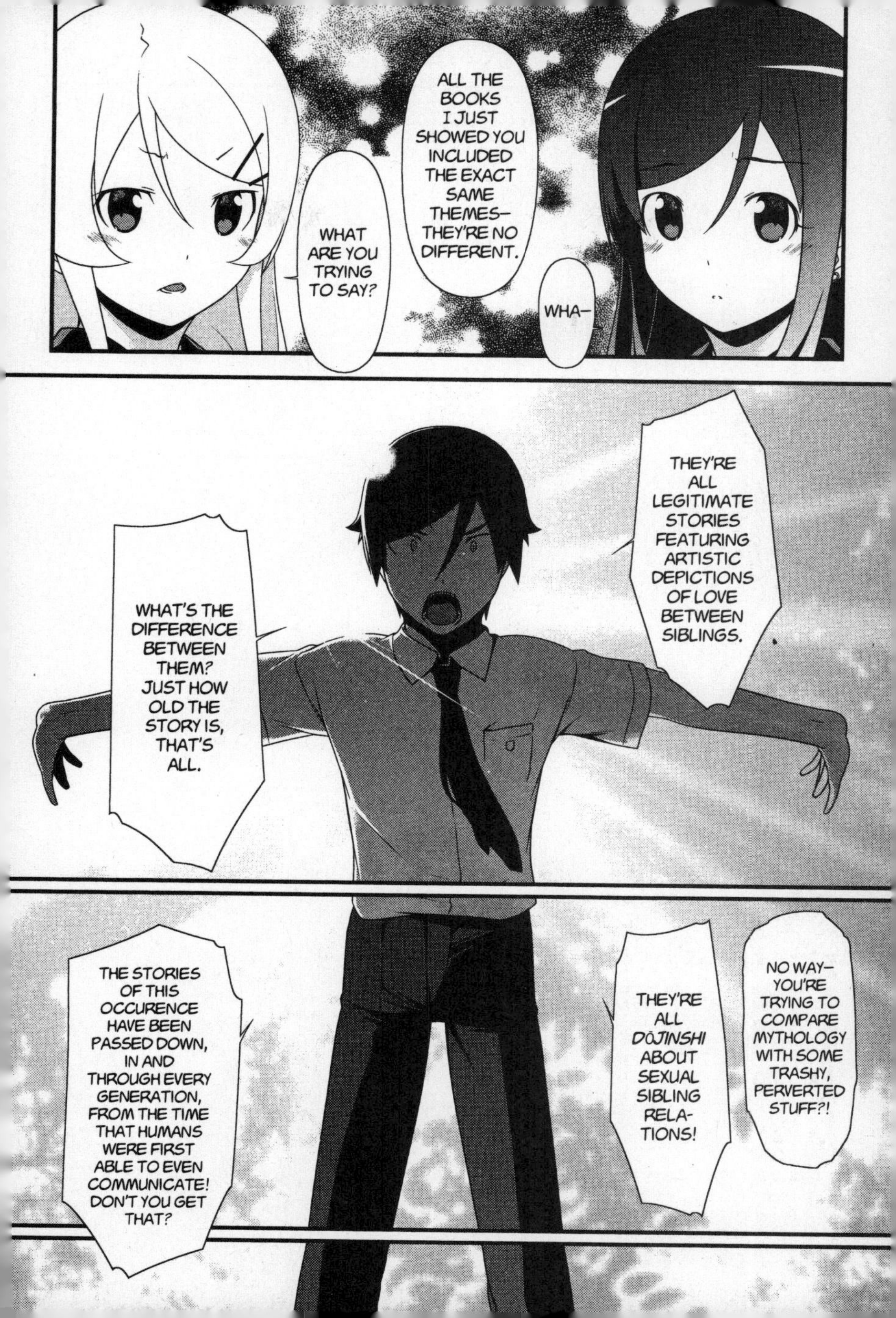
WHA-
ALL THE BOOKS I JUST SHOWED YOU INCLUDED THE EXACT SAME THEMES—THEY'RE NO DIFFERENT.
WHAT ARE YOU TRYING TO SAY?
THEY'RE ALL LEGITIMATE STORIES FEATURING ARTISTIC DEPICTIONS OF LOVE BETWEEN SIBLINGS.
WHAT'S THE DIFFERENCE BETWEEN THEM? JUST HOW OLD THE STORY IS, THAT'S ALL.
NO WAY—YOU'RE TRYING TO COMPARE MYTHOLOGY WITH SOME TRASHY, PERVERTED STUFF?!
THEY'RE ALL DŌJINSHI ABOUT SEXUAL SIBLING RELA-TIONS!
THE STORIES OF THIS OCCURENCE HAVE BEEN PASSED DOWN, IN AND THROUGH EVERY GENERATION, FROM THE TIME THAT HUMANS WERE FIRST ABLE TO EVEN COMMUNICATE! DON'T YOU GET THAT?

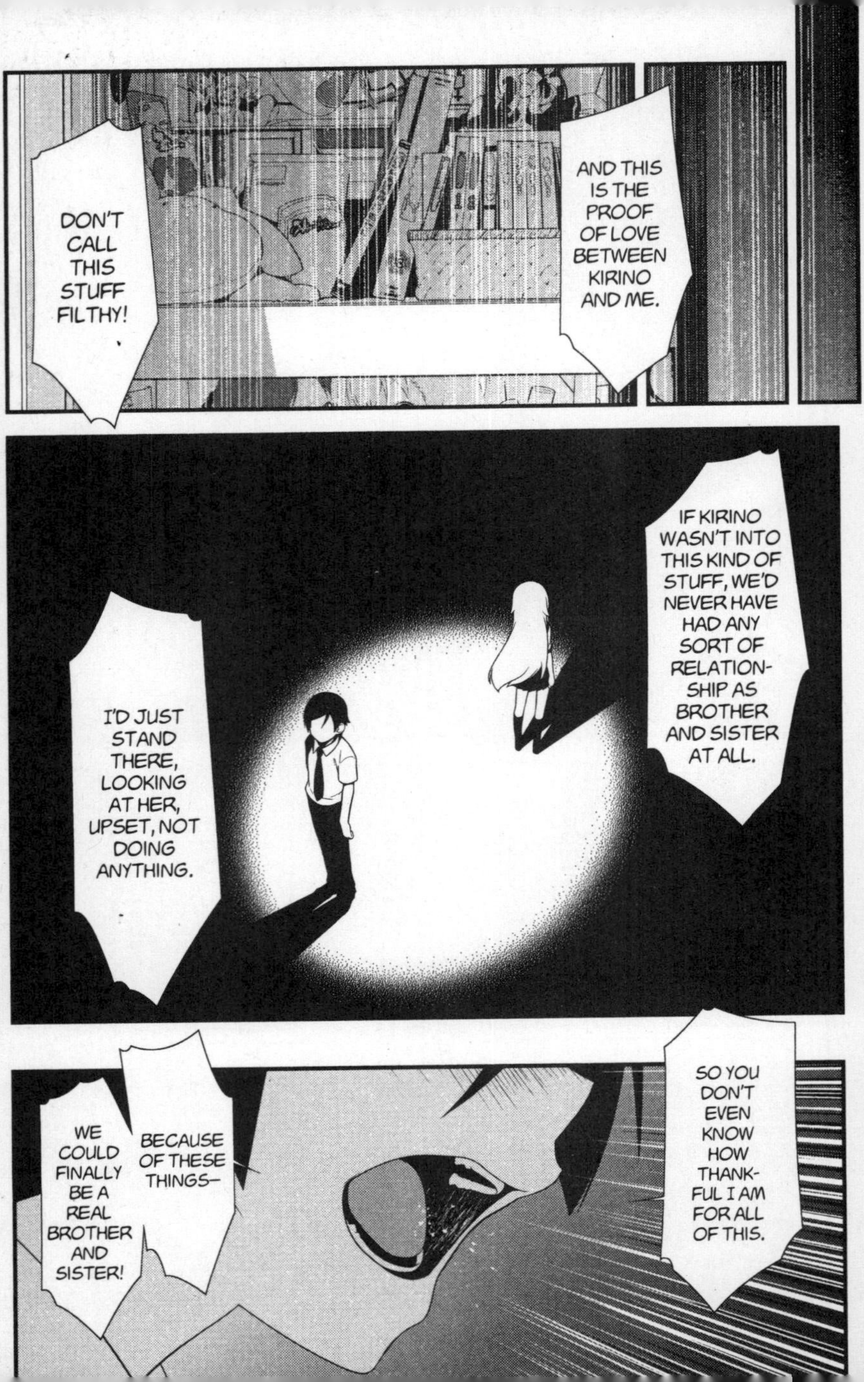
AND THIS IS THE PROOF OF LOVE BETWEEN KIRINO AND ME.
DON'T CALL THIS STUFF FILTHY!
IF KIRINO WASN'T INTO THIS KIND OF STUFF, WE'D NEVER HAVE HAD ANY SORT OF RELATION-SHIP AS BROTHER AND SISTER AT ALL.
I'D JUST STAND THERE, LOOKING AT HER, UPSET, NOT DOING ANYTHING.
SO YOU DON'T EVEN KNOW HOW THANK-FUL I AM FOR ALL OF THIS.
BECAUSE OF THESE THINGS—
WE COULD FINALLY BE A REAL BROTHER AND SISTER!

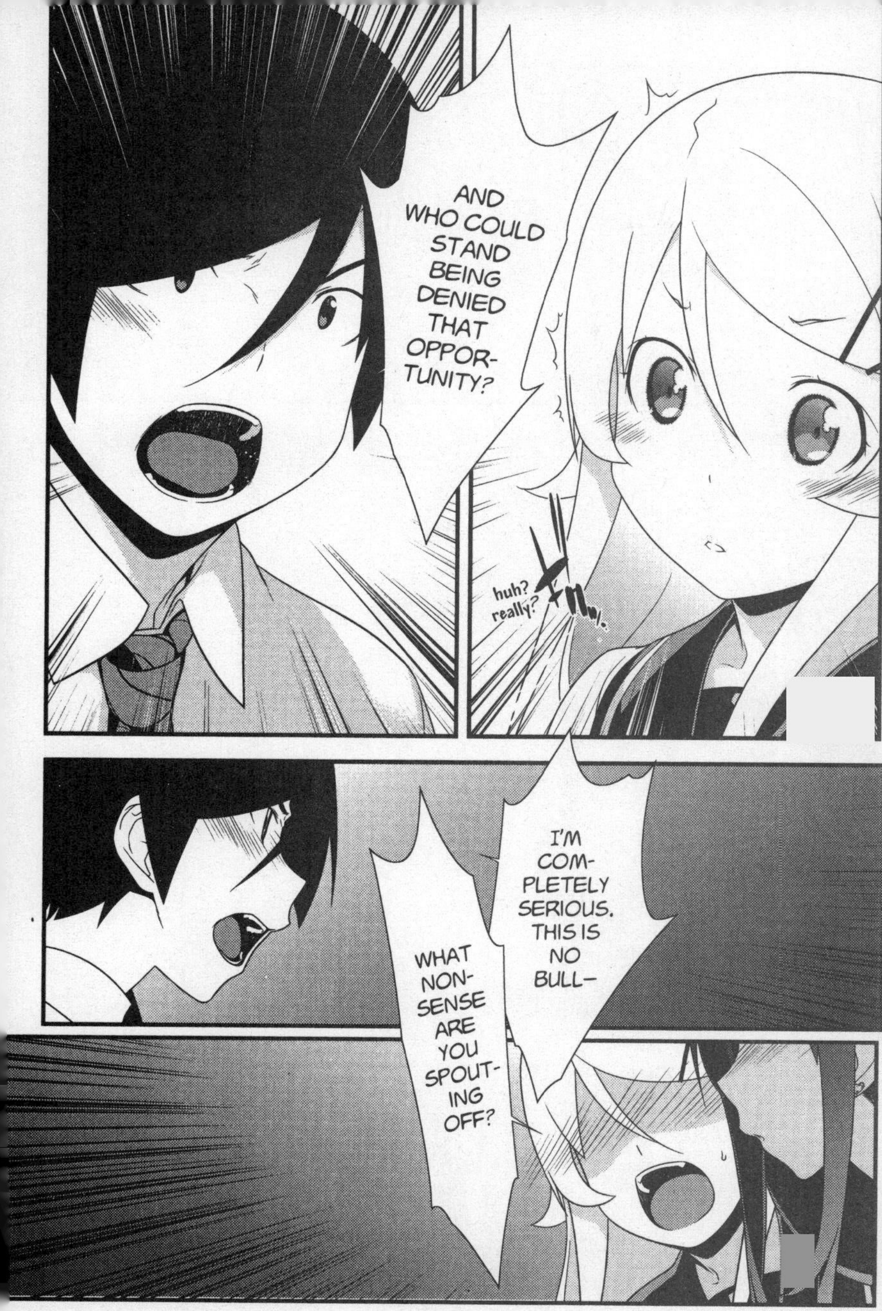
AND WHO COULD STAND BEING DENIED THAT OPPOR-TUNITY?
huh? really?
I'M COM-PLETELY SERIOUS. THIS IS NO BULL-
WHAT NON-SENSE ARE YOU SPOUT-ING OFF?

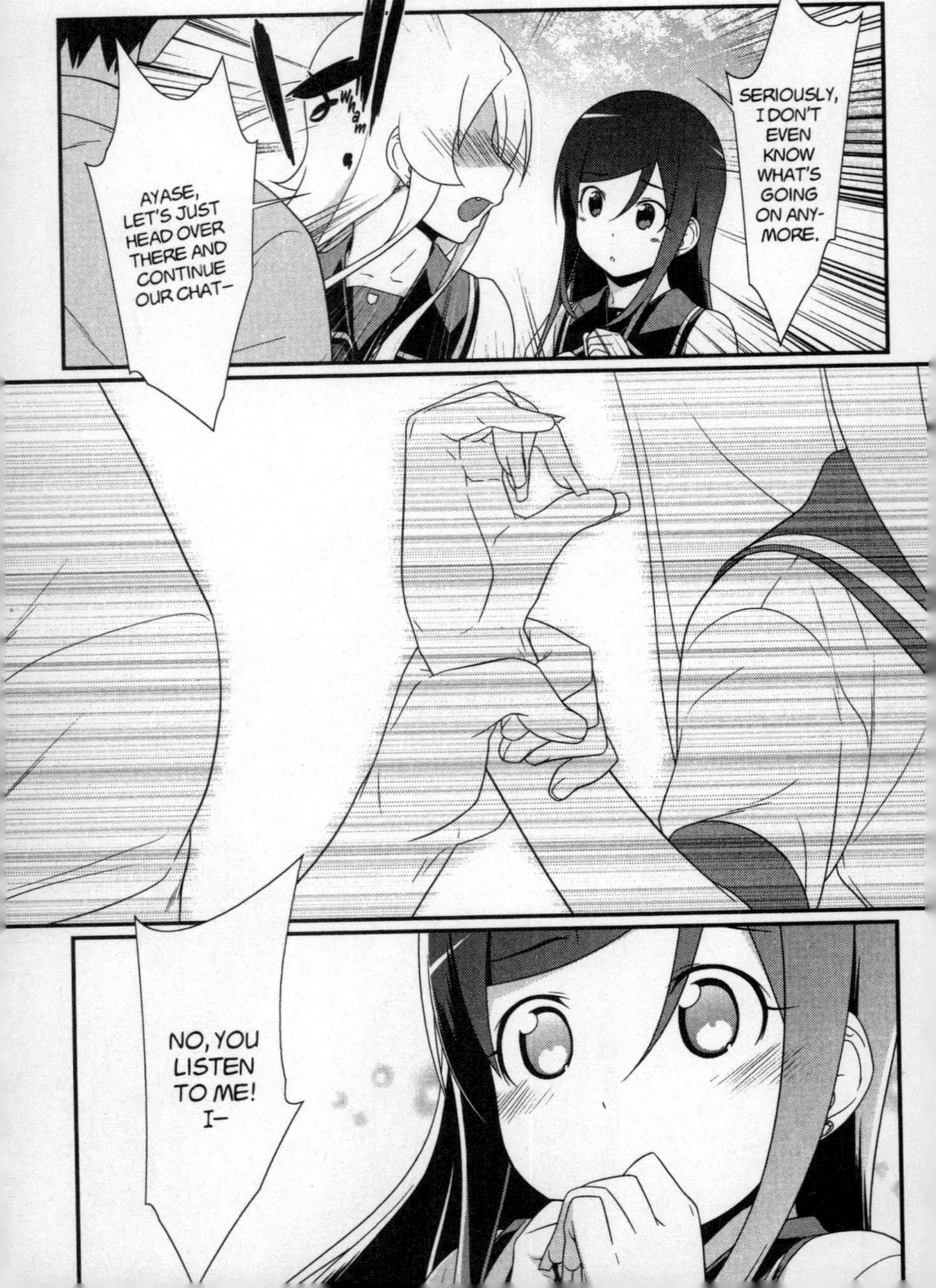
SERIOUSLY, I DON'T EVEN KNOW WHAT'S GOING ON ANY-MORE.
wham
AYASE, LET'S JUST HEAD OVER THERE AND CONTINUE OUR CHAT–
NO, YOU LISTEN TO ME! I–

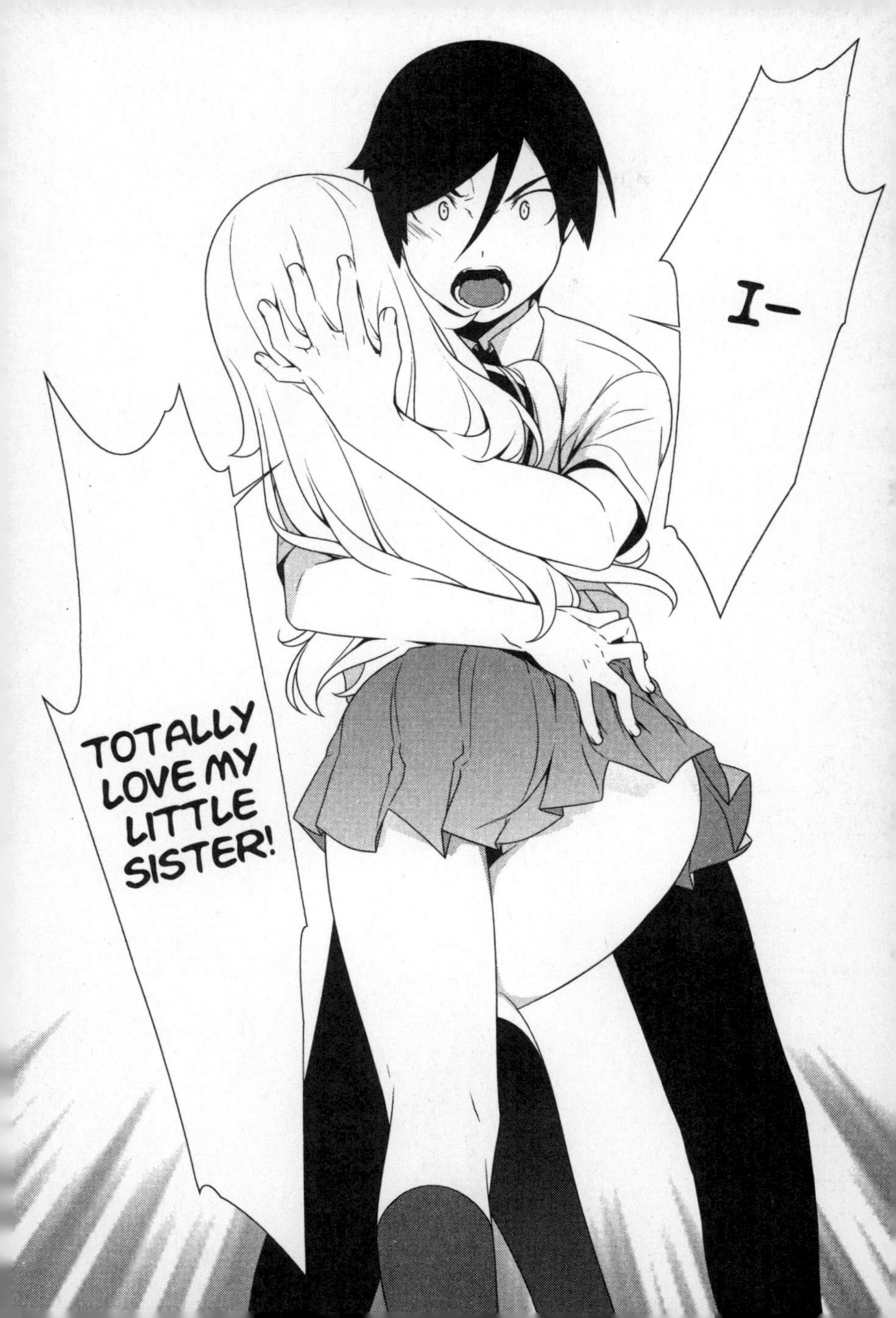
I-
TOTALLY LOVE MY LITTLE SISTER!

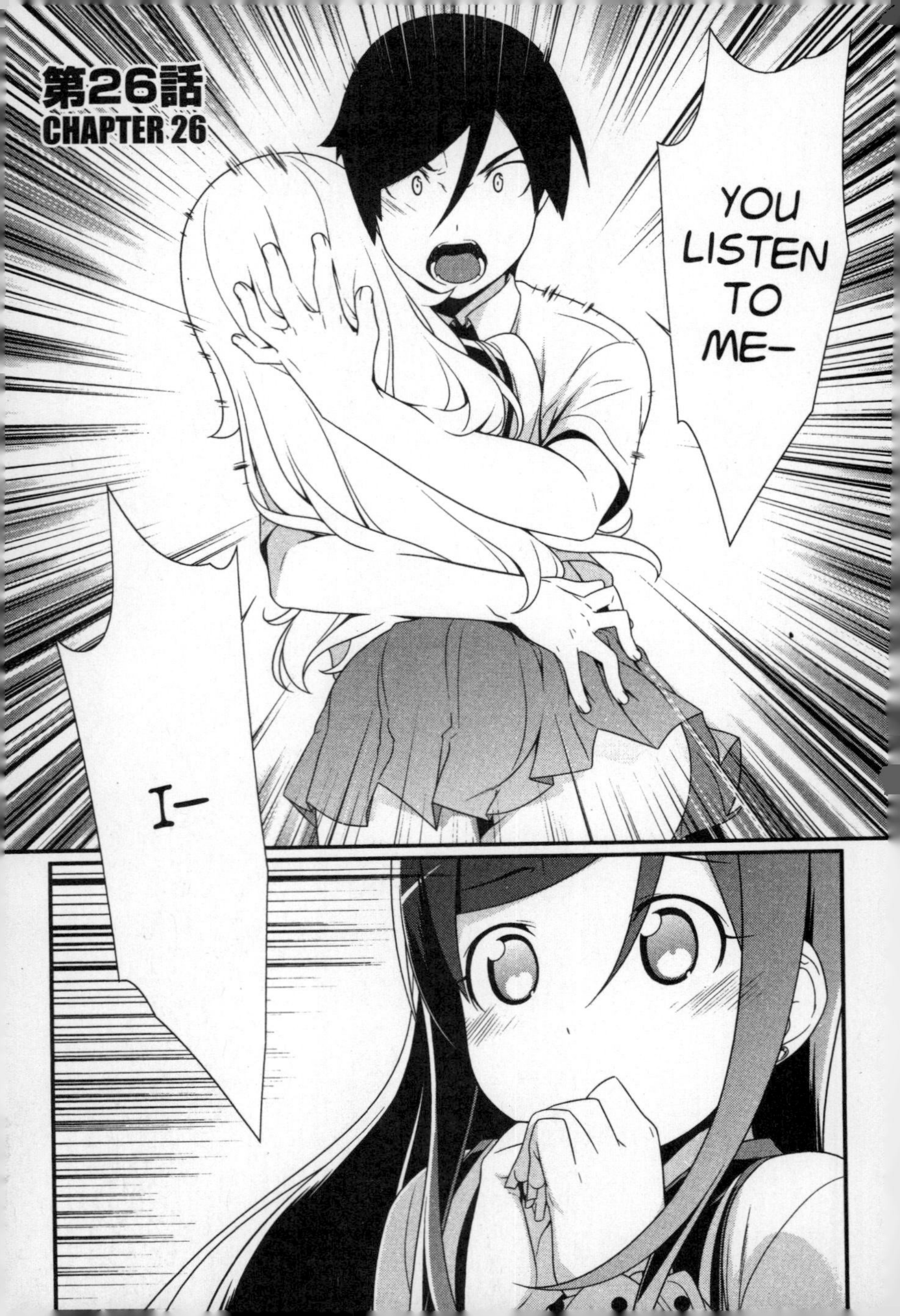
第26話
CHAPTER 26
YOU LISTEN TO ME–
I–

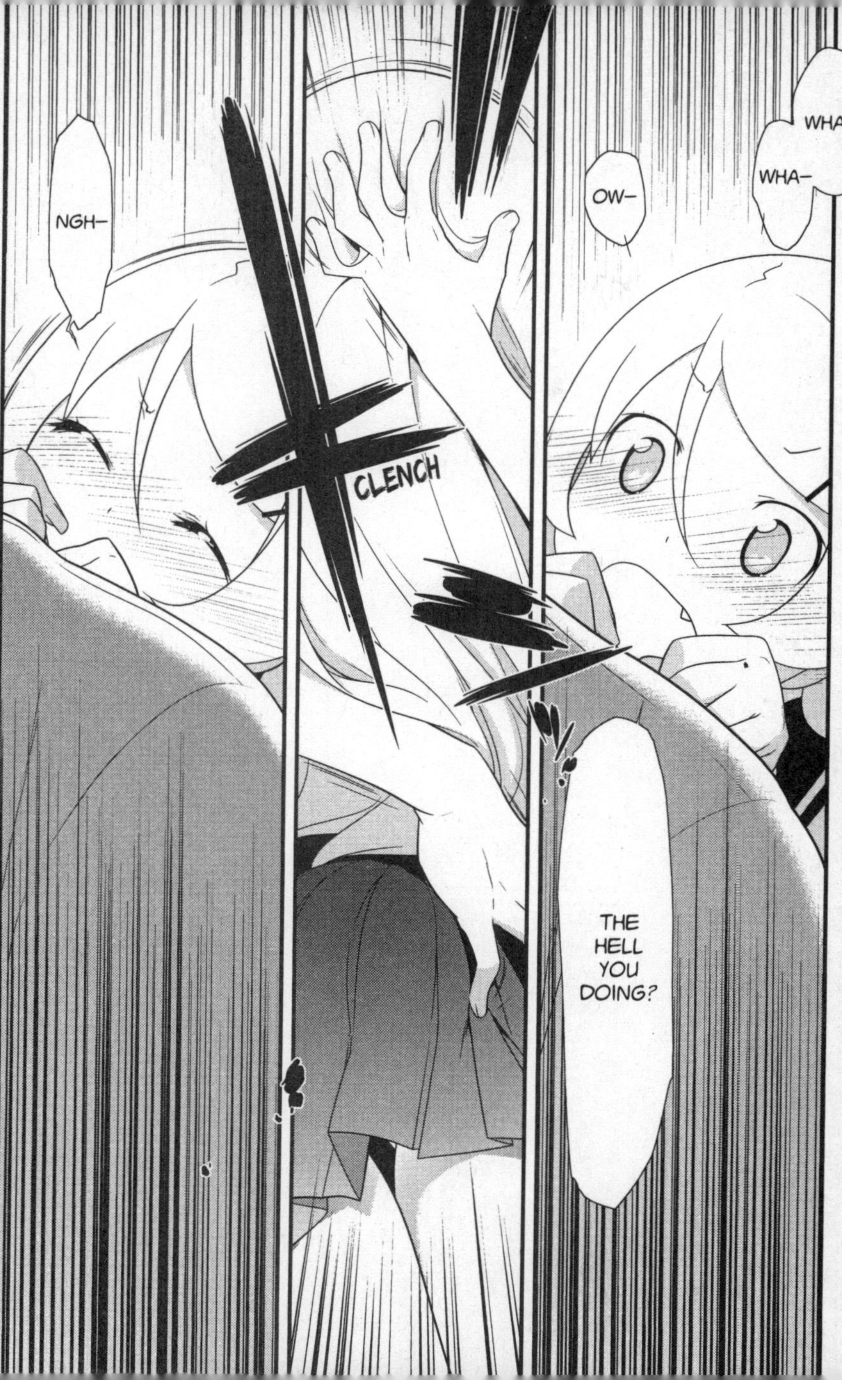
WHA-
WHA-
OW-
THE HELL YOU DOING?
CLENCH
NGH-

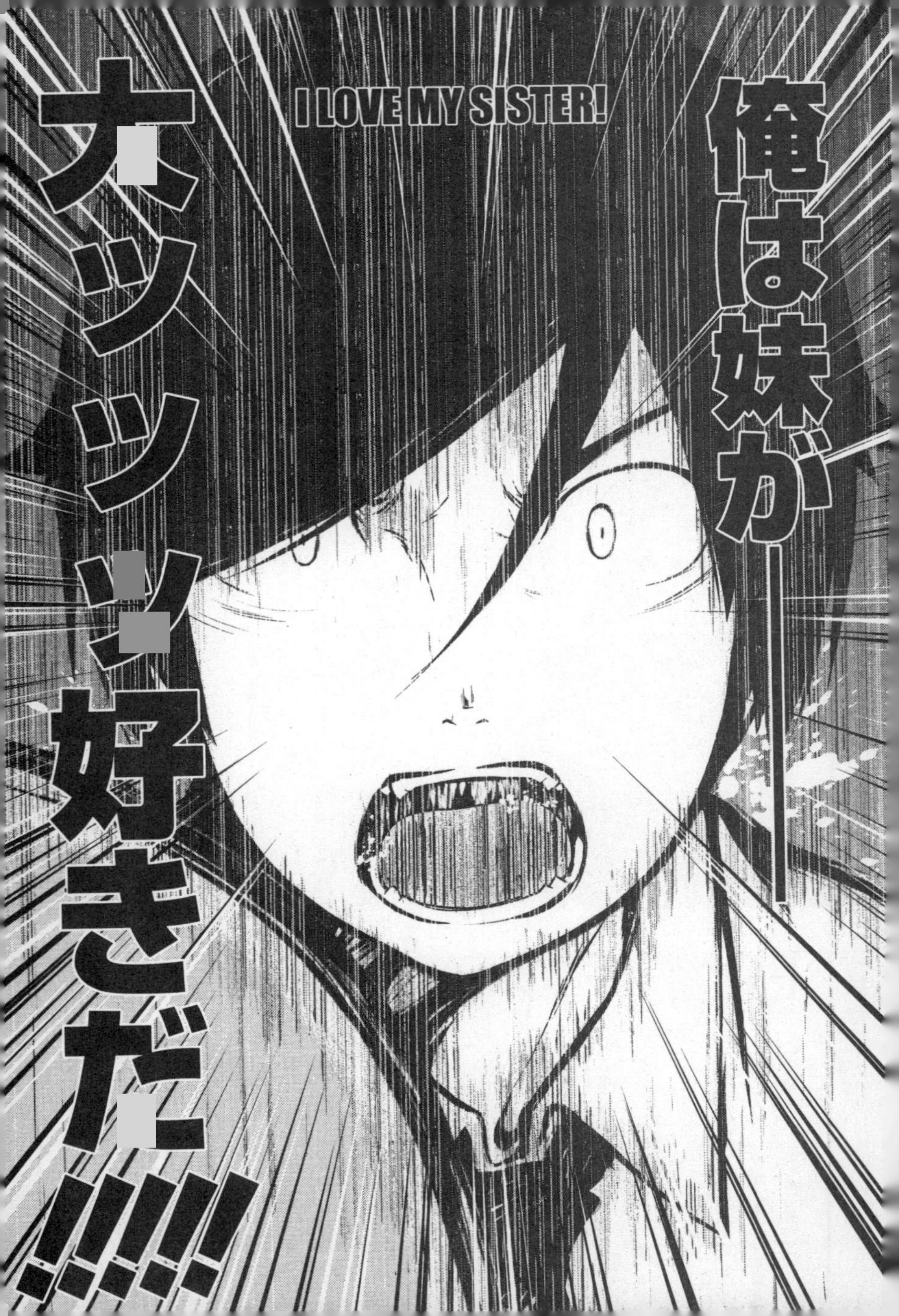

俺は妹が――
I LOVE MY SISTER!
大ッッッ好きだ!!!!

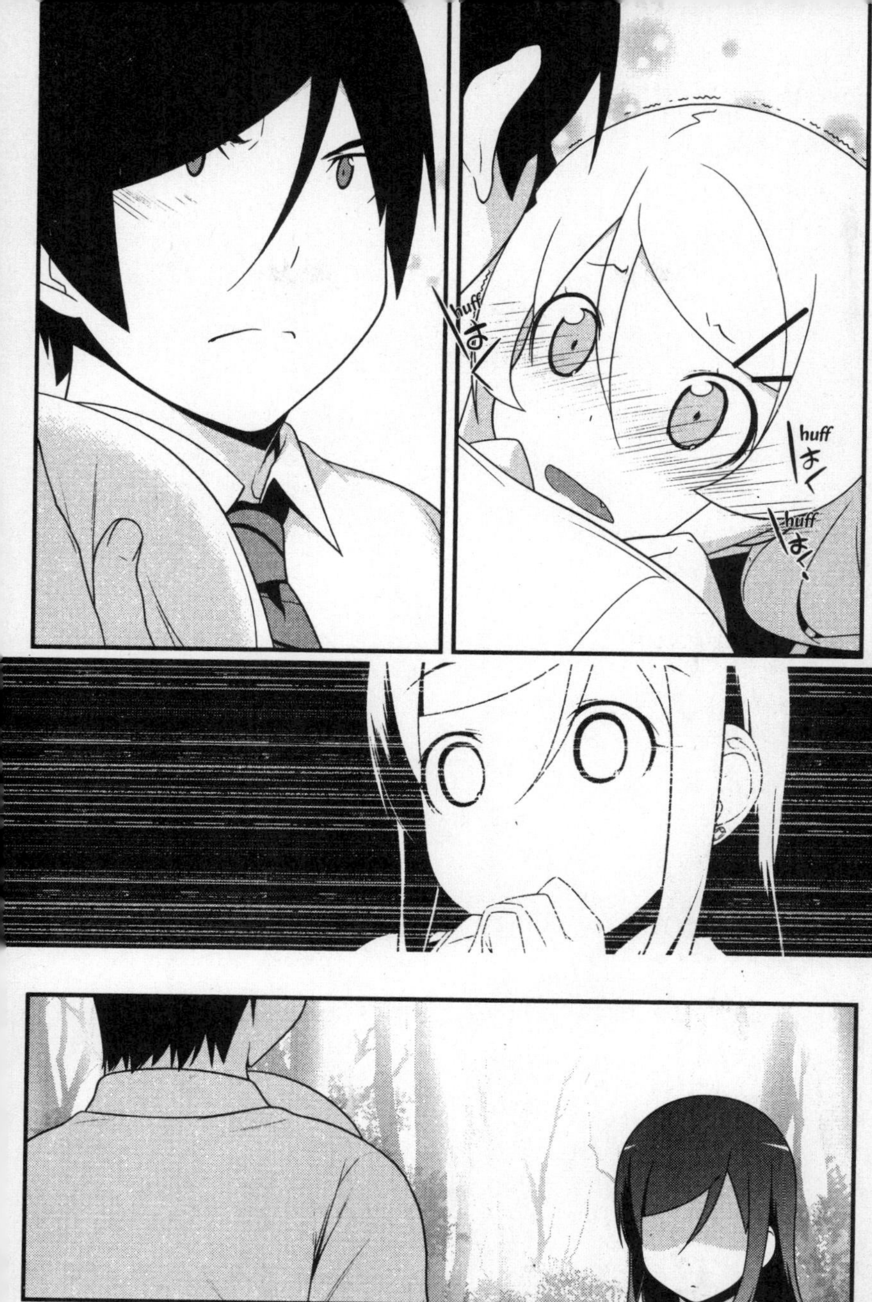
huff はく
huff はく
huff はく

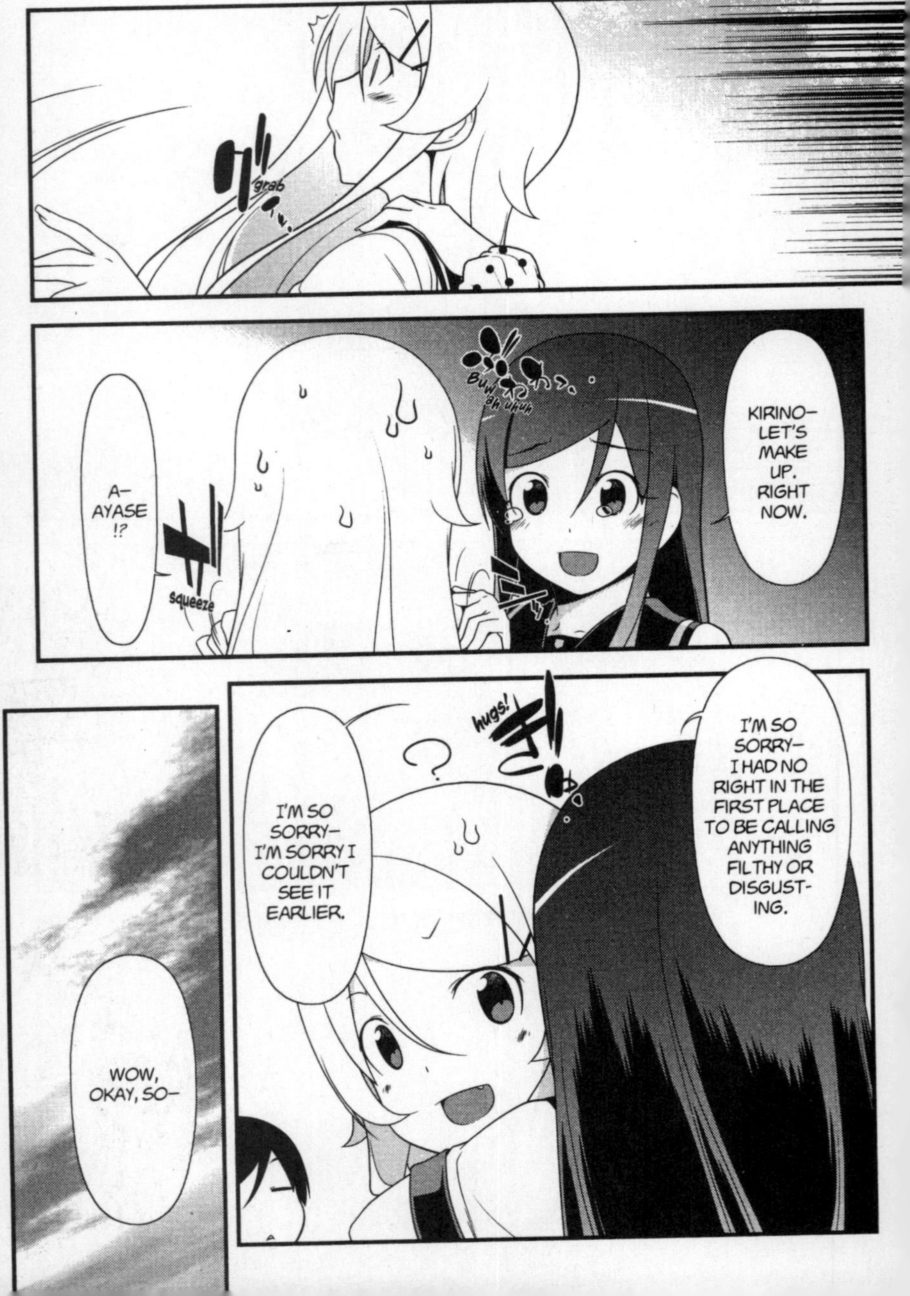
grab
KIRINO— LET'S MAKE UP. RIGHT NOW.
squeeze
A— AYASE !?
hugs!
I'M SO SORRY— I HAD NO RIGHT IN THE FIRST PLACE TO BE CALLING ANYTHING FILTHY OR DISGUST-ING.
I'M SO SORRY— I'M SORRY I COULDN'T SEE IT EARLIER.
WOW, OKAY, SO—

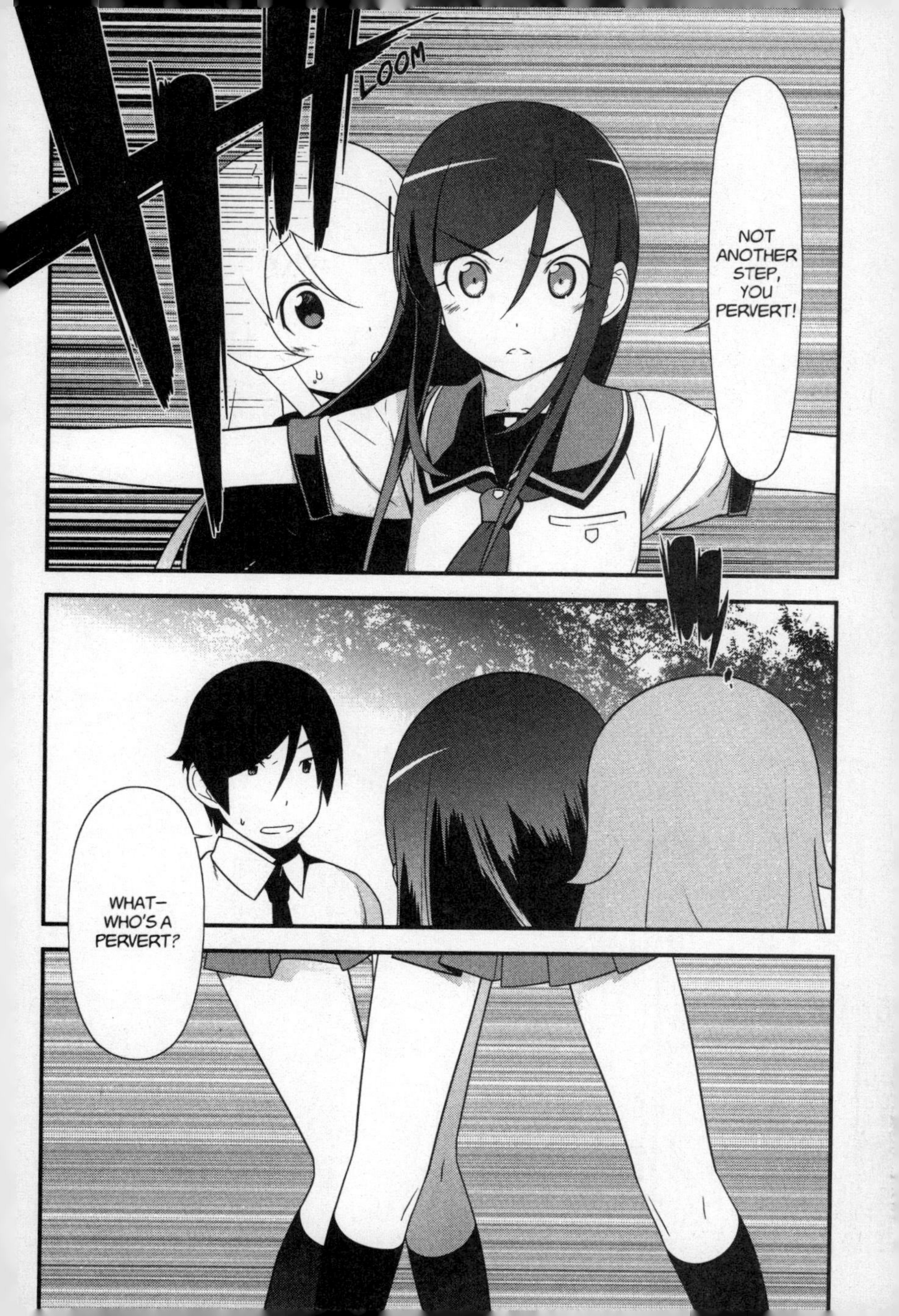
LOOM
NOT ANOTHER STEP, YOU PERVERT!
WHAT— WHO'S A PERVERT?

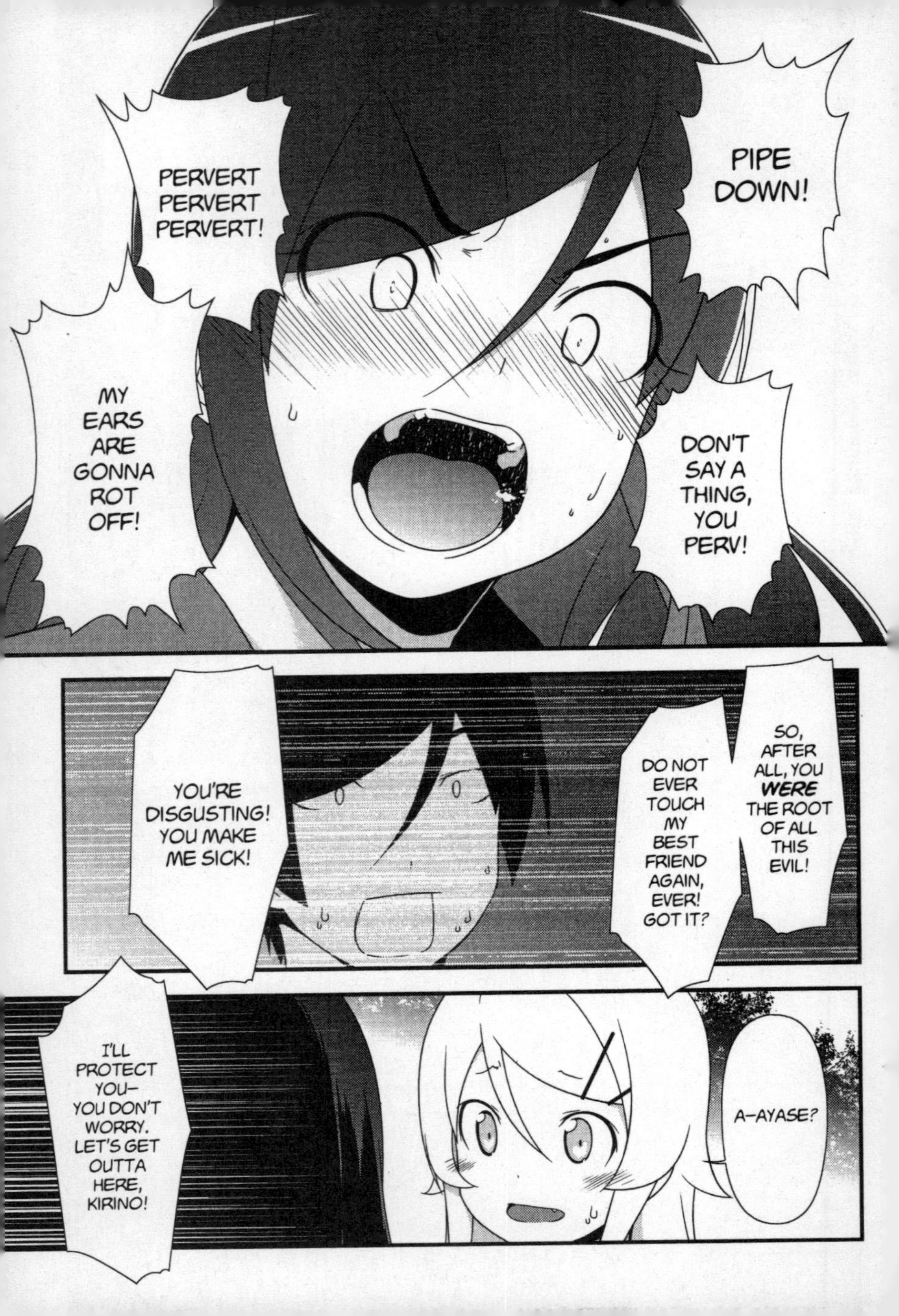
PIPE DOWN!
PERVERT PERVERT PERVERT!
DON'T SAY A THING, YOU PERV!
MY EARS ARE GONNA ROT OFF!
SO, AFTER ALL, YOU *WERE* THE ROOT OF ALL THIS EVIL!
DO NOT EVER TOUCH MY BEST FRIEND AGAIN, EVER! GOT IT?
YOU'RE DISGUSTING! YOU MAKE ME SICK!
A-AYASE?
I'LL PROTECT YOU— YOU DON'T WORRY. LET'S GET OUTTA HERE, KIRINO!

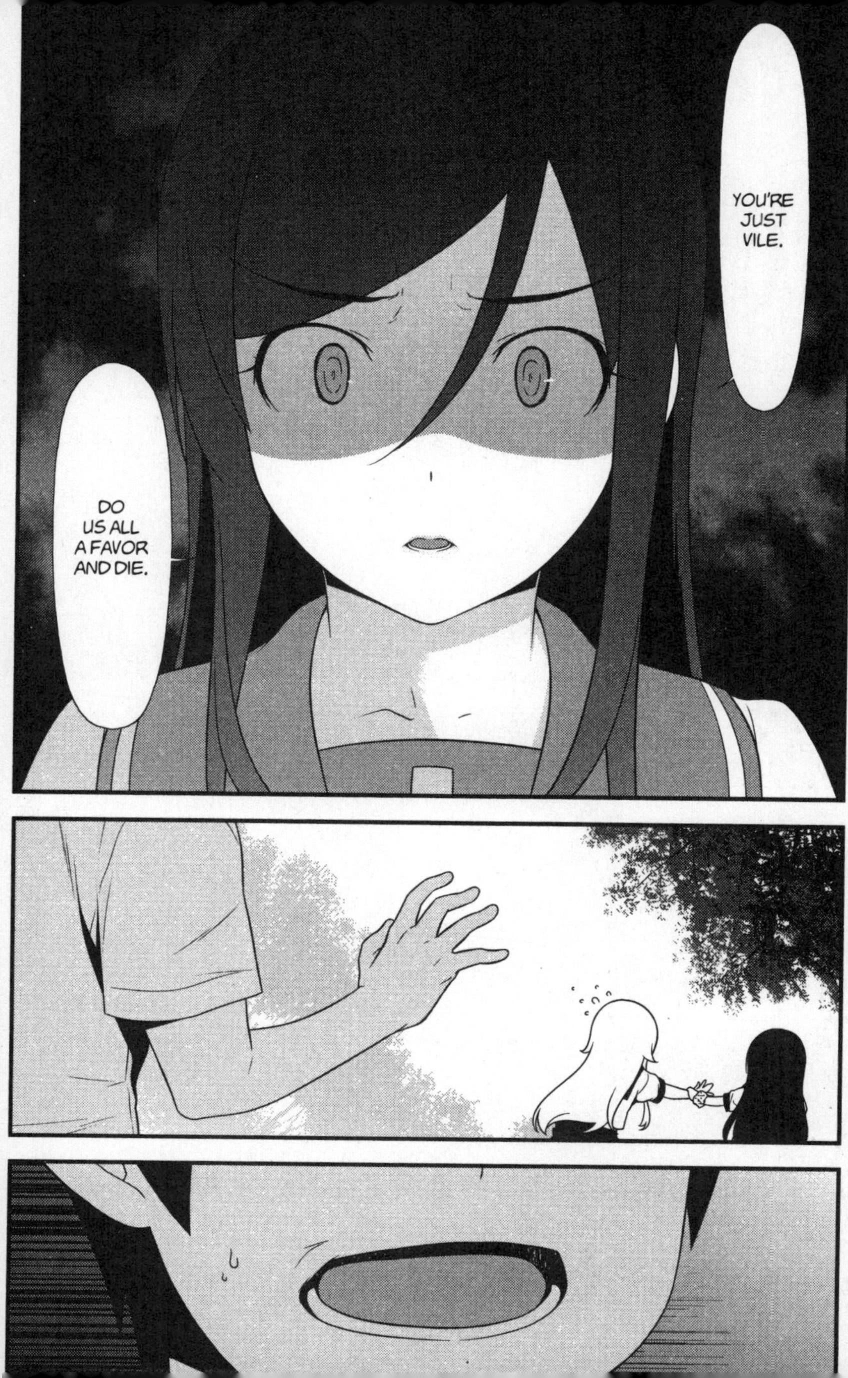
YOU'RE JUST VILE.
DO US ALL A FAVOR AND DIE.

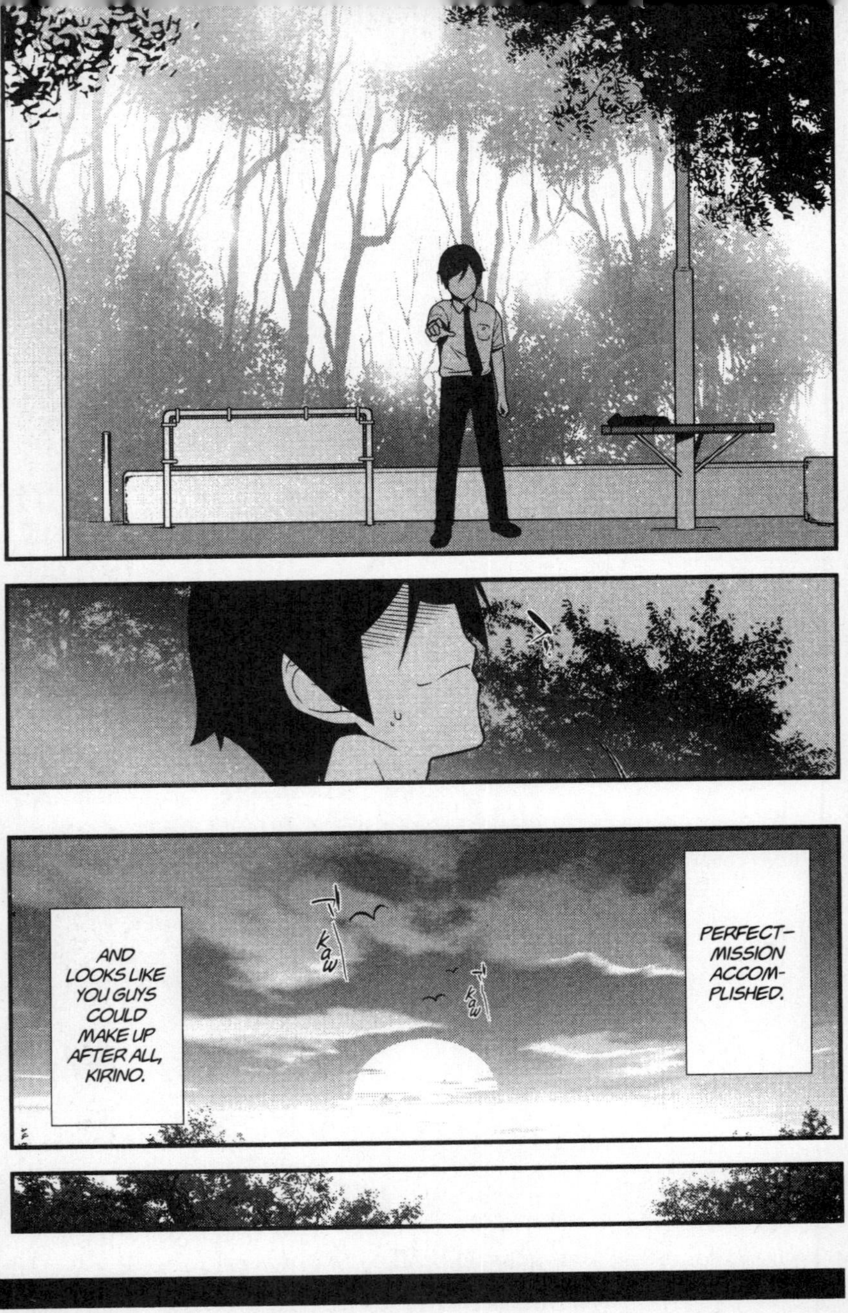
PERFECT—MISSION ACCOMPLISHED.
kaw
kaw
AND LOOKS LIKE YOU GUYS COULD MAKE UP AFTER ALL, KIRINO.

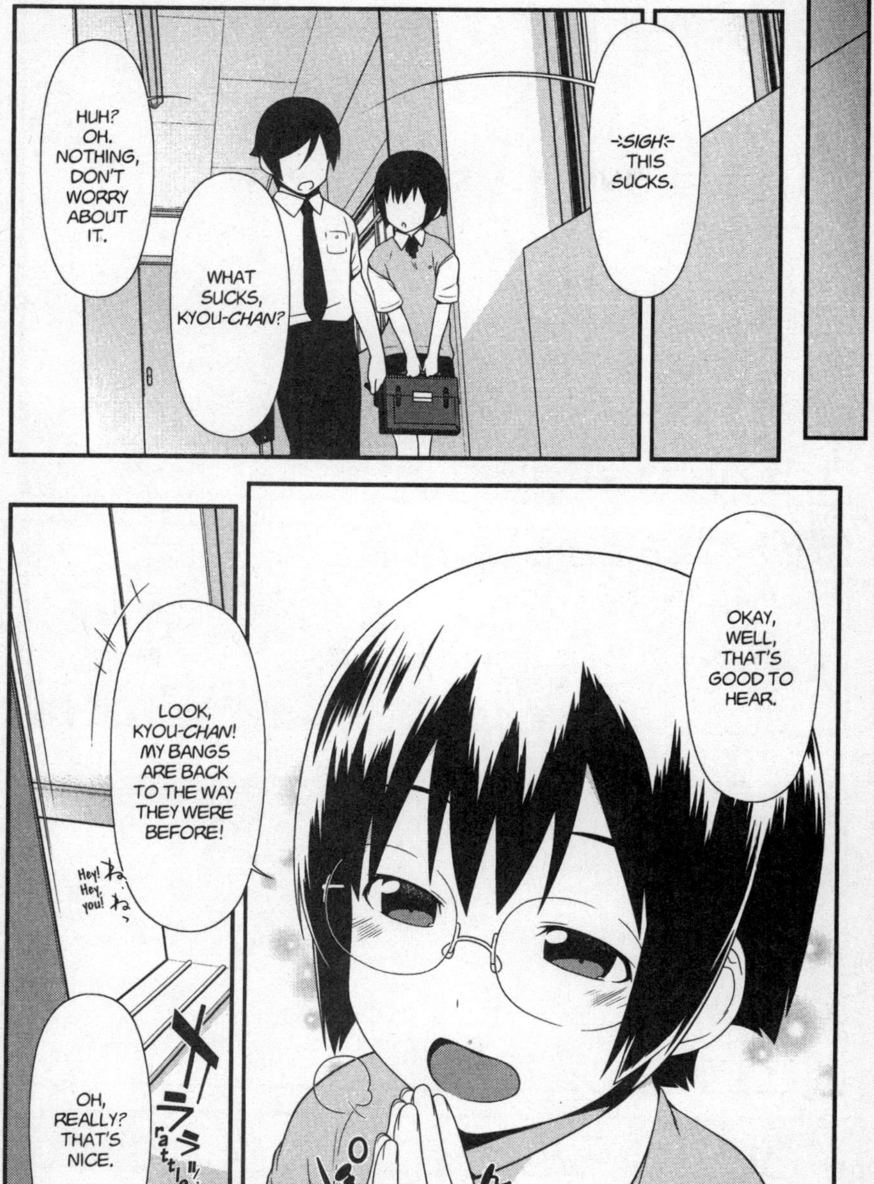

-SIGH- THIS SUCKS.
WHAT SUCKS, KYOU-CHAN?
HUH? OH. NOTHING, DON'T WORRY ABOUT IT.
OKAY, WELL, THAT'S GOOD TO HEAR.
clap
LOOK, KYOU-CHAN! MY BANGS ARE BACK TO THE WAY THEY WERE BEFORE!
Hey! Hey, you!
OH, REALLY? THAT'S NICE.
rattle

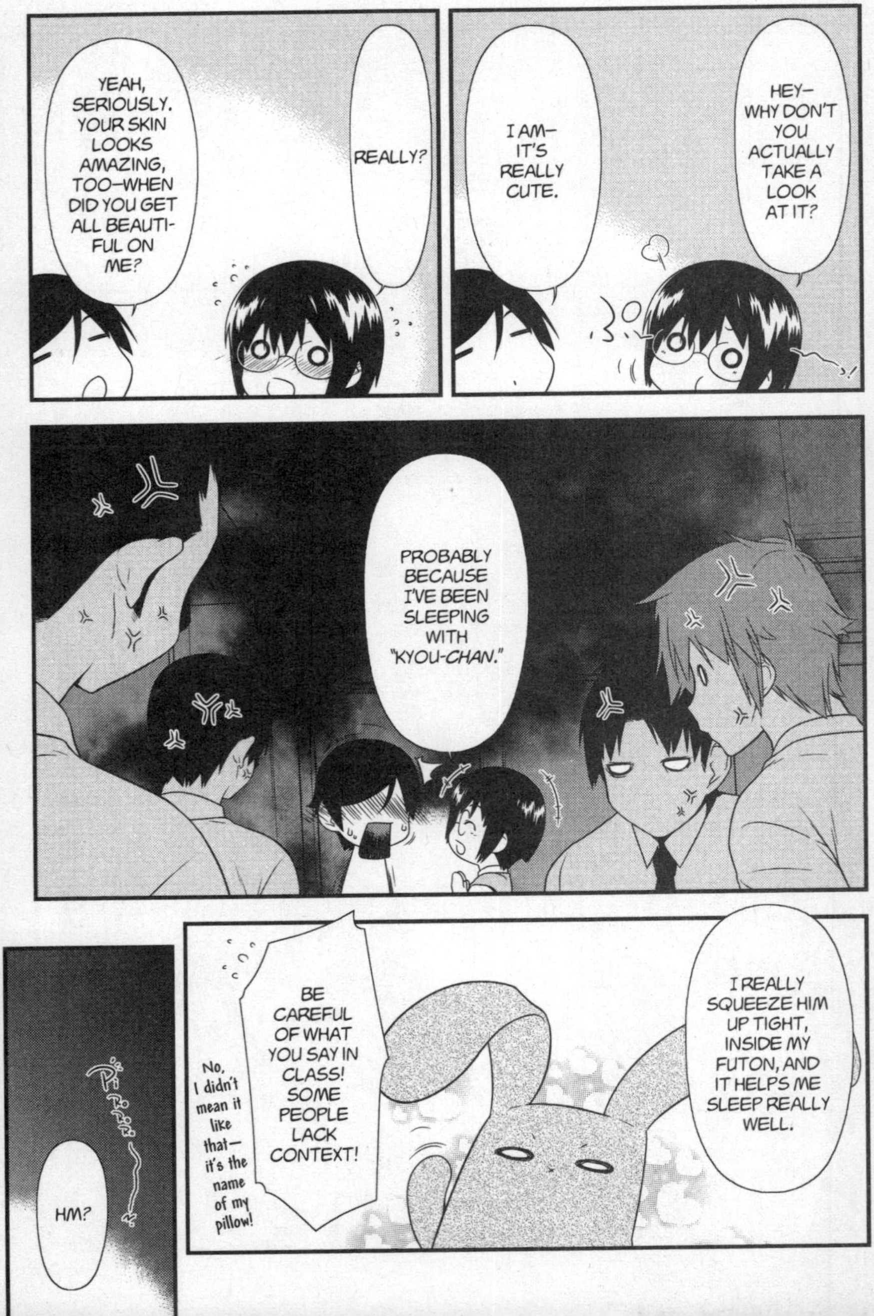
HEY— WHY DON'T YOU ACTUALLY TAKE A LOOK AT IT?
I AM— IT'S REALLY CUTE.
REALLY?
YEAH, SERIOUSLY. YOUR SKIN LOOKS AMAZING, TOO—WHEN DID YOU GET ALL BEAUTI-FUL ON ME?
PROBABLY BECAUSE I'VE BEEN SLEEPING WITH "KYOU-CHAN."
I REALLY SQUEEZE HIM UP TIGHT, INSIDE MY FUTON, AND IT HELPS ME SLEEP REALLY WELL.
BE CAREFUL OF WHAT YOU SAY IN CLASS! SOME PEOPLE LACK CONTEXT!
No, I didn't mean it like that—it's the name of my pillow!
HM?

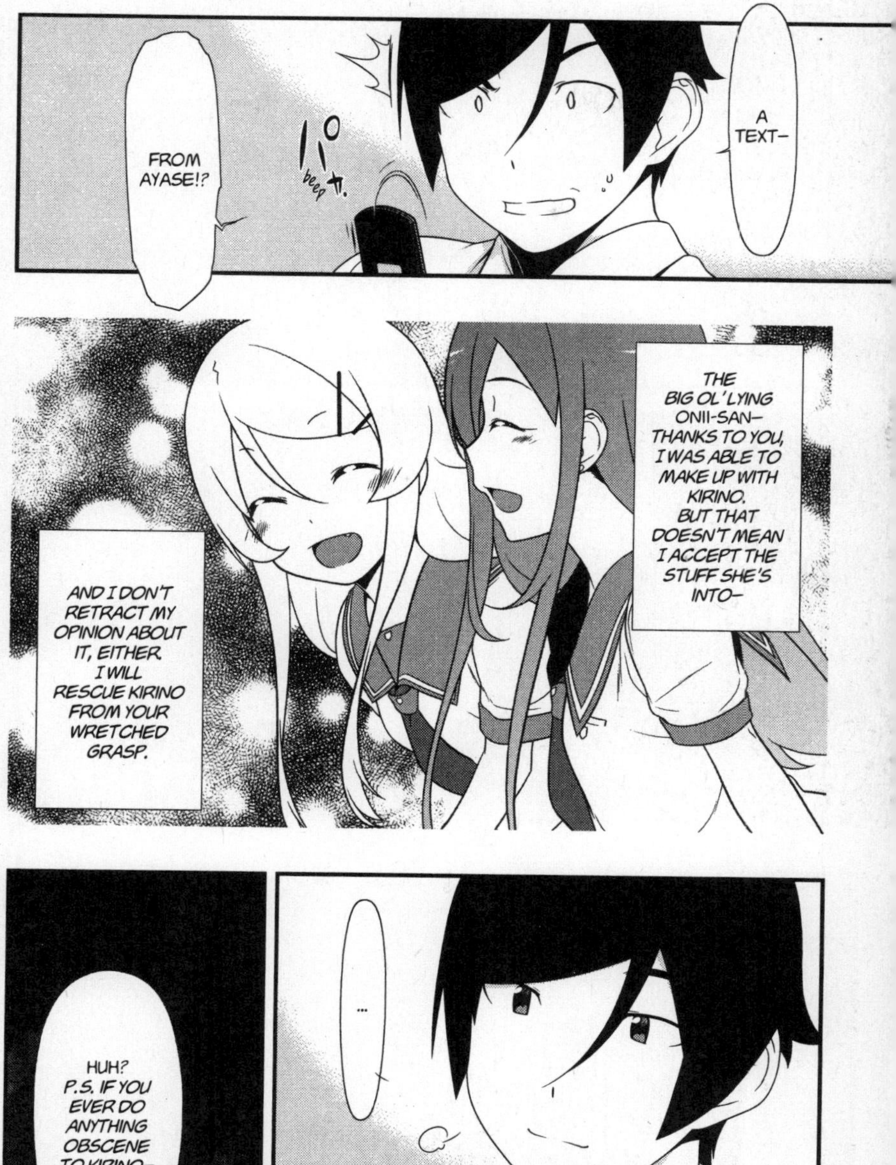
A TEXT—
FROM AYASE!?
beep
THE BIG OL' LYING ONII-SAN— THANKS TO YOU, I WAS ABLE TO MAKE UP WITH KIRINO. BUT THAT DOESN'T MEAN I ACCEPT THE STUFF SHE'S INTO—
AND I DON'T RETRACT MY OPINION ABOUT IT, EITHER. I WILL RESCUE KIRINO FROM YOUR WRETCHED GRASP.
...
HUH? P.S. IF YOU EVER DO ANYTHING OBSCENE TO KIRINO—

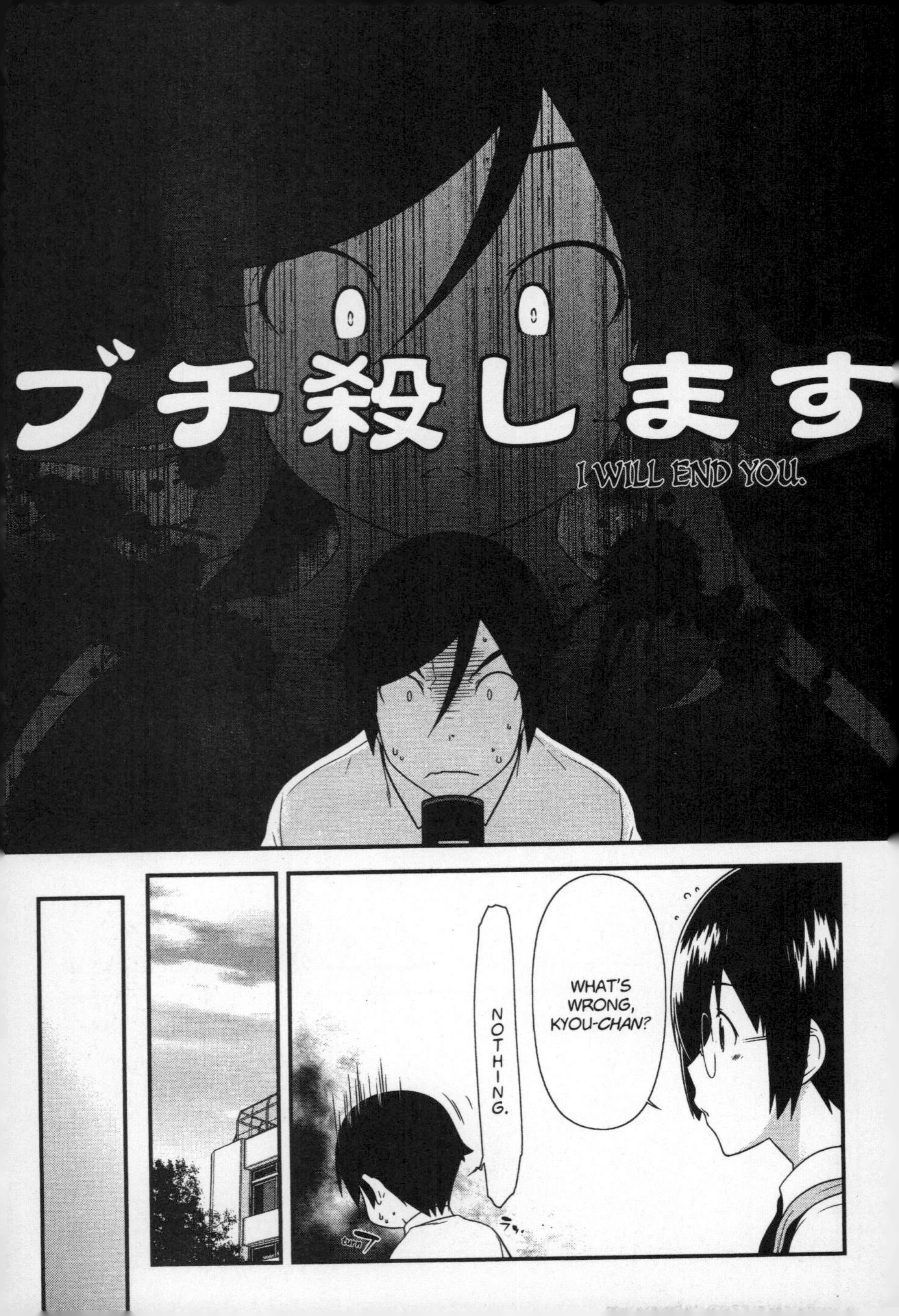
ブチ殺します
I WILL END YOU.
WHAT'S WRONG, KYOU-CHAN?
NOTHING.
turn

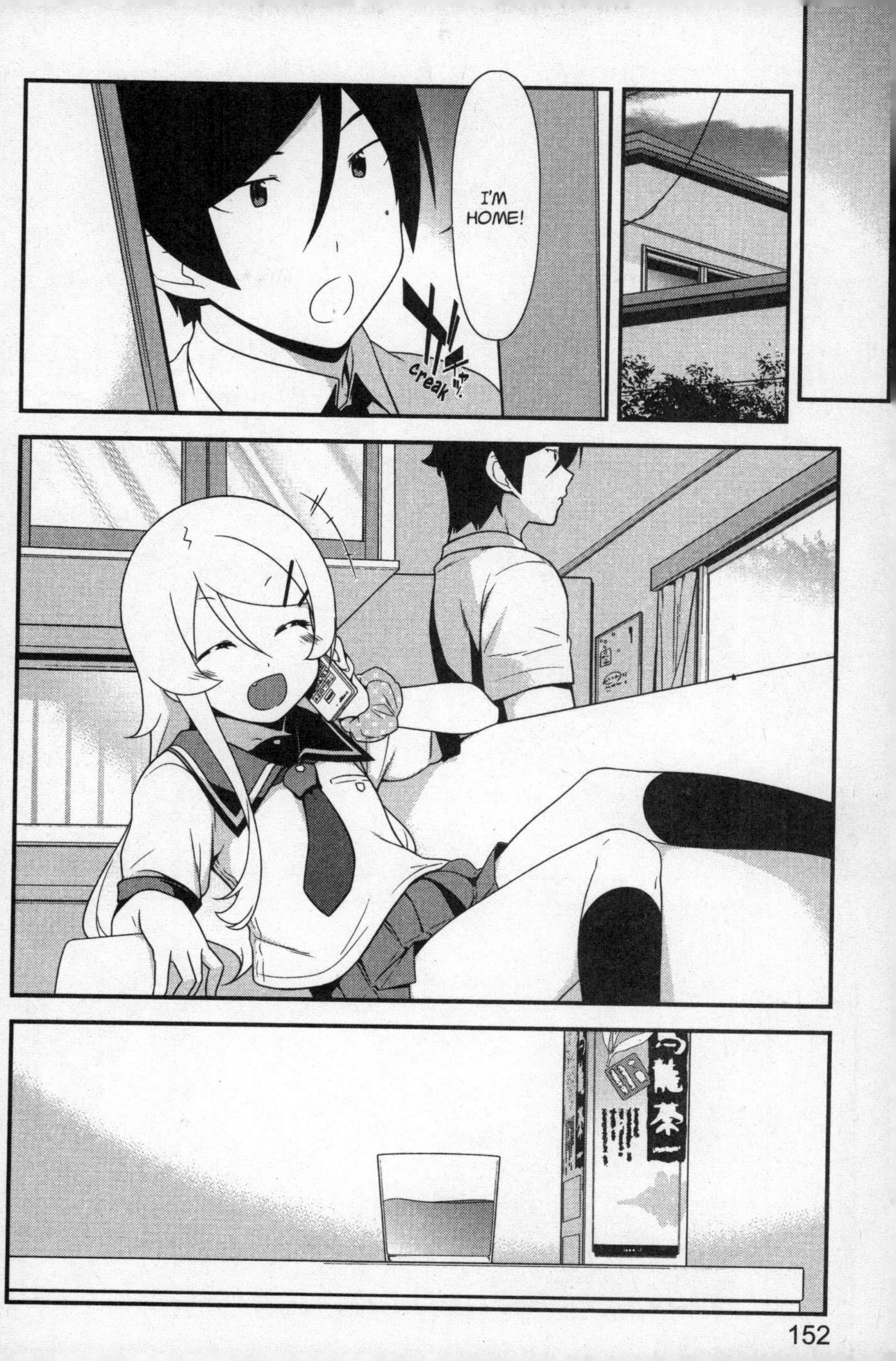
I'M HOME!
creak

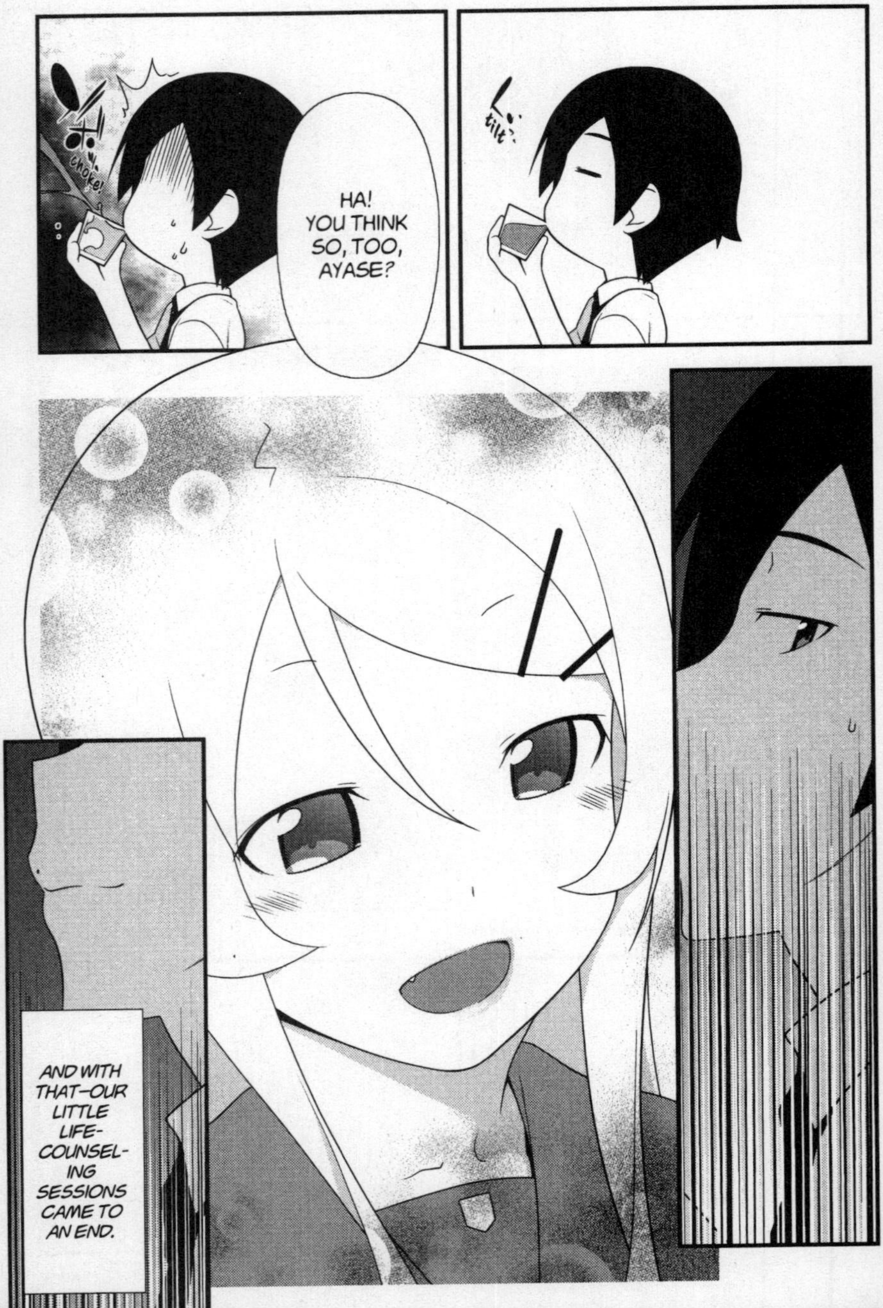
tilt?
choke!
HA! YOU THINK SO, TOO, AYASE?
AND WITH THAT—OUR LITTLE LIFE-COUNSELING SESSIONS CAME TO AN END.

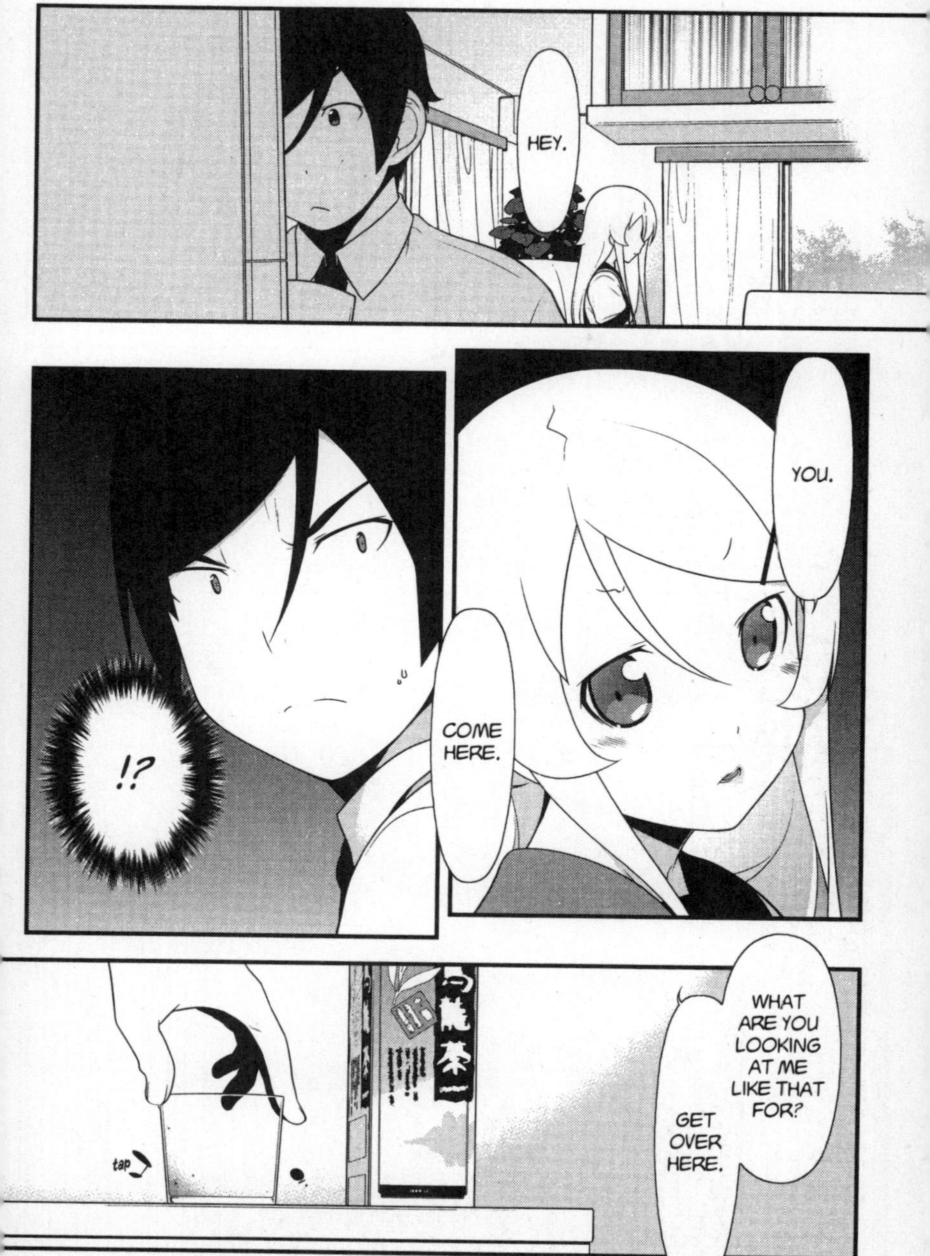
HEY.
YOU.
COME HERE.
!?
WHAT ARE YOU LOOKING AT ME LIKE THAT FOR?
GET OVER HERE.
tap

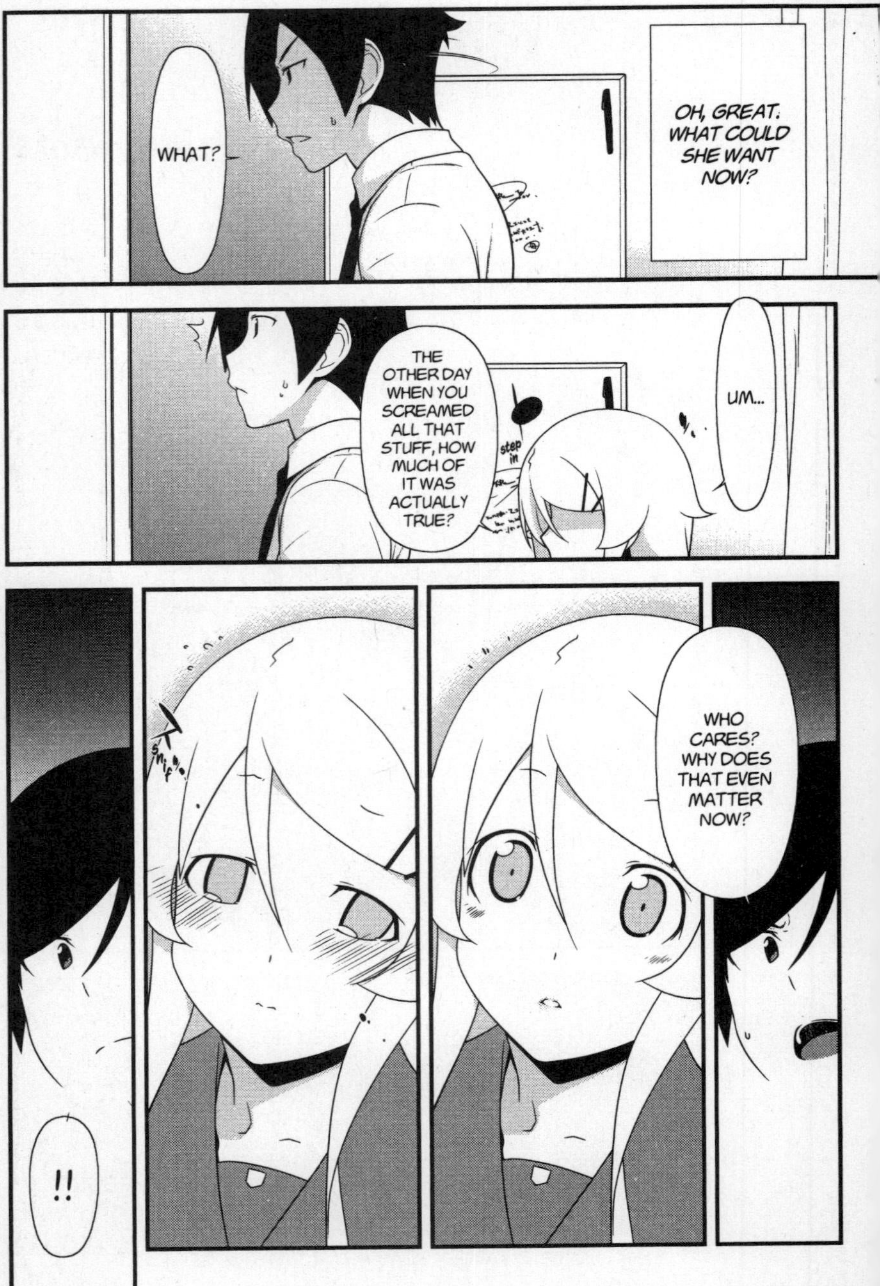
OH, GREAT. WHAT COULD SHE WANT NOW?
WHAT?
UM...
THE OTHER DAY WHEN YOU SCREAMED ALL THAT STUFF, HOW MUCH OF IT WAS ACTUALLY TRUE?
step in
WHO CARES? WHY DOES THAT EVEN MATTER NOW?
sniff
!!

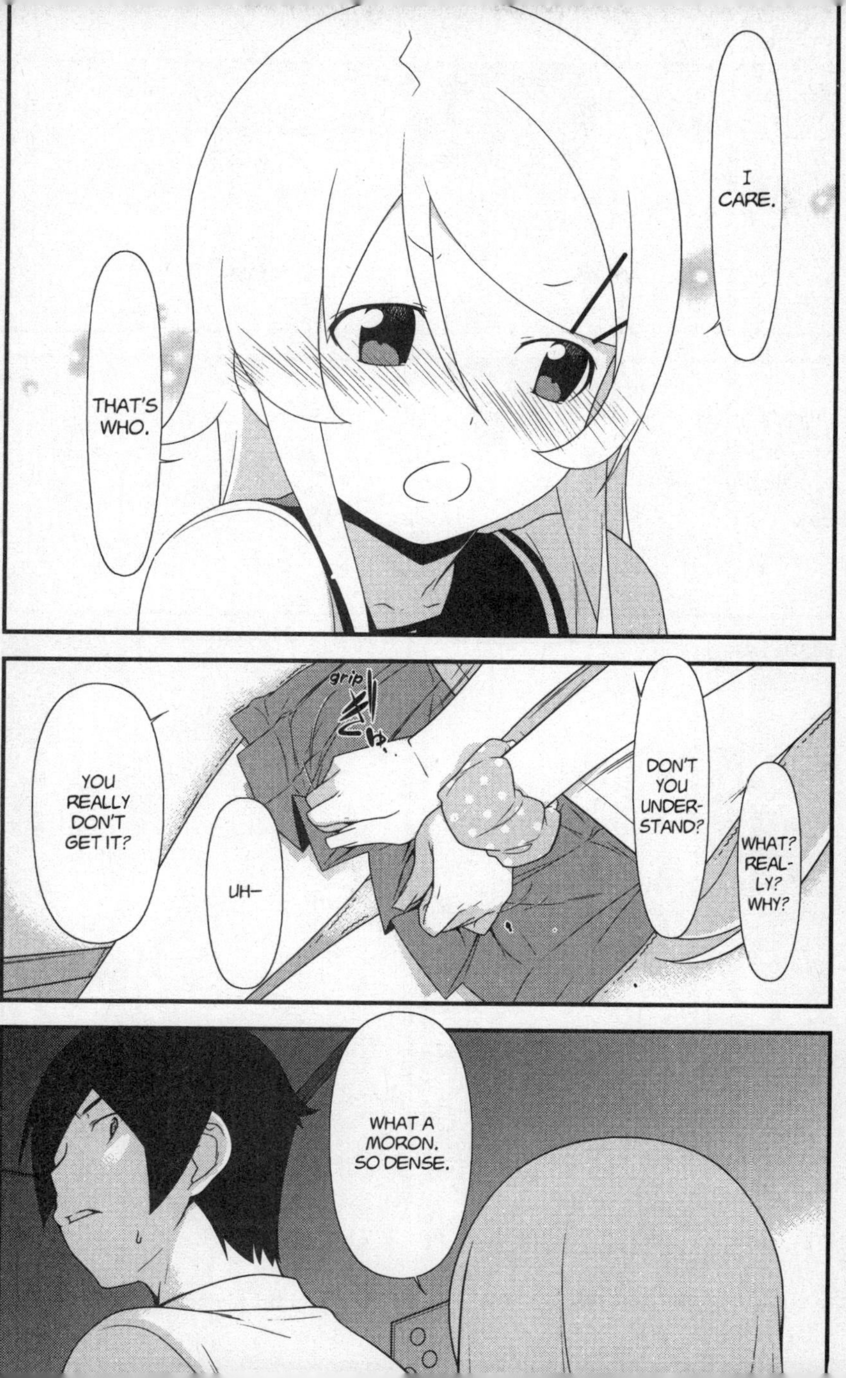
I CARE.
THAT'S WHO.
DON'T YOU UNDERSTAND?
WHAT? REAL-LY? WHY?
grip
UH–
YOU REALLY DON'T GET IT?
WHAT A MORON. SO DENSE.

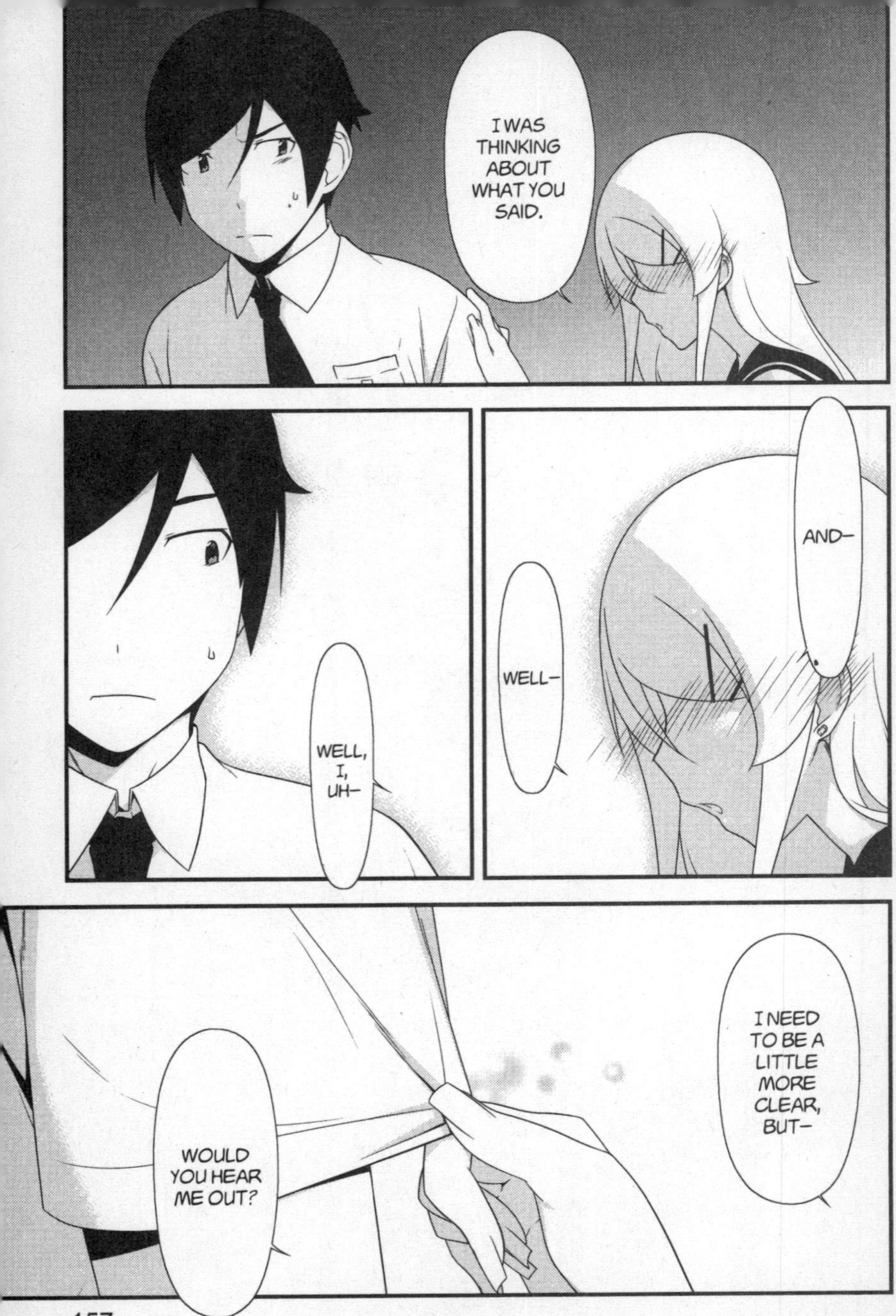
I WAS THINKING ABOUT WHAT YOU SAID.
AND—
WELL—
WELL, I, UH—
I NEED TO BE A LITTLE MORE CLEAR, BUT—
WOULD YOU HEAR ME OUT?

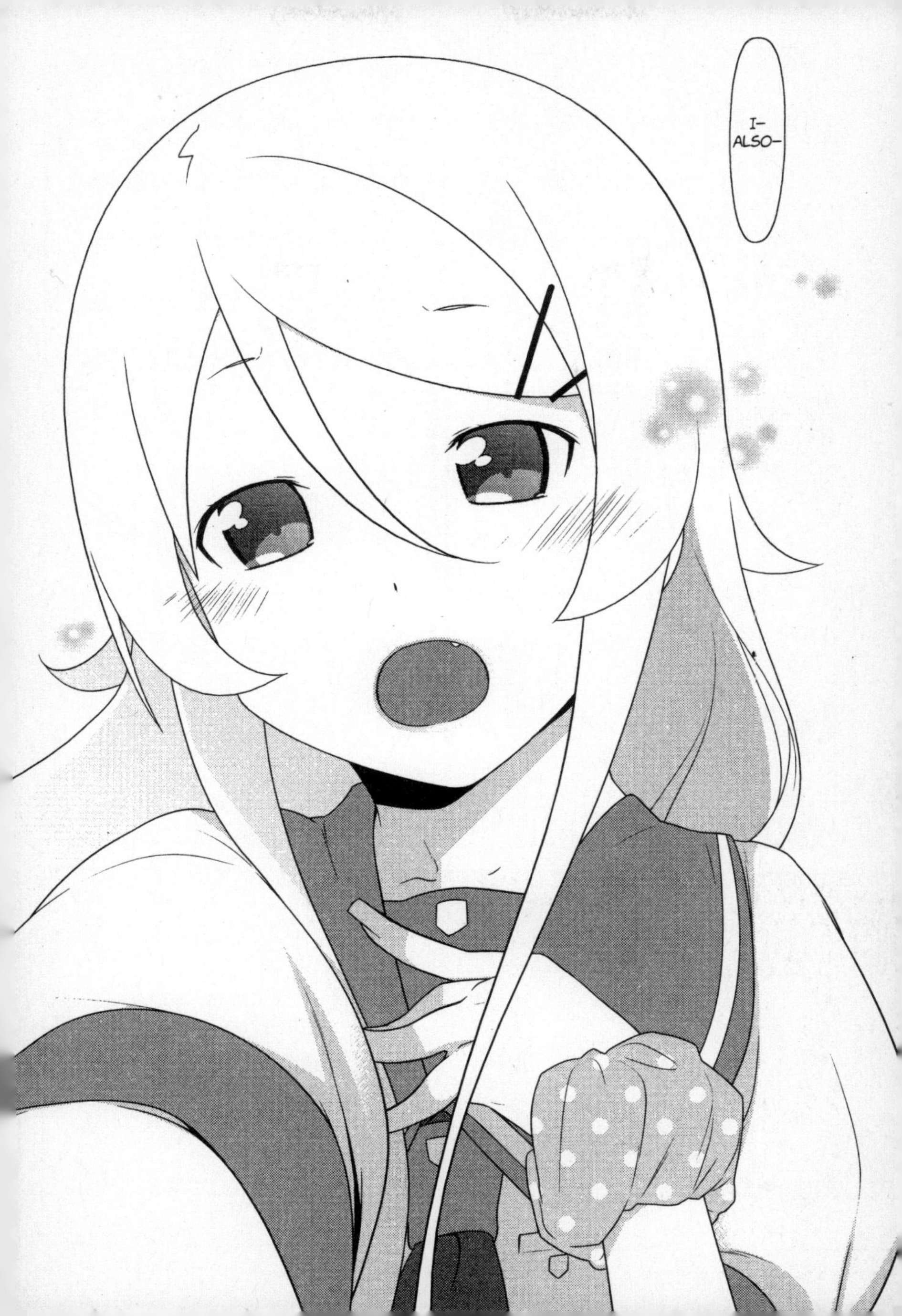
I— ALSO—

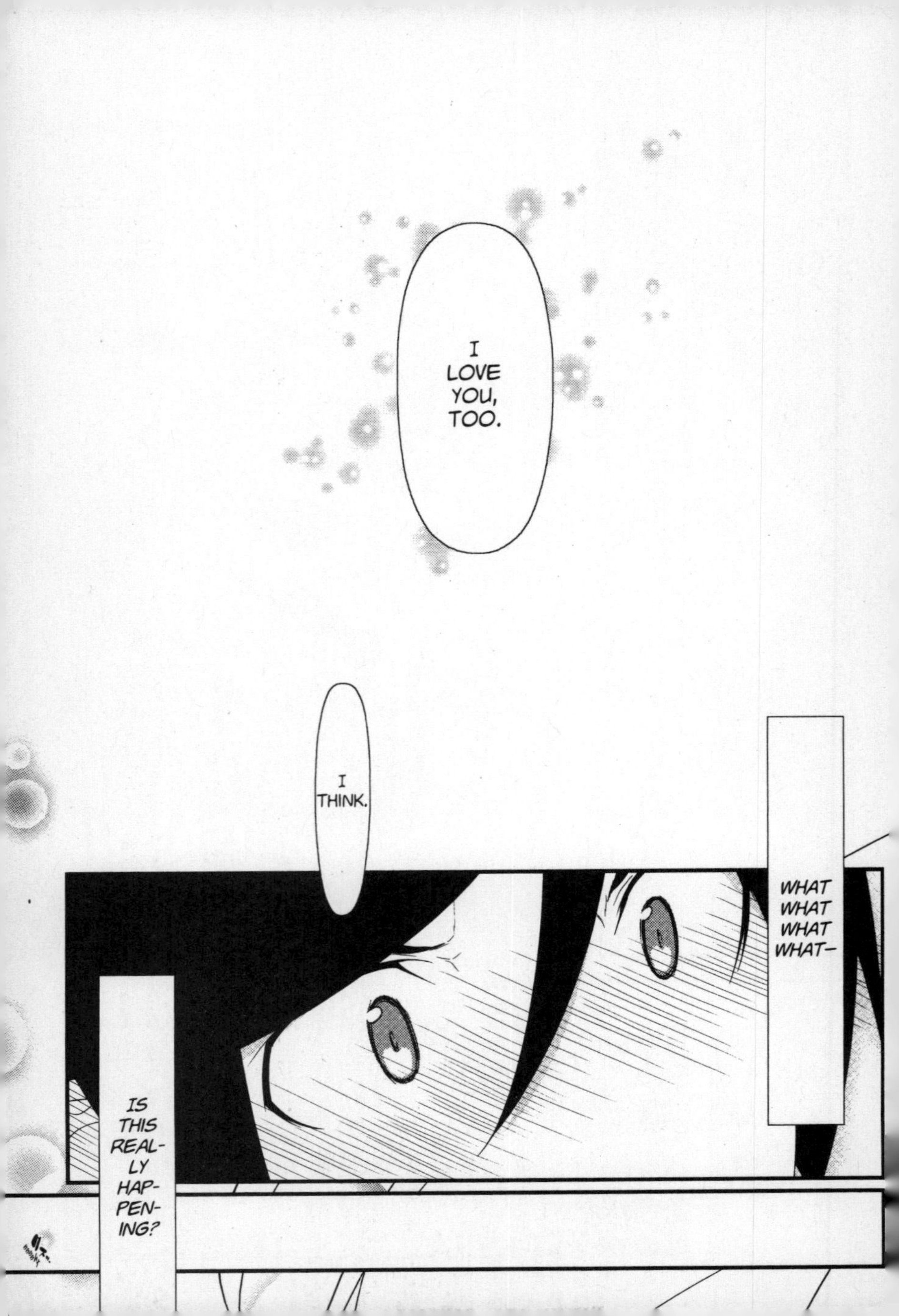
I LOVE YOU, TOO.
I THINK.
WHAT WHAT WHAT WHAT–
IS THIS REALLY HAPPENING?

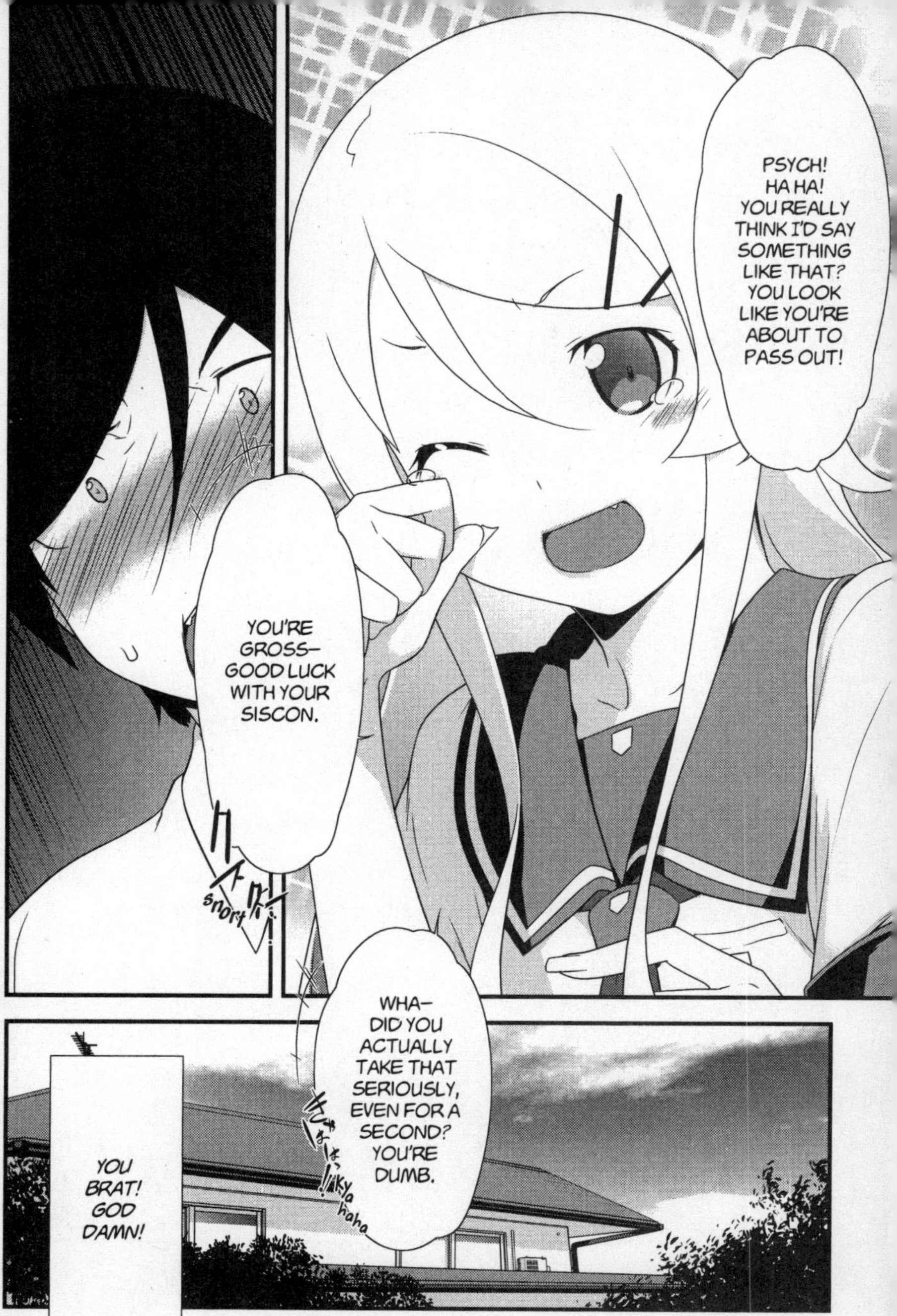
PSYCH! HA HA! YOU REALLY THINK I'D SAY SOMETHING LIKE THAT? YOU LOOK LIKE YOU'RE ABOUT TO PASS OUT!
YOU'RE GROSS– GOOD LUCK WITH YOUR SISCON.
snort
WHA– DID YOU ACTUALLY TAKE THAT SERIOUSLY, EVEN FOR A SECOND? YOU'RE DUMB.
kya haha
YOU BRAT! GOD DAMN!

Thanks for purchasing this volume of
Oreimo—I really appreciate it.
It's me, Ikeda Sakura.

Here we are, at the fourth volume of this book.
Once again, thanks for everything, and
I hope that reading this brings you at least a
little happiness. And, to everyone that took
part in helping me make this book what you
see here, thank you so much.

This book has all the material through the
second light novel. For the most part, all of the
major characters have been depicted here, but
I wonder what will happen from here on out?

I actually don't know, either.

I think I'd like to continue on from here,
so if you're willing to walk that road
with me, I'd appreciate it.

—*Ikeda Sakura*

Designer
Heather Doornink

Editor
Jemiah Jefferson

Publisher
Mike Richardson

English-language version produced by Dark Horse Comics

Published by
Dark Horse Manga
A division of Dark Horse Comics, Inc.
10956 SE Main Street
Milwaukie, OR 97222
DarkHorse.com

To find a comics shop in your area, call the Comic Shop Locator Service toll-free
at 1-888-266-4226.

First edition: September 2013
ISBN 978-1-61655-221-3

10 9 8 7 6 5 4 3 2 1
Printed in the United States of America

c/o Dark Horse Comics ♥ 10956 SE Main St. ♥ Milwaukie OR 97222 ♥ oreimo@darkhorse.com

THE OFF-KAI

Hello,

I recently picked up volumes 1 and 2 of Oreimo and I've really enjoyed them a lot. I've been a huge fan of the series since I first watched the anime back in October of 2010, and since then I've come to really love it. Seeing both volumes at the local Chapters bookstore, I had to pick them up; I was not going to pass up reading the manga.

So recently finishing the second volume, I was reading the Off-Kai section and the subject of translation and localization was talked about. Reading both volumes and taking careful note of the dialogue by each character, I've gotta say that it really fits. Usually when I'm watching anime subbed online I'm not a huge fan of localization, as it can seem out of place, but reading it in Oreimo worked very well.

True, maybe it's because that's how teens do talk these days. I know students in my school really say some wild things and have quite the colorful vocabulary, but all things considered, I think the people at Dark Horse did a fine job with making the dialogue fit the characters and display how teens talk.

I'm really enjoying what Dark Horse has done here, bringing such a popular manga to North America. I'm really happy that I can finally own this myself. Oh, and before I close this, I have to say that my favorite character has to be Kirino. As much as she can be a bitch, I still think she's so awesome and totally cute. Kuroneko is also very cool too, and I love her a lot, but Kirino takes the top spot.

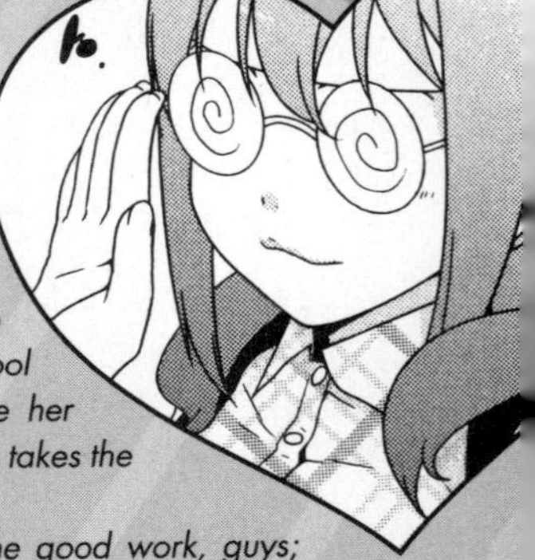

Keep up the good work, guys; you're doing a excellent job and I'm super excited for the coming volumes! By the way, will Dark Horse be releasing the entire series of Oreimo? I'm currently watching season 2 online, and wondering if all the events that happen [in the anime series] will, in manga form, be released over here sometime in the future?

Thanks once again!
—Nick (via e mail)

Thanks for the props, Nick; they are very welcome as well as wonderful. Our whole team working on *Oreimo* read and appreciated your message; on behalf of us all, YOU ROCK. I'm also glad to hear that you're watching season 2 of the anime series (currently streaming on Crunchyroll for viewers in the US); I haven't had time to jump in yet, having my hands full

with all manner of life stuff (and also other TV shows—and fanfic, and fan art, and . . . you get the picture) but when I do, I will probably do the same thing as I did with season 1 and watch all of them in one long, compulsive, "just one more/ OMG I love this *so much*" binge and stay up way too late and show up at work all bleary eyed and dehydrated. I have done everything I can to capture the spirit of the anime, from Kyousuke's laconic, skeptical drawl (well peppered with occasional profanity!), to Kirino's mega-intense geekery in the face of *Siscalypse* and *Meruru*, to Ayase's Jekyll-and-Hyde duality. (Man, she is scary.) *Oreimo*'s strength is not only in its message and humor, but in the complexity of its characters, their emotions, relationships, and inner lives painfully exposed and defended against all attackers. If you have yet to see the animated series, I can't recommend it highly enough, and it makes a great companion to the manga.

As for future *Oreimo* at Dark Horse, I am unfortunately unable to say at the moment, but I am hopeful that we will secure the rights to more of this wonderful story. As you may well know, the light-novel series from which both anime and manga have been adapted has recently published its twelfth and final volume, and this volume of the manga only addresses the first two of those books. Therefore, there is a lot more material to adapt—and I certainly hope that happens!

Until next time,
♥ Jemiah

OREIMO

Ordinary teenage guy Kyousuke doesn't get along with his ill-tempered little sister Kirino, but when he discovers Kirino's secrets—she's not only a fashion model and a great student, but she's really into silly anime and X-rated video games!—he finds himself charged with protecting and defending her right to be just the person she is.

This hilarious, charming hit series is filled with surprises and outrageous laughs. Who says girls can't be *otaku*, too?

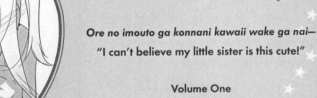

Ore no imouto ga konnani kawaii wake ga nai—
"I can't believe my little sister is this cute!"

Volume One
ISBN 978-1-59582-956-6

Volume Two
ISBN 978-1-61655-055-4

Volume Three
ISBN 978-1-61655-181-0

$10.99 each

Available at your local comics shop or bookstore! · To find a comics shop in your area, call 1-888-266-4226.
For more information or to order direct: ·On the web: DarkHorse.com · E-mail: mailorder@darkhorse.com · Phone: 1-800-862-0052 Mon.–Fri. 9 AM to 5 PM Pacific Time.

Oreno Imouto ga Konnani Kawaii wakeganai © FUSHIMI / SAKURA IKEDA. Originally published in Japan by ASCII MEDIA WORKS Inc., Tokyo. Dark Horse Manga™ is a trademark of Dark Horse Comics, Inc. All rights reserved. (BL 7100)

CLAMP

Chobits
ちょびっツ

BOOK 1

In near-future Japan, the hottest style for your personal computer, or "persocom," has the appearance of an attractive android! Hideki, a poor student trying to get into a Tokyo university, has neither money nor a girlfriend—then finds a persocom seemingly discarded in an alley. Hideki takes the cute, amnesiac robot home and names her "Chi."

But who is this strange new persocom in his life? Instead of having a digital assistant, Hideki finds himself having to teach Chi how to get along in the everyday world, even while he and his friends try to solve the mystery of her origins. Is she one of the urban-legendary *Chobits*—persocoms built to have the riskiest functions of all: real emotions and free will?

A crossover hit for both female and male readers, CLAMP's best-selling manga ever in America is finally available in omnibus form! Containing sixteen bonus color pages, *Chobits* Volume 1 begins an engaging, touching, exciting story.

ISBN 978-1-59582-451-6
$24.99

AVAILABLE AT YOUR LOCAL COMICS SHOP OR BOOKSTORE
To find a comics shop in your area, call 1.888.266.4226. For more information or to order direct: •On the web: DarkHorse.com •E-mail: mailorder@darkhorse.com •Phone: 1.800.862.0052 Mon.–Fri. 9 AM to 5 PM Pacific Time.

DARK HORSE MANGA
DarkHorse.com

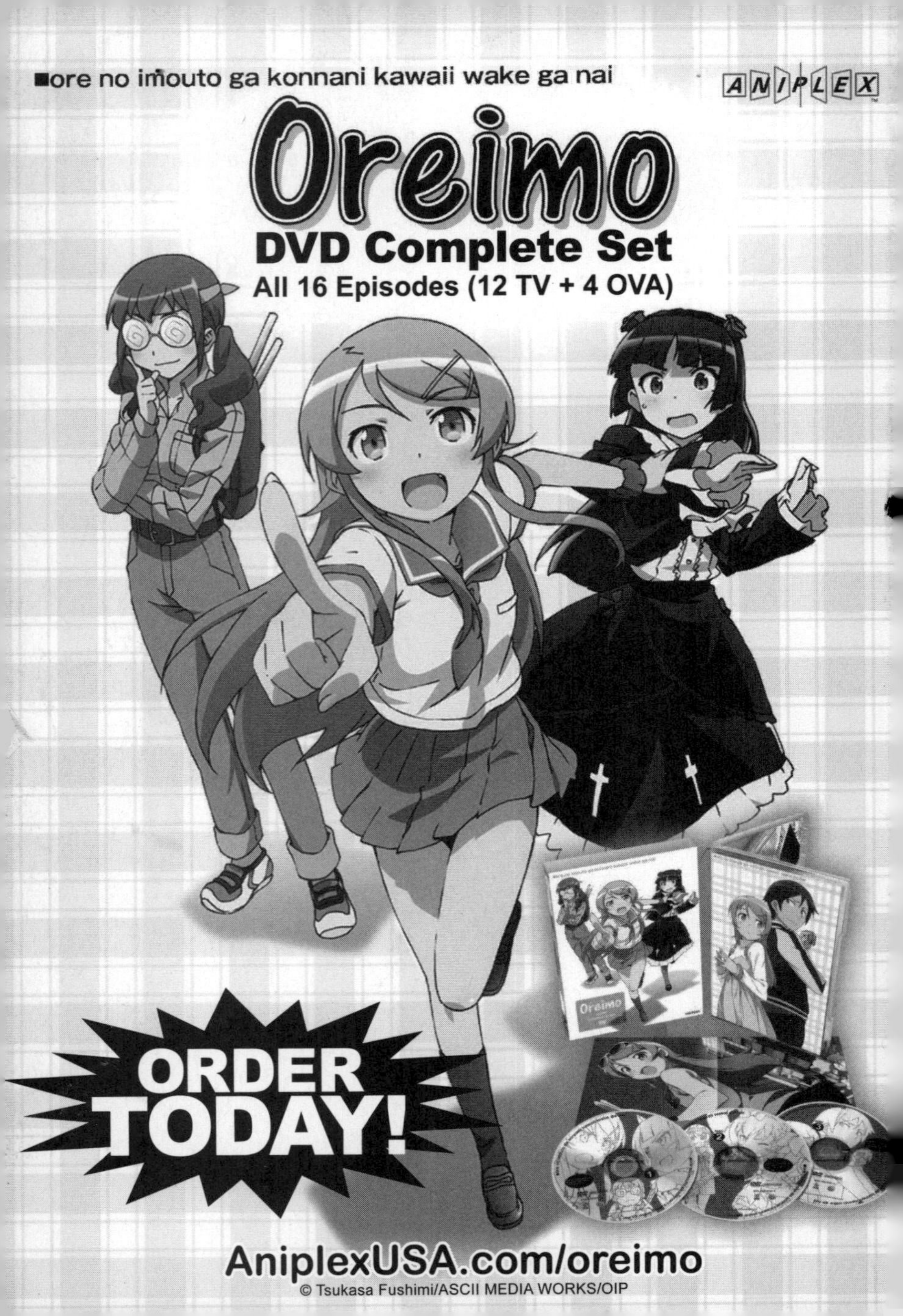

STOP! YOU'RE READING THE WRONG WAY!

This manga volume is translated into English, but arranged in right-to-left reading format to maintain the artwork's visual orientation as originally drawn and published in Japan. If you've never read comics this way before, take a look at the diagram to give yourself an idea of how to go about it. Start in the upper-right corner, and read each word balloon and panel moving right to left. It may take a little getting used to, but you should get the hang of it quickly. Have fun!

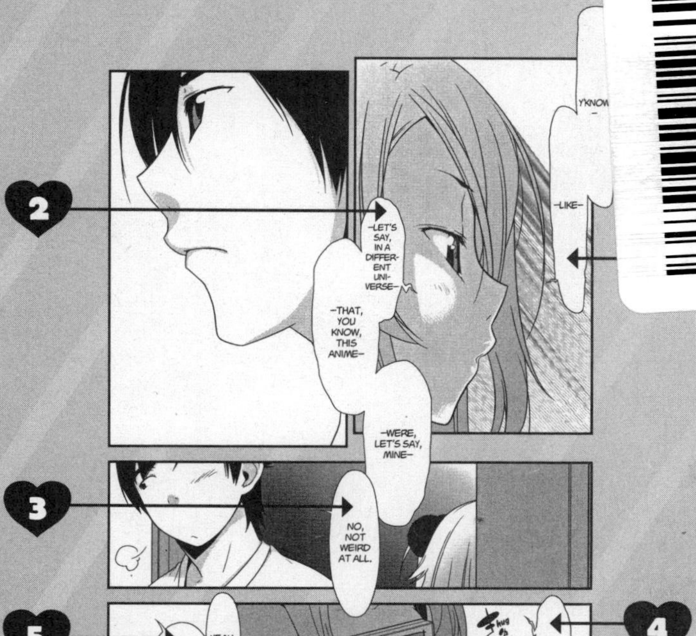

Y'KNOW
—
-LIKE-
2
-LET'S SAY, IN A DIFFERENT UNIVERSE-
-THAT, YOU KNOW, THIS ANIME-
-WERE, LET'S SAY, MINE-
3
NO, NOT WEIRD AT ALL.
4
hug
DO YOU- REALLY THINK SO?
I MEAN, REALLY?
5
YEAH.
I MEAN, I'M NOT THE KIND OF PERSON WHO MAKES FUN OF WHAT OTHER PEOPLE ARE INTO.